THE
STOCK MARKET BAROMETER

WILEY INVESTMENT CLASSICS

THE
STOCK MARKET BAROMETER

William Peter Hamilton

A Marketplace Book

JOHN WILEY & SONS, INC.
New York • Chichester • Weinheim • Brisbane • Singapore • Toronto

Library of Congress Cataloging-in-Publication Data:
Hamilton, William Peter, 1867–
    The stock market barometer / William Peter Hamilton,
       p. cm.—(A marketplace book) (Wiley investment classics)
    Originally published: New York : Harper & Brothers, c1922.
    Includes index.
    ISBN 0-471-24738-3 (cloth : alk. paper).—ISBN 0-471-24764-2
(pbk. : alk. paper)
    1. Stock market. 2. Stock price forecasting. 3. Dow Jones industrial average. I. Title. II. Series. III. Series: Wiley
HG4551.H3 1998
332.64'273—dc21'   97-42291
                                      CIP

Printed in the United States of America.

10 9 8 7 6 5 4 3 2

To
My Old Friend and Colleague

HUGH BANCROFT

without whose suggestion and encouragement
this book would not have
been written

LIST OF CONTENTS

FOREWORD

We live in a time when anything (and, unfortunately, anyone) that is old is considered outdated, useless, and the worst of all possible adjectives—irrelevant. Ours is a society that worships the new, one that measures shelf life in nanoseconds.

This "disdain-for-the-past" mentality also permeates our financial markets. Indeed, rare is the mutual-fund manager today who regards the study of market history as a worthwhile pastime. After all, today's stock market is an extremely complex, high-octane creature that bears little resemblance to the stock market of even 5 or 10 years ago, let alone the markets at the turn of the century. Why waste your time reviewing the past for tools that can't possibly be used in today's market ? The only useful investment tools today are those that fit on a hard drive, right ?

Hard drives didn't exist in Charles Dow or William Peter Hamilton's day nearly 100 years ago. Yet, these two men developed and refined a market-forecasting tool that is still better than anything I've ever seen on Wall Street.

I was introduced to the Dow Theory—the "stock market barometer" developed by Charles Dow (the founder and first editor of *The Wall Street Journal)* about which William Peter Hamilton writes in these pages—when I started my investment career more than 15 years ago as an editor of *Dow Theory Forecasts* investment newsletter. At that time, I was a bit surprised to discover that the primary market forecasting tool used by my new employer was a theory whose origins date to the turn of the century. Surely a simple theory that focuses exclusively on the movements of the Dow Jones Industrial and Transportation Averages (the Transports were called the "Rails" in Hamilton's day) would have little forecasting ability in today's complex and fast-moving stock market.

Fifteen years later, I'm here to tell you that if you used only the Dow Theory to discern market trends, you'd be doing better than most Wall Street "experts." But don't take my word for it. *The Hulbert Financial Digest,* the "Siskel & Ebert" of the financial newsletter business, rates *Dow Theory Forecasts* as one of the top five market timers for the five years ended June 1997. For 15-year performance, *Dow Theory Forecasts* ranked second among all market timers and first among those that do not use margin to boost their returns. That *Dow Theory Forecasts* racked up such an impressive record using, exclusively, the Dow Theory for market timing, tells you a lot about the power of the Theory.

In *The Stock Market Barometer,* Hamilton lays out very clearly the principles behind the Dow Theory:

- The market represents everything everybody knows, hopes, believes, and anticipates.
- The market consists of three trends—the daily, secondary, and primary trends—and it is the primary trend that truly matters to long-term investors.
- The movements of the Dow Industrial and Transportation Averages provide the keys for discerning future market direction.

But these pages hold much more than blueprint for the Dow Theory. Hamilton provides his thoughts on a range of topics, including market manipulation ("In a primary bull or bear market the actuating forces are above and beyond manipulation"), speculation ("When speculation is dead this country will be dead also"), even government regulation ("If there is one lesson which should have been burned in upon the public mind in the past decade, it is that when government interferes with private enterprise, even where that enterprise is directed to the development of a public utility, it can do incalculable harm and very little good"). What will strike you is how fresh many of these views are today despite having been written many decades ago.

I'm sure Hamilton chose carefully when using the term "barometer" in the book's title. Successfully predicting the weather using a barometer has its limitations. Likewise, Hamilton understood that any tool to predict market movements, including the Dow Theory, has its shortcomings. "Heaven forbid that I should attempt to found a school of economists prepared to die for the thesis that the world wabbles along on a theory of averages," Hamilton writes.

Yet, for all its warts, the Dow Theory has passed the most important test of all—the test of time. If you are a serious student of investing, you owe it to yourself to "go back to the future" and read this book.

CHARLES B. CARLSON
Market Commentary Editor,
Dow Theory Forecasts

PREFACE

A preface is too often an apology, or at best an explanation of what should be sufficiently clear. This book requires no apology, and if it fails to explain itself the fault is that of the author. But acknowledgment must be made most gratefully to Clarence W. Barron, president of Dow, Jones & Co., and to Joseph Cashman, manager of that great financial news service, for permission to use the indispensable Dow-Jones stock-price averages, and to my old comrade in Wall Street newspaper work, Charles F. Renken, compiler of those averages, for the charts here used in illustration.

W. P. H.

THE
STOCK MARKET BAROMETER

Chapter I

CYCLES AND STOCK MARKET RECORDS

AN English economist whose unaffected humanity always made him remarkably readable, the late William Stanley Jevons, propounded the theory of a connection between commercial panics and spots on the sun. He gave a series of dates from the beginning of the seventeenth century, showing an apparent coincidence between the two phenomena. It is entirely human and likable that he belittled a rather ugly commercial squeeze of two centuries ago because there were not then a justifying number of spots on the sun. Writing in the New York *Times* early in 1905, in comment on the Jevons theory, I said that while Wall Street in its heart believed in a cycle of panic and prosperity, it did not care if there were enough spots on the sun to make a straight flush. Youth is temerarious and irreverent. Perhaps it would have been more polite to say that the accidental periodic association proved nothing, like the exact coincidence of presidential elections with leap years.

Cycles and the Poets

Many teachers of economics, and many business men without pretension even to the more modest title

1

of student, have a profound and reasonable faith in a cycle in the affairs of men.   It does not need an understanding of the Einstein theory of relativity to see that the world cannot possibly progress in a straight line in its moral development.   The movement would be at least more likely to resemble the journey of our satellite around the sun, which, with all its planetary attendants, is moving toward the constellation of Vega.   Certainly the poets believe in the cycle theory. There is a wonderful passage in Byron's "Childe Harold" which, to do it justice, should be read from the preceding apostrophe to Metella's Tower.   This was Byron's cycle:

> "Here is the moral of all human tales,
> 'Tis but the same rehearsal of the past;
> First freedom and then glory; when that fails
> Wealth, vice, corruption, barbarism at last,
> And history, with all her volumes vast,
> Hath but one page."

There seems to be a cycle of panics and of times of prosperity.   Anyone with a working knowledge of modern history could recite our panic dates—1837, 1857, 1866 (Overend-Gurney panic in London), 1873, 1884, 1893, 1907, if he might well hesitate to add the deflation year of 1920.   Panics, at least, show a variable interval between them, from ten to fourteen years, with the intervals apparently tending to grow longer. In a subsequent chapter we shall analyze this cycle theory, to test its possible usefulness.

Periodicity

But the pragmatic basis for the theory, a working hypothesis if nothing more, lies in human nature itself. Prosperity will drive men to excess, and repentance for the consequence of those excesses will produce a corresponding depression. Following the dark hour of absolute panic, labor will be thankful for what it can get and will save slowly out of smaller wages, while capital will be content with small profits and quick returns. There will be a period of readjustment like that which saw the reorganization of most of the American railroads after the panic of 1893. Presently we wake up to find that our income is in excess of our expenditure, that money is cheap, that the spirit of adventure is in the air. We proceed from dull or quiet business times to real activity. This gradually develops into extended speculation, with high money rates, inflated wages and other familiar symptoms. After a period of years of good times the strain of the chain is on its weakest link. There is a collapse like that of 1907, a depression foreshadowed in the stock market and in the price of commodities, followed by extensive unemployment, often an actual increase in savings-bank deposits, but a complete absence of money available for adventure.

Need for a Barometer

Read over Byron's lines again and see if the parallel is not suggestive. What would discussion of business be worth if we could not bring at least a little of the poet's imagination into it? But unfortunately crises are brought about by too much imagination. What we need are soulless barometers, price indexes and averages to tell us where we are going and what we may expect. The best, because the most impartial, the most remorseless of these barometers, is the recorded average of prices in the stock exchange. With varying constituents and, in earlier years, with a smaller number of securities, but continuously these have been kept by the Dow-Jones news service for thirty years or more.

There is a method of reading them which has been fruitful of results, although the reading has on occasion displeased both the optimist and the pessimist. A barometer predicts bad weather, without a present cloud in the sky. It is useless to take an axe to it merely because a flood of rain will destroy the crop of cabbages in poor Mrs. Brown's backyard. It has been my lot to discuss these averages in print for many years past, on the tested theory of the late Charles H. Dow, the founder of *The Wall Street Journal.* It might not be becoming to say how constantly helpful the analysis of the price movement proved. But one who ventures on that discussion, who reads that barometer, learns to keep in mind the natural indignation against himself for the destruction of Mrs. Brown's cabbages.

Dow's Theory

Dow's theory is fundamentally simple. He showed that there are, simultaneously, three movements in progress in the stock market.   The major is the primary movement, like the bull market which set in with the re-election of McKinley in 1900 and culminated in September, 1902, checked but not stopped by the famous stock market panic consequent on the Northern Pacific corner in 1901; or the primary bear market which developed about October, 1919, culminating June-August, 1921.

It will be shown that this primary movement tends to run over a period of at least a year and is generally much longer.   Coincident with it, or in the course of it, is Dow's secondary movement, represented by sharp rallies in a primary bear market and sharp reactions in a primary bull market.   A striking example of the latter would be the break in stocks on May 9, 1901. In like secondary movements the industrial group (taken separately from the railroads) may recover much more sharply than the railroads, or the railroads may lead, and it need hardly be said that the twenty active railroad stocks and the twenty industrials, moving together, will not advance point for point with each other even in the primary movement.   In the long advance which preceded the bear market beginning October, 1919, the railroads worked lower and were comparatively inactive and neglected, obviously because at that time they were, through government ownership and guaranty, practically out of the speculative field and not exercising a normal influence on the speculative barometer.   Under the resumption of private ownership they will tend to regain much of their old significance.

The Theory's Implications

Concurrently with the primary and secondary movement of the market, and constant throughout, there obviously was, as Dow pointed out, the underlying fluctuation from day to day. It must here be said that the average is deceptive for speculation in individual stocks. What would have happened to a speculator who believed that a secondary reaction was due in May, 1901, as foreshadowed by the averages, if of all the stocks to sell short on that belief he had chosen Northern Pacific? Some traders did, and they were lucky if they covered at sixty-five points loss.

Dow's theory in practice develops many implications. One of the best tested of them is that the two averages corroborate each other, and that there is never a primary movement, rarely a secondary movement, where they do not agree. Scrutiny of the average figures will show that there are periods where the fluctuations for a number of weeks are within a narrow range; as, for instance, where the industrials do not sell below seventy or above seventy-four, and the railroads above seventy-seven or below seventy-three. This is technically called "making a line," and experience shows that it indicates a period either of distribution or of accumulation. When the two averages rise above the high point of the line, the indication is strongly bullish. It may mean a secondary rally in a bear market; it meant, in 1921, the inauguration of a primary bull movement, extending into 1922.

If, however, the two averages break through the

lower level, it is obvious that the market for stocks has reached what meteorologists would call "saturation point." Precipitation follows—a secondary bear movement in a bull market, or the inception of a primary downward movement like that which developed in October, 1919. After the closing of the Stock Exchange, in 1914, the number of industrials chosen for comparison was raised from twelve to twenty and it seemed as if the averages would be upset, especially as spectacular movements in stocks such as General Electric made the fluctuations in the industrials far more impressive than those in the railroads. But students of the averages have carried the twenty chosen stocks back and have found that the fluctuations of the twenty in the previous years, almost from day to day, coincided with the recorded fluctuations of the twelve stocks originally chosen.

Dow-Jones Averages the Standard

The Dow-Jones average is still standard, although it has been extensively imitated. There have been various ways of reading it; but nothing has stood the test which has been applied to Dow's theory. The weakness of every other method is that extraneous matters are taken in, from their tempting relevance. There have been unnecessary attempts to combine the volume of sales and to read the average with reference to commodity index numbers. But it must be obvious that the averages have already taken those things into account, just as the barometer considers everything which affects the weather. The price movement represents the aggregate knowledge of Wall Street and, above all, its aggregate knowledge of coming events.

Nobody in Wall Street knows everything. I have known what used to be called the "Standard Oil crowd," in the days of Henry H. Rogers, consistently wrong on the stock market for years together. It is one thing to have "inside information" and another thing to know how stocks will act upon it. The market represents everything everybody knows, hopes, believes, anticipates, with all that knowledge sifted down to what Senator Dolliver once called, in quoting a *Wall Street Journal* editorial in the United States Senate, the bloodless verdict of the market place.

Chapter II

WALL STREET OF THE MOVIES

WE shall prove, by strict analysis, the fidelity of the stock market barometer, tested over a long period of years. With the aid of Dow's theory of the price movement we shall examine the major swings upwards or downwards, extending from less than a year to three years or more; their secondary interruption in reactions or rallies, as the case may be; and the relatively unimportant but always present daily fluctuation. We shall see that all these movements are based upon the sum of Wall Street's knowledge of the business of the country; that they have no more to do with morality than the precession of the equinoxes, and that manipulation cannot materially deflect the barometer.

Movies and Melodrama

But, to judge from some of my correspondence, the case must not even be argued, because it is alleged that Wall Street does not come into court with clean hands. It has seemed, in the past, at least discouraging to point out how the dispassionate, the almost inhuman, movement of the market has nothing whatever to do with the occasional scandals which disfigure the record of every market for anything anywhere. But the proportion of people who only feel is, to those who think, overwhelming. The former are in such a

9

majority that concession must be made to them, although I still decline to apologize for the stock market. I should as soon think of apologizing for the meridian of Greenwich. To quote one of the best known of Grover Cleveland's useful platitudes, it is a condition and not a theory which confronts us.

In the popular imagination there is a fearful and wonderful picture of Wall Street—something we may call the Wall Street of the movies. What the English call the cinema is our modern substitute for the conventional melodrama of our grandfathers. Its characters are curiously the same. Its villains and vampires are not like anything in real life; but they behave as consistent villains or vampires ought to behave if they are to satisfy critics who never saw a specimen of either. Many years ago Jerome K. Jerome wrote a chapter on stage law. He showed that on the English stage the loss of a three-and-six-penny marriage certificate invalidated the marriage. In the event of death the property of the testator went to the person who could secure possession of the will. If the rich man died without a will the property went to the nearest villain. In those days lawyers looked like lawyers— on the stage. The detective looked like a gimlet-eyed sleuth, and a financier looked so like a financier that it positively seemed to hurt his face.

Financiers of Fiction

Our modern financier on the screen looks like that, especially in the "close-ups." But he is no new creation.

I remember reading a magazine story, a score of years ago, of a stock market coup by a great "manipulator," of the type of James R. Keene. The illustrations were well drawn and even thrilling. In one of them Keene, or his prototype, was depicted bending dramatically over a Consolidated Stock Exchange ticker! It is to be presumed that he was smashing the market with ten-share lots. Only a Keene could do it, and only a Keene of the movies at that. Doubtless the author of the story, Mr. Edwin Lefevre, who was dissipating his talents in hazy financial paragraphs for the New York *Globe* at that time, felt that he had been artistically frustrated. But perhaps he had himself to thank. Here is his own description of such a manipulator. It is in a short story published in 1901, called *The Break in Turpentine:*

"Now, manipulators of stocks are born, not made. The art is most difficult, for stocks should be manipulated in such wise that they will not look manipulated. Anybody can buy stocks or can sell them. But not every one can sell stocks and at the same time convey the impression that he is buying them, and that prices therefore must inevitably go much higher. It requires boldness and consummate judgment, knowledge of technical stock market conditions, infinite ingenuity and mental agility, absolute familiarity with human nature, a careful study of the curious psychological phenomena of gambling and long experience with the Wall Street public and with the wonderful imagination of the American people; to say nothing of knowing thoroughly the various brokers to be employed, their capabilities, limitations and personal temperaments; also, their price."

That is professedly fiction, and, incidentally, more true and respectable as art than the product of the melodrama or the screen. It lays no stress on the deeper knowledge of values and business conditions necessary to assure the existence of the kind of market which alone makes manipulation possible. Truth is stranger than fiction, and perhaps harder to write, although the remark is open to an obvious retort.

Silk Hats and Strained Faces

Not long ago there appeared a letter to a popular newspaper, notorious for what may be called the anti-Wall Street complex. It professed to give, in a series of gasps, the impressions of a Western stranger on visiting Wall Street. One of these "flashlights" was, "silk hats and strained faces." Let me be exact. I have seen a silk hat in Wall Street. It was when Mayor Seth Low opened the new Stock Exchange in 1901. My stenographer, bless her honest heart, said it was real stylish. But financiers of the movies tend to wear silk hats, just as the heroes in melodrama, even when reduced to penury and rags, wore patent-leather shoes. A screen financier without a silk hat would be like an egg without salt. We cannot otherwise infer, as we are required, that he is a bad egg.

"A Long Way Back for Soup"

Only a few years ago there was a severely localized scandal over a "corner" in a stock called Stutz Motor, for which no true market had been established. Nobody was hurt except a few speculators who chose to sell the thing short. They paid up without whining. But it formed an irresistible text for a popular attack upon Wall Street. One of the New York newspapers said that the incident was only in a piece with "the Metropolitan Traction corruptionists, the New Haven wreckers, the Rock Island wreckers, and" what it called, with a free rendering of history, "the life insurance corruptionists." This was in a newspaper professing to sell news. It did not tell its readers that the last of the Metropolitan Street Railway financing happened twenty years before. Even the foolish and indefensible capitalization of the surface lines of New York, unloaded on what was then called the Interborough Metropolitan Company, was fifteen years old. The life insurance investigation, which, incidentally, neither charged nor proved "corruption," went back sixteen years. Even the last essay in misjudged New Haven financing, a comparatively minor matter, occurred fully eleven years earlier; that of Rock Island, nineteen years before; while that favorite charge against Wall Street, the recapitalization of the Chicago & Alton, was carried through in 1899 and not a soul saw anything wrong with it until 1907. I suppose I write myself down a hopeless reactionist when I say that, with the fullest knowledge of the facts, I cannot see anything reprehensible in it now.

Widows and Orphans

Even an incident so spectacular as the Northern Pacific corner, with the purely stock market panic which it produced, cannot be pleaded as an example of a kind of manipulation which would disable our barometer. That particular panic occurred in the course of a primary bull market. It produced merely a severe secondary reaction, for the upward movement was resumed and did not culminate until sixteen months afterwards. That incident of 1901, however, is still alive and kicking, so far as the politicians who denounce Wall Street are concerned. It is remarkable that all the stock affected in these bygone incidents is alleged to have been held by widows and orphans. I wish somebody would marry that widow and adopt, or even spank, the orphan. After depriving their trustees of the commonest business sense they have no right to come around in this indelicate way and remind us of our crimes. There is a lucrative engagement waiting for them elsewhere—in the movies.

Dow's Theory True of any Stock Market

Let us be serious, and get back to our text. The law that governs the movement of the stock market, formulated here, would be equally true of the London Stock Exchange, the Paris Bourse or even the Berlin Boerse. But we may go further. The principles underlying that law would be true if those Stock Exchanges and ours were wiped out of existence. They would come into operation again, automatically and inevitably, with the re-establishment of a free market in securities in any great Capital. So far as I know, there has not been a record corresponding to the Dow-Jones averages kept by any of the London financial publications.   But the stock market there would have the same quality of forecast which the New York market has if similar data were available.

It would be possible to compile from the London Stock Exchange list two or more representative groups of stocks and show their primary, their secondary and their daily movements over the period of years covered by Wetenhall's list and the London Stock Exchange official list.   An average made up of the prices of the British railroads might well confirm our own.   There is in London a longer and more diversified list of industrial stocks to draw upon.   The averages of the South African mining stocks in the Kaffir market, properly compiled from the first Transvaal gold rush in 1889, would have an interest all their own.   They would show how gold mining tends to flourish when other industries are stagnant or even prostrated.   The comparison of that average with the movement of securities held for fixed income would be highly instructive to the economist.   It would demonstrate in the most vivid way the relation of the purchasing power of gold to bonds held for investment. It would prove conclusively the axiom that the price of securities held for fixed income is in inverse ratio to the cost of living, as we shall see for ourselves in a later chapter.

The Fact Without the Truth is False

It is difficult, and with many observers it has proved impossible, to regard Wall Street comprehendingly from the inside. Just as it will be shown that the market is bigger than the manipulator, bigger than all the financiers put together, so it is true that the stock market barometer is in a way bigger than the stock market itself. A modern writer, G. K. Chesterton, has said that the fact without the truth is sterile, that the fact without the truth is even false. It was not until Charles H. Dow propounded his theory of the price movement that any real attempt had been made to elicit and set forth the truth contained in the fact of the stock market. Can we make it possible for the man whose business brings him into the midst of that whirling machinery to understand the power which moves it, and even something of the way that power is generated? Apparently the only picture which has hitherto reached the popular retina is the distorted image which we have called the Wall Street of the movies.

Homage Vice Pays to Virtue

Why does the swindling oil-stock promoter circularize his victims from some reputable address in the financial district, and use all sorts of inducements to get his stock quoted in the financial columns of reputable metropolitan newspapers? Would he do that if the public he addresses, the investor and the speculator,—the investor in embryo,—really believed that Wall Street was the sink of iniquity which the country politician depicts? If that were truly the case the shady promoter would seek other quarters. But he uses the financial district because he knows that its credit and integrity are the best in the world. Hypocrisy is the tribute which vice pays to virtue. He would have no use for a Wall Street as rotten as himself. Indeed, if the financial district were one tithe as corrupt as the demagogues who abuse it there would be no problem for them to propound. The money center of the United States would fall to pieces of its own rottenness. All this is true, and yet if the exact contrary were the case the theory of the stock-market movement would still be valid.

Rhodes and Morgan

It will not be charged that the writer is like the dyer's hand, subdued to what he works in, if his illustrations have been chosen mainly from the financial district. There is a Wall Street engaged upon tasks so serious, so exacting, that it has neither time nor inclination to be crooked. If it is true, as we have seen, that nobody can know all the facts which at any one time influence the stock-market movement, it is true, as any of us can record from personal experience, that some have far more knowledge than others. The men who really know lift you out of this scuffle of petty criticism and recrimination. When they are rich men their wealth is incidental, the most obvious means to larger ends, but not an end in itself.

When I was following my profession in South Africa, a quarter of a century ago, I was thrown in contact with Cecil John Rhodes. He had definite ideas and large conceptions, far above the mere making of money. Money was necessary to the carrying out of his ideas, to the extension of white civilization from the Cape to Cairo, with a railroad as the outward and visible sign of something of even spiritual significance. In the respect of intuitive intelligence I have met only one man like him—the late J. Pierpont Morgan. It was impossible to follow the rapidity of their mental processes. There was something phenomenal about it, like the performances of mathematically gifted children who can give you the square root of a number in thousands with a few moments of mental calculation. Other well-known men—speaking perhaps from the point of view of a reporter—seemed to have mental processes much like our own. Most of the great captains of industry I have met, like James J. Hill and Edward H. Harriman, had a quality essential to a first-rate thinker. They could eliminate the irrelevant. They could grasp the fundamental fact in a page of verbiage. But Rhodes and Morgan could do more. They could reason to an often startling but sound conclusion before you could state the premises.

Not Indescribable

And these men were rich, almost fortuitously. They had great tasks to accomplish, and it was necessary that they should have the financial means which made achievement possible. In the past few years we have heard a great deal about "ideals," and found that most of them were half-digested opinions. But there is a

Wall Street with an ideal. There has usually been,
and I hope there always will be, the right man to take
the right objective view at the right moment. Not
long ago I heard a lecturer setting forth what he called
the "indescribable" beauties of the Grand Canyon of
the Colorado. In the space of an hour and a quarter
he proved conclusively that those beauties were indescribable, at least so far as he was concerned. But
Milton could have described them, or the Psalmist.
Perhaps any reasonably intelligent man could give you
an idea of that natural wonder if he set forth simply
the spiritual truth in the physical fact before him.

The Unchangeable

I feel I have said before, perhaps in editorials you
read to-day, and forget to-morrow, what I am saying
now. The problems of humanity do not change, because human nature is what it has been as far back
as human record tells. "Cycles" are as old as organ-
ized humanity. The changes we see are superficial,
especially where sincere and intelligent men so legislate
that they may the better live together in peace and
good will. The human heart is essential to all progress. Reform starts there, and not in the halls of
legislation.

The Bells of Trinity

Facing the western end of Wall Street, casting its
shadow from the setting sun upon the most criticized
and least understood section of a great nation, stands
the spire of Trinity. We have often heard its bells

ringing the old familiar Christmas hymns. The shep-
herds will be watching their flocks again, all seated
on the ground. It may well be that, hearing those
bells, the glory of the Lord shall in some manner shine
round about us. There is little that laws can do to
make men happier or richer or more contented. There
is no form of government to-day, without its parallel,
and warning, in the past. There is none in the past
of which it could not be said that only righteousness
exalteth a nation. Wall Street knows as well as the
most disinterested of its critics that goodness and justice and sacrifice and love are the foundation of all
good government, because in that spirit alone a people
truly governs itself.

We have said that the laws we are studying are
fundamental, axiomatic, self-evident. And in this
higher truth surely there is something permanent which
would remain if the letter of the Constitution of the
United States had become an interesting study for the
archeologist, and the surviving writings of our day
were classical in a sense their authors never dreamed.
Such a foundation is permanent because truth has in it
the element of the divine.

Chapter III

CHARLES H. DOW, AND HIS THEORY

TO judge from a large number of letters received from readers of past discussions on Dow's theory of the averages, and on panic and prosperity cycles generally, that theory is assumed to be something in the nature of a sure way to make money in Wall Street. It may be said at once that it bears no resemblance to any "martingale" or system of beating the bank. Some of the questions show more intelligence and understanding than this, and one of them at least deserves an extended reply.

A Newspaper Man, and More

"Who was Dow, and where can I read his theory?" Charles H. Dow was the founder of the *Dow-Jones* financial news service in New York, and founder and first editor of *The Wall Street Journal*. He died in December, 1902, in his fifty-second year. He was an experienced newspaper reporter, with an early training under Samuel Bowles, the great editor of the Springfield *Republican*. Dow was a New Englander, intelligent, self-repressed, ultra-conservative; and he knew his business. He was almost judicially cold in the consideration of any subject, whatever the fervor of discussion. It would be less than just to say that never saw him angry; I never saw him even excited.

His perfect integrity and good sense commanded the confidence of every man in Wall Street, at a time when there were few efficient newspaper men covering the financial section, and of these still fewer with any deep knowledge of finance.

Dow also had the advantage of some years experience on the floor of the Stock Exchange. It came about in a rather curious way. The late Robert Goodbody, an Irishman, a Quaker and an honor to Wall Street, came over from Dublin to America. As the New York Stock Exchange requires that every member shall be an American citizen, Charles H. Dow became his partner. During the time necessary for Robert Goodbody to naturalize, Dow held a seat in the Stock Exchange and executed orders on the floor. When Goodbody became an American citizen Dow withdrew from the Exchange and returned to his more congenial newspaper work.

Dow's Caution, and His Theory

Knowing and liking Dow, with whom I worked in the last years of his life, I was often, with many of his friends, exasperated by his overconservatism. It showed itself particularly in his editorials in *The Wall Street Journal*, to which it is now necessary to allude because they are the only written record of Dow's theory of the price movement. He would write a strong, readable and convincing editorial, on a public question affecting finance and business, and in the last paragraph would add safeguards and saving clauses which not merely took the sting out of it but took the "wallop" out of it. In the language of the prize ring, he pulled his punches.

He was almost too cautious to come out with a flat, dogmatic statement of his theory, however sound it was and however close and clear his reasoning might be. He wrote, mostly in 1901 and the first half of 1902, a number of editorials dealing with methods of stock speculation. His theory must be disinterred from those editorials, where it is illustrative and incidental and never the main subject of discussion. It is curious also that in one of his earliest statements of the price movement he makes an indefensible claim. Under the caption "Swings Within Swings," in the Review and Outlook of *The Wall Street Journal* of January 4, 1902, he says:

"Nothing is more certain than that the market has three well defined movements which fit into each other. The first is the daily variation due to local causes and the balance of buying or selling at that particular time. The secondary movement covers a period ranging from ten days to sixty days, averaging probably between thirty and forty days. The third swing is the great move covering from four to six years."

Where Dow Went Wrong

Remember that Dow wrote this twenty years ago, and that he had not the records for analysis of the stock market movement which are now available. The extent of the primary movement, as given in this quotation, is proved to be far too long by subsequent experience; and a careful examination has shown me that the major swing before Dow wrote was never "from four to six years," rarely three years and oftener less than two.

But Dow always had a reason for what he said, and his intellectual honesty assures those who knew him that it was at least an arguable reason. It was based upon his profound belief in the recurrence of financial crises, at periodic intervals (as shown by recorded financial history), of a little more than ten years. Dow assumed for that period one primary bull market and one primary bear market, and therefore split the ten-year period in half. It was rather like the little boy who, being asked to name ten arctic animals, submitted "five seals and five polar bears!"

Panic Dates of Jevons

In the opening chapter we spoke of historic panics, of Professor Stanley Jevons, and of his theory connecting such crises with the recurrence of spots on the sun and their assumed influence upon the weather and crops. I said that the reasoning was about as good as associating presidential elections with leap years. But here are the dates of commercial crises in England as recorded by Jevons, and it is fair to say that they are sufficiently impressive. These years are 1701, 1711, 1712, 1731–32, 1742, 1752, 1763, 1772–3, 1783, 1793, 1804–5, 1815, 1825, 1836, 1847, 1857, 1866, and 1873.

As Dow says in an editorial quoting these dates, published in *The Wall Street Journal* on July 9, 1902:

"This makes a very good showing for the ten-year theory and is supported, to a considerable extent, by what has occurred in this country during the past century."

Dow's account of the successive crises in this country (he had personal experience of three of them—1873, 1884 and 1893) was so good and interesting that it is well worth quoting here. So far as Jevons's dates are concerned, it is curious to note that he omitted one serious crisis near the beginning of his list. That occurred in 1715, and was precipitated by the Scottish invasion of England in that year to restore the Stuarts to the English throne. It is rather human of Jevons to omit it, if, as I suspect, there were not enough spots on the sun in that year to fit the parallel.

Dow on Our Own Crises

Here is Dow's account of our own crises:

"The first crisis in the United States during the nineteenth century came in 1814, and was precipitated by the capture of Washington by the British on the 24th of August in that year. The Philadelphia and New York banks suspended payments, and for a time the crisis was acute. The difficulties leading up to this period were the great falling off in foreign trade caused by the embargo and non-intercourse acts of 1808, the excess of public expenditures over public receipts, and the creation of a large number of state banks taking the place of the old United States Bank. Many of these state banks lacked capital and issued currency without sufficient security.

1819, 1825, and 1837

"There was a near approach to a crisis in 1819 as the result of a tremendous contraction of bank circulation. The previous increase of bank issues had prompted speculation, the contraction caused a serious fall in the prices of commodities and real estate. This, however, was purely a money panic as far as its causes were concerned.

"The European crisis in 1825 caused a diminished demand for American products and led to lower prices and some money stringency in 1826. The situation, however, did not become very serious and was more in the nature of an interruption to progress than a reversal of conditions.

"The year 1837 brought a great commercial panic, for which there was abundant cause. There had been rapid industrial and commercial growth, with a multitude of enterprises established ahead of the time. Crops were deficient, and breadstuffs were imported. The refusal of the government to extend the charter of the United States Bank had caused a radical change in the banking business of the country, while the withdrawal of public deposits and their lodgment with state banks had given the foundation for abnormal speculation.

1847, 1857, and 1866

"The panic in Europe in 1847 exerted but little influence in this country, although there was a serious loss in specie, and the Mexican war had some effect in checking enterprises. These effects, however, were neutralized somewhat by large exports of breadstuffs and later by the discovery of gold in 1848–9.

"There was a panic of the first magnitude in 1857, following the failure of the Ohio Life Insurance and Trust Company in August. This panic came unexpectedly, although prices had been falling for some months. There had been very large railroad building, and the proportion of specie held by banks was very small in proportion to their loans and deposits. One of the features of this period was the great number of failures. The banks generally suspended payments in October.

"The London panic in 1866, precipitated by the failure of Overend, Gurney & Co., was followed by heavy fall in prices in the Stock Exchange here. In April there had been a corner in Michigan Southern and rampant speculation generally, from which the relapse was rather more than normal.

1873, 1884, and 1893

"The panic of September, 1873, was a commercial as well as a Stock Exchange panic. It was the outcome of an enormous conversion of floating into fixed capital. Business had been expanded on an enormous scale, and the supply of money became insufficient for the demands made upon it. Credit collapsed, and the depression was extremely serious.

"The year 1884 brought a Stock Exchange smash but not a commercial crisis. The failure of the Marine Bank, Metropolitan Bank and Grant & Ward in May was accompanied by a large fall in prices and a general check which was felt throughout the year. The Trunk Line war, which had lasted for several years, was one of the factors in this period.

"The panic of 1893 was the outcome of a number of causes—uncertainty in regard to the currency situation, the withdrawal of foreign investments and the fear of radical tariff legislation. The anxiety in regard to the maintenance of the gold standard was undoubtedly the chief factor, as it bore upon many others."

A Weak Prediction

With a caution in prediction which is not merely New England but almost Scottish, Dow, in a typical final paragraph, goes on to say:

"Judging by the past and by the developments of the last six years, it is not unreasonable to suppose that we may get at least a Stock Exchange flurry in the next few years."

So far from being unreasonable, it was not even a daring guess. It was more than a "flurry" in 1907, five years after, when the New York banks resorted to clearing-house certificates and the stock market grazed a panic by a bare five minutes. But the prediction was made during a primary upward swing which culminated in September of the year 1902, three months before Dow died.

Events soon disproved Dow's five-year primary swings, arrived at by splitting the assumed ten-year cycle in half. There was a primary bear market from September, 1902, lasting nearly a year. A primary bull market originated in September, 1903, becoming definitely marked by June, 1904, and culminating in January, 1907—a period of three years and four months; while the primary bear market which followed it and covered the period of the crisis of 1907 lasted until the following December—a period of eleven months.

Nelson's Book on Speculation

All that Dow ever printed is in *The Wall Street Journal,* and only by search through the precious files of Wall Street's Bible can his theory of the stock market price movement be reconstructed. But at the end of 1902 the late S. A. Nelson wrote and published an unpretentious book called *The A B C of Stock Speculation.* It is long out of print, but may occasionally be picked up from the second-hand booksellers. He tried to persuade Dow to write the book, and, failing that, he incorporated in it all that he could find of what Dow had said on stock speculation in *The Wall Street Journal.* Of the thirty-five chapters in the book, fifteen (Chapters V to XIX inclusive) are editorials, some slightly abridged, from *The Wall Street*

Journal, covering such subjects as 'Scientific Speculation," "Methods of Reading the Market," "Methods
of Trading" and market swings generally—all of them
interesting but not suitable for entire reproduction
here, although they will be sufficiently quoted in subsequent chapters.

Nelson's is a conscientious and sensible little book.
He was a conscientious and sensible little man—one
we loved and laughed at, for young reporters could
not take him as seriously as he took himself. His
autographed copy lies before me as I write, and I can
see his pathetic figure and earnest, strained face—he
was dying of tuberculosis—as I read his rather conventional discussions on the morality of speculation.
He died not long after, far away from his beloved
Wall Street, but it was he who evolved the name of
"Dow's Theory." It was an honorable ascription, to
which Dow is fully entitled; for if many people had
recognized meaning in traceable movements in the
stock market—the great and useful barometer of
trade—it was Dow who first formulated those ideas
in a practical way.

Chapter IV

DOW'S THEORY, APPLIED TO SPECULATION

WE have seen in past discussions of Dow's theory of the stock-market price movement that the essence of it could be summed up in three sentences. In an editorial published December 19, 1900, he says, in *The Wall Street Journal*:

"The market is always to be considered as having three movements, all going on at the same time. The first is the narrow movement from day to day. The second is the short swing, running from two weeks to a month or more; the third is the main movement, covering at least four years in its duration."

It has already been shown that his third and main movement may complete itself in much less than Dow's assumed four years, and also how an attempt to divide the ten-year period of the panic cycle theory into a bear and bull market of approximately five years each led to an unconscious exaggeration. That, however, is immaterial. Dow had successfully formulated a theory of the market movements of the highest value, and had synchronized those movements so that those who came after him could construct a business barometer.

The Truth Beneath Speculation

This is the essence of Dow's theory, and it need hardly be said that he did not see, or live to see, all

that it implied. He never wrote a single editorial on
the theory alone, but returns to it to illustrate his discussions on stock-market speculation, and the underlying facts and truths responsible not only for speculation (using the word in its best and most useful
sense) but for the market itself.

It is not surprising that *The Wall Street Journal*
received many inquiries as to the assumptions it made
on the basis of Dow's major premise. On January 4,
1902, Dow replies to a pertinent question, and any
thoughtful reader of these pages should be able to
answer it himself. The correspondent asks him, "For
some time you have been writing rather bullish on the
immediate market, yet a little bearish in a larger
sense. How do you make this consistent?" Dow's
reply was, of course, that he was bullish after the
secondary swing but that he did not think, in view of
stock values from earnings of record, that a bull market which had then been operative sixteen months
could run much further. It was a curious contraction,
incidentally, of his own minimum four-year estimate,
but that major upward swing as a matter of fact ran
until the following September. It may be said that
such a swing always outruns values. In its final stage
it is discounting possibilities only.

A Useful Definition

In the same editorial Dow goes on to give a useful
definition from which legitimate inferences may drawn.
He says:

"It is a bull period as long as the average of one high point exceeds that of previous high points.   It is a bear period when the low point becomes lower than the previous low points.   It is often difficult to judge whether the end of an advance has come because the movement of prices is that which would occur if the main tendency had changed.   Yet, it may only be an unusually pronounced secondary movement."

This passage contains, by implication, both the idea of "double tops" and "double bottoms" (which I frankly confess I have not found essential or greatly useful) and the idea of a "line," as shown in the narrow fluctuation of the averages over a recognized period, necessarily one either of accumulation or distribution.   This has been found to be of the greatest service in showing the further persistence of the main movement, or the possible termination of the secondary movement, so apt to be mistaken for the initiation of a new major trend.   I shall, in a later chapter, analyze such a "line," made in the stock market in 1914.

Successful Forecast

In subsequent discussions there will be no difficulty in showing, from the various studies in the price movement since 1902, standing for record in the columns of *The Wall Street Journal,* that the method for a forecast of the main market movement and for a correct discrimination between that and the secondary movement had been provided in Dow's theory, and that it has been used with surprising accuracy.   A prophet, especially in Wall Street, takes his life in his hands.   If his predictions are always of the ros whatever the facts of the situation may be, he will at worst be merely called a fool for his pains. The charge against him will be far more serious if he sees that a boom nas overrun itself, and says so. If he is bearish and right he will be accused of unworthy motives. He will even be held contributory to the decline which he foresaw, although his motives may have been of the highest and he may have not a penny of interest in the market either way.

"Recalling" a Prophet

Is the American public so ungrateful to its Micaiahs and Cassandras as this? Yes, indeed, and more so. It does not like unpleasant truths. In 1912, when Colonel C. McD. Townsend of the United States Engineers, an army man with a brilliant record then and since, was president of the Mississippi River Commission, he predicted, from the height of the water in the upper rivers, one of the greatest Mississippi floods. He warned the city of New Orleans that the flood might be expected in a month's time, recommending the most vigorous and immediate steps to lessen the calamity. Was New Orleans grateful? Its citizens held an indignation meeting to demand from President Taft the recall of this "calamity howler" and "dangerous alarmist." Mr. Taft characteristically kept his head, and Colonel Townsend was not removed. A good deal of property in the Mississippi Valley was "removed," and it is needless to record that New Orleans did not escape. The railroads and great industrial concerns, where they were likely to be affected, took the warning seriously, with advantage to themselves. The mayor of New Orleans subsequently rescinded the resolution, with an apology. Anyone who knows one of the ablest and least advertised engineers in the United States Army will readily understand that Townsend regarded the mayor and the previous mass meeting with equal indifference.

Synchronizing the Price Movement

It has been said before that Dow's theory is in no sense to be regarded as a gambler's system for beating the game. Any trader would disregard it at his peril, but Dow himself never considered it in that light, as I can testify from many discussions with him. I was writing the stock market paragraphs of the Dow-Jones news service and *The Wall Street Journal* in those days, and it was, of course, essential that I should thoroughly understand so scientific a method of synchronizing the market movement. Many men in Wall Street knew Dow and set their experience at his service. His mind was cautious to a fault, but logical and intellectually honest. I did not always agree with him and he was oftener right than I. When he was wrong it was clearly from lack of accurate data such as is now available.

Necessary Knowledge

It would perhaps be well to point out here that a knowledge of the major movement of the market, whether up or down, is necessary for the successful flotation of any largely capitalized enterprise. In a future discussion it will be convenient and highly interesting to illustrate, from James R. Keene's own admissions, how he distributed Amalgamated Copper to an oversanguine public at a time when the *Boston News Bureau,* to its everlasting honor, was warning New England investors to have nothing to do with that property at anything like the prices asked, or allow themselves to be deceived by the quarterly dividend of 1½ per cent and a half per cent extra. That rate was retained at a time when *The Wall Street Journal* was openly calling the company a "blind pool," and showing, as the *Boston News Bureau* had shown, that neither the conditions of the copper trade nor the capitalization itself justified the flotation price. But Keene could never have distributed the stock except during the known major swing of a great bull market. He had exactly the same condition to help him in the much more formidable, and creditable, task of distributing the enormous capitalization of the United States Steel Corporation. That stock could never have been sold, and its sale would never have been attempted, in the subsequent bear market of 1903.

An Instructive Editorial

It would be unfair to Dow if the reader were not given the opportunity of extracting for himself some light on Dow's own application of his theory, or at any rate some idea of his method in the series of editorials which, as I have said before, dealt primarily with stock speculation as such and only incidentally with rules for reading the market. Here is an editorial, almost in full, published on July 20, 1901, only ten weeks after the panic which resulted from the Northern Pacific corner. At the time he wrote he did not see clearly that it was not a culmination of a major swing but a peculiarly violent secondary reaction in a primary bull market. He speaks first of individual stocks:

"There is what is called the book method. Prices are set down, giving each change of one point as it occurs, forming thereby lines having a general horizontal direction but running into diagonals as the market moves up and down. There come times when a stock with a good degree of activity will stay within a narrow range of prices, say two points, until there has formed quite a long horizontal line of these figures. The formation of such a line sometimes suggests that stock has been accumulated or distributed, and this leads other people to buy or sell at the same time. Records of this kind kept for the last fifteen years seem to support the theory that the manipulation necessary to acquire stock is oftentimes detected in this way.

"Another method is what is called the theory of double tops. Records of trading show that in many cases when a stock reaches top it will have a moderate decline and then go back again to near the highest figures. If after such a move, the price again recedes, it is liable to decline some distance.

"Those, however, who attempt to trade on this theory alone find a good many exceptions and a good many times when signals are not given.

Trading on Averages

"There are those who trade on the theory of averages. It is true that in a considerable period of time the market has about as many days of advance as it has of decline.   If there come a series of days of advance, there will almost surely come the balancing days of decline.

"The trouble with this system is that the small swings are always part of the larger swings, and while the tendency of events equally liable to happen is always toward equality, it is also true that every combination possible is liable to occur, and there frequently come long swings, or, in the case of stock trading, an extraordinary number of days of advance or decline which fit properly into the theory when regarded on a long scale, but which are calculated to upset any operations based on the expectation of a series of short swings.

"A much more practicable theory is that founded on the law of action and reaction.   It seems to be a fact that a primary movement in the market will generally have a secondary movement in the opposite direction of at least three-eighths of the primary movement.   If a stock advances ten points, it is very likely to have a relapse of four points or more.   The law seems to hold good no matter how far the advance goes.   A rise of twenty points will not infrequently bring a decline of eight points or more.

"It is impossible to tell in advance the length of any primary movement, but the further it goes, the greater the reaction when it comes, hence the more certainty of being able to trade successfully on that reaction.

"A method employed by some operators of large experience is that of responses.   The theory involved is this: The market is always under more or less manipulation.   A large operator who is seeking to advance the market does not buy everything on the list, but puts up two or three leading stocks either by legitimate buying or by manipulation.   He then watches the effect on the other stocks.   If sentiment is bullish, and people are disposed to take hold, those who see this rise in two or three stocks immediately begin to buy other stocks and the market rises to a higher level.   This is the public response, and is an indication that the leading stocks will be given another lift and that the general market will follow.

"If, however, leading stocks are advanced and others do not follow, it is evidence that the public is not disposed to buy. As soon as this is clear the attempt to advance prices is generally discontinued. This method is employed more particularly by those who watch the tape. But it can be read at the close of the day in our record of transactions by seeing what stocks were put up within specified hours and whether the general market followed or not. The best way of reading the market is to read from the standpoint of values. The market is not like a balloon plunging hither and thither in the wind. As a whole, it represents a serious, well-considered effort on the part of far-sighted and well-informed men to adjust prices to such values as exist or which are expected to exist in the not too remote future. The thought with great operators is not whether a price can be advanced, but whether the value of property which they propose to buy will lead investors and speculators six months hence to take stock at figures from ten to twenty points above present prices.

"In reading the market, therefore, the main point is to discover what a stock can be expected to be worth three months hence and then to see whether manipulators or investors are advancing the price of that stock toward those figures. It is often possible to read movements in the market very clearly in this way. To know values is to comprehend the meaning of movements in the market."

There are assumptions here to which modifications might be offered, but there is no need. It would be impossible to show, except by the research of records covering at least half a century, that there are as many days of advance as of decline. The information would be valueless if obtained. It amounts to saying that heads and tails will equalize themselves if a coin is spun a sufficient number of times.

But what may be commended is Dow's clarity and

sterling good sense. What he had to say was worth saying and he stopped when he had said it—a rare virtue in editorial writing. His feeling for the essential fact and for the underlying truth, without which the fact is bare and impertinent, will be readily remarked. He dealt with speculation as a fact, and could still show forth its truth without profitless moralizing, or confusing it with gambling. It will be well to imitate his point of view in further discussion, both on his theory and on the immense and useful significance of the stock market generally.

Chapter V

MAJOR MARKET SWINGS

IT may be said, in continuing the discussion of what Charles H. Dow actually published in the columns of *The Wall Street Journal,* on his now well-known theory of the stock price movement as shown by the averages, and it must be emphasized, that he was consciously devising a scientific barometer for practical use. Remember the difference between the thermometer and a barometer. The thermometer records actual temperature at the moment, just as the stock ticker records actual prices. But it is essentially the business of a barometer to predict. In that lies its great value, and in that lies the value of Dow's Theory. The stock market is the barometer of the country's, and even of the world's, business, and the theory shows how to read it.

The Averages Sufficient in Themselves

It stands alone in this respect, for a sufficient reason. Wall Street has been called "the muddy source of the nation's prosperity," and we need not concern ourselves with question-begging adjectives. The sum and tendency of the transactions in the Stock Exchange represent the sum of all Wall Street's knowledge of the past, immediate and remote, applied to the discounting of the future. There is no need to add to the averages, as some statisticians do, elaborate compilations of commodity price index numbers, bank clearings, fluctuations in exchange, volume of domestic and foreign trade or anything else. Wall Street considers all these things. It properly regards them as experience of the past, if only of the immediate past, to be used for estimating the future. They are merely creating causes of the weather predicted.

It is a common superstition, exemplified in the Pujo Committee's inquiry into some supposed supercontrol of banking and finance, that "powerful interests" in Wall Street exist which have a sort of monopoly of knowledge and use it to their own nefarious ends. The stock market is bigger than all of them, and the financial interests of Wall Street are seldom combined except momentarily to stop a panic, as in the crisis of 1907. Taken separately, or even in temporary alliance, these interests are often wrong in their estimate of the stock market. In the days of H. H. Rogers and the supposedly all-powerful activities of what was called the Standard Oil group, I have known that group wrong on stocks for months and even years together. There was no shrewder judge of business conditions as affecting great enterprises than Henry H. Rogers, but I have heard him argue seriously that it was not he that was wrong but the stock market and the headstrong public.

Bigger Than any Manipulation

In the price movements, as Dow correctly saw, the sum of every scrap of knowledge available to Wall

Street is reflected as far ahead as the clearest vision in Wall Street can see. The market is not saying what the condition of business is to-day. It is saying what that condition will be months ahead. Even with manipulation, embracing not one but several leading stocks, the market is saying the same thing, and is bigger than the manipulation. The manipulator only foresees values which he expects and hopes, sometimes wrongly, the investing public will appreciate later. Manipulation for the advance is impossible in a primary bear market. Any great instances of designed manipulation—and they are few in number—occurred in a primary bull market, necessarily so because the market sees more than the manipulator. A personal experience of not only Wall Street but other great markets has taught that manipulation in a falling market is practically non-existent. The bear trader carries his own letter of marque, and fights for his own hand. A major bear swing has always been amply justified by future events, or for exception, as in 1917, by terrifying future possibilities.

Writing in a Bull Market

Starting feebly near the end of June, 1900, with a pitifully small volume of transactions, four months before the re-election of McKinley, a bull market developed which covered a period of more than twenty-six months. This was interrupted by the May panic of 1901, arising out of the Northern Pacific corner, proving to be only a secondary downward swing of a typical, if violent, kind. It was during the course of this bull market that Dow wrote the editorials in *The Wall Street Journal* to which reference has here been freely made because they contain the substance of his theory. He had designed a barometer for practical use, and it is characteristic of the man that he proceeded to apply it, to find out if it had the vital quality of dependable forecast. It is a pity that he could not have lived to test it in the twelve months' bear market which followed. All subsequent market swings, up or down, have proved the value of his method.

Throughout that bull market his forecasts were remarkably accurate, if necessarily general and not applied to particular stocks or small groups. He was correct in the essential matter of the adjustment of prices to values. His concluding editorials were published in July, 1902, not long before his death. In those he foresaw that prices were outrunning values, and that within a few months the market would begin to predict a contraction in railroad earnings, at least a slower development in the great industrial groups, and contraction of trade elsewhere.

Primary Movements

It will be well to give here the major swings from the time Dow wrote to the end of the bear market which culminated in 1921. They are as follows:

1. Up.   June, 1900, to Sept., 1902.
2. Down. Sept., 1902, to Sept., 1903.
3. Up.   Sept., 1903, to Jan., 1907.
4. Down. Jan., 1907, to Dec., 1907.

5.	Up.	Dec., 1907, to Aug., 1909.
6.	Down.	Aug., 1909, to July, 1910.
7.	Up.	July, 1910, to Oct., 1912.
8.	Down.	Oct., 1912, to Dec., 1914.
9.	Up.	Dec., 1914, to Oct., 1916.
10.	Down.	Oct., 1916, to Dec., 1917.
11.	Up.	Dec., 1917, to Oct.-Nov., 1919.
12.	Down.	Nov., 1919, to June-Aug., 1921.
13.	Up.	Aug., 1921, to Mar., 1923.
14.	Down.	Mar., 1923, to Oct., 1923.
15.	Up.	Oct., 1923, to

If the late J. Pierpont Morgan said that he was "a bull on the United States," this exhibit confirms his judgment. In that period of twenty-three years the bull markets lasted rather less than twice as long as the bear markets. The average duration of seven major bull swings is twenty-five months; while the average duration of seven major bear swings is fifteen months.

It will be noted from the table that the longest major swing upward was that from September 22, 1903, to January 5, 1907. The actual top of the averages was January 22, 1906, with a subsequent irregular decline of some months and a like irregular recovery, all within the year 1906, to a figure close to the old high point. This is therefore taken as the end of that primary movement, although the secondary swing of 1906 was by far the most extended of which we have any record. This exceptional year, of which the San Francisco earthquake was the feature, will be fully discussed in a subsequent chapter. The other five bull markets show periods of from something over nineteen months to a few days less than twenty-seven months.

Startling Predictions

The longest of the six bear markets here illustrated extended to nearly twenty-seven months, including the outbreak of the Great War and the hundred days' closing of the Stock Exchange, culminating immediately before Christmas, 1914. That was a black Christmas, as some of us may happen to remember; but it was followed, in 1915, by the tremendous boom in the production of material for the combatants in a war which America had not then entered—a boom which the stock market predicted with the greatest accuracy at a time when the business of the country was hardly beginning to grasp its significance.

Two of these six bear markets did not last quite a year, one of them less than a month more, and one of them less than fifteen months. There seems sufficient material here to say that a bear market is normally appreciably shorter than a bull market; perhaps as secondary downward swings in a primary rising average are short and sharp, with a halting recovery consuming a longer time than the decline.

The Market Is Always Right—

It will be shown at a later stage that throughout these great market movements it was possible from the stock market barometer to predict, some valuable distance ahead, the development of the business of the country. These discussions would fail in their purpose if they did not make the subject clear to the unfinancial layman—interesting to the man who never bought

a share of speculative stock in his life.   A barometer
is a necessity for all vessels at sea, from the smallest
coasting schooner to the *Aquitania*.   It means as much,
and even more, to the "Bolivar" of Kipling's ballad,
"swamping in the sea," watching, in dispair,

> "Some damned liner's lights go by, like a grand hotel"

as it does to the navigating officers on the liner's
bridge.   There is no business so small that it can afford
to disregard the stock market barometer.   Certainly
there is no business so large that it dare disregard it.
Indeed the most serious mistakes in the management
of great business have come from a failure of these
navigators of the great liners of the sea of commerce
to take heed when the passionless, disinterested stock
market called their attention to bad weather ahead.

—and Never Thanked

When, in the United States Senate, the late Senator
Dolliver, reading an editorial of *The Wall Street Journal,* said,   "Listen to the bloodless verdict of the
market place," he saw the merciless accuracy of that
verdict; because it is, and necessarily must be, based
upon all the evidence, even when given by unconscious
and unwilling witnesses.

No wonder the rural politician can so easily make
Wall Street the scapegoat for depressing conditions,
affecting his farmer constituents no more than the rest
of us.   Wall Street is guilty in their eyes, for they are
willing enough to hold Wall Street responsible for a

condition which it merely foresaw and predicted. It was said in a preceding chapter that the prophet of calamity will make himself hated in any case, and hated all the more if his predictions come true. But Wall Street's predictions do come true. Its predictions of prosperity, duly fulfilled as we have seen, are forgotten. Its predictions of adversity are remembered, and by none more than the man who ignored those predictions and is therefore the more bound to find somebody other than himself to blame.

Wall Street the Farmer's Friend

Wall Street is often called "provincial" by politicians and others actuated by an unreasoning sectional jealousy of the necessary financial center of the country. The country can have only one such center, although the framers of the Federal Reserve Act, overloading it with sectional politics, tried hard to make twelve. The farmers say, or their political spokesman says, "What does Wall Street know about farming?" Wall Street knows more than all the farmers put together ever knew, with all the farmers have forgotten. It can, moreover, refresh its memory instantly at any moment. It employs the ablest of the farmers, and its experts are better even than those of our admirable, and little appreciated, Department of Agriculture, whose publications Wall Street reads even if the farmer neglects them.

The stock market which began to break at the end of October and the beginning of November, 1919,

when the farmer was insanely pooling his wheat for
$3 a bushel and his cotton for forty cents a pound,
knew more than the farmer about cotton and wheat.
And that barometer was telling him then to get out,
to sell what he had at the market price and to save
himself while there was yet time. He blames Wall
Street and the Federal Reserve banking system and
everyone but his own deluded and prejudiced self.
He thinks he can change it all by getting his Congress-
man to take an axe to break the barometer. He is
trying to break the barometers of the grain trade in
Chicago and Minneapolis, the barometers of the cotton
trade in New Orleans and New York. Twenty years
ago, at the demand of her farmers, Germany broke
her grain barometer, with destructive legislation.
What was the consequence? She had to construct a
new barometer on the old plan, and it was the farmers
who paid for it in advance out of their own pockets.
The Germans have learned to let free markets alone,
a thing the British always knew, and built up the greatest empire, with the widest commerce the world ever
saw, on exactly that knowledge.

Chapter VI

A UNIQUE QUALITY OF FORECAST

THERE are two Wall Streets. One of them is the Wall Street of fact, slowly arriving at definition out of a chaos of misconception. The other is the Wall Street of fiction; the Wall Street of sensational newspapers, of popularity-hunting politicians; the Wall Street of false dramatic interpretation, whose characters are no more real than the types of the old-fashioned melodrama of fifty years ago—those caricatures which have had an astonishing and unintelligent revival on the moving-picture screen. It was felt that our second chapter might well be devoted to that popular misconception, Wall Street of the movies.

Major Movements Are Unmanipulated

One of the greatest of misconceptions, that which has militated most against the usefulness of the stock market barometer, is the belief that manipulation can falsify stock market movements otherwise authoritative and instructive. The writer claims no more authority than may come from twenty-six years of stark intimacy with Wall Street, preceded by practical acquaintance with the London Stock Exchange, the Paris Bourse and even that wildly speculative market in gold shares, "Between the Chains," in Johannesburg in 1895. But in all that experience, for what it

49

may be worth, it is impossible to recall a single instance of a major market movement which depended for its impetus, or even for its genesis, upon manipulation. These discussions have been made in vain if they have failed to show that all the primary bull markets and every primary bear market have been vindicated, in the course of their development and before their close, by the facts of general business, however much over-speculation or over-liquidation may have tended to excess, as they always do, in the last stage of the primary swing.

A Financial Impossibility

This is a sweeping statement, but I am convinced of its fundamental truth. When James R. Keene took up the task of marketing two hundred and twenty thousand shares of Amalgamated Copper, for the people who had brought about that amalgamation but had not been able to float the stock, it is estimated that in the course of distribution he must have traded in at least seven hundred thousand shares of that stock. He carried the price to above par to realize a net of ninety to ninety-six for his employers. This was a relatively small stock capitalization; but let us assume that some syndicate, larger than any that the stock market has ever seen, necessarily involving the co-operation of all the great banking institutions, under-took to manufacture the general bull market without which Keene's efforts would have been worse than wasted. Let us concede that this super-syndicate could afford to ignore the large number of active securities

outside of the forty active stocks taken in our railroad
and industrial averages and defy all trained public
opinion. Let us assume that they had accumulated for
the rise, against all their previous practice and conviction, without, by some miracle, arousing suspicion,
not two hundred and twenty thousand shares of stock,
but a hundred times that number.

Anybody who learned in the little red school house
that two and two make four must see that we are here
leading ourselves into an arithmetical impossibility.
This syndicate would presumably not be content with
less than a forty-point net profit, and its actual trades,
before it had established a broad general market even
equivalent to that Keene established for Amalgamated
Copper, alone would therefore amount to something
like one hundred and twenty million shares, which,
taking them at par, would involve financing to the
amount of many billions of dollars—so much financing,
in fact, that the great banks concerned would presumably relinquish all their other business and confine
themselves to the syndicate operations alone. Such a
syndicate could not have done this, or a tithe of this,
at any time during the existence of our national banking system. Does anybody think it would be possible
to undertake such a panic-breeding operation with the
assistance of the Federal Reserve system?

Where Manipulation Was Possible

To state the terms of a corresponding bear operation, where every wealthy member of the syndicate is

necessarily already a large holder in stocks, bonds, real estate and industrial production, would reduce the whole thing to the wildest absurdity. My mind refuses even to grasp it. Keene, in a broad bull market, to distribute a number of shares amounting to one-twenty-fifth of the common stock alone of the United States Steel Corporation, had behind him all the wealth and influence of the powerful Standard Oil group. When he distributed United States Steel common and preferred he had behind him not only the great Morgan banking influences but those of every group that came into that steel combination, with the general approval of a public which correctly recognized a wonderful and even unprecedented expansion in production and trade. But even with that backing could he have multiplied his efforts a hundredfold? The merchant, the banker, the manu-facturer who studies the stock market barometer with reference to the major swings, can dismiss from his mind altogether the idea that they are falsified by manipulation.

Roger W. Babson's Theory

But the idea is widely held. There is no intention here to arouse or encourage controversy, and if I take an example from Roger W. Babson and his book on *Business Barometers,* he will, I am sure, readily understand that it is not intended in criticism or depreciation of his highly sincere work. It is only fair to Mr. Babson to say, also, that the extract I give

here was published in 1909 (the italics are Mr.
Babson's):

"A slowly sagging market usually means that the ablest speculators expect in the near future a period of depression in
general business; and a slowly rising market usually means that
prosperous business conditions may be expected, *unless the decline
or rise is artificial and caused by manipulation.*   In fact, if it
were not for manipulation, merchants could almost rely on the
stock market alone as a barometer, and let these large market
operators stand the expense of collecting the data necessary for
determining fundamental conditions.   Unfortunately, however,
it is impossible by studying the stock market alone to distinguish
between artificial movements and natural movements; therefore,
although bankers and merchants may watch the stock market as
one of the barometers, yet they should give to it only a fair and
proportional amount of weight."
—*Business Barometers Used in the Accumulation of
Money,* by Roger W. Babson; second edition, 1910.

Mr. Babson's Chart

What sort of barometer should we have if we had
to make allowances for a tube of mercury that was
too short, or for a general lack of accuracy in the
delicate and sensitive mechanism of the aneroid?   The
stock market barometer is not perfect, or, to put it
more correctly, the adolescent science of reading it is
far from having attained perfection.   But it is not
imperfect in the sense Mr. Babson here assumes.   It
does discharge its function of prediction, when viewed
over any reasonable length of time, with almost
uncanny accuracy.   Let us take a few examples from
Mr. Babson's own picture chart, those composite
"plots" above and below a consistently rising line rep-

resenting the steady increase in a growing country's wealth, and we shall see how the stock market predicted each of them before Mr. Babson had the material to draw them in the squares of his instructive and striking chart. To those who are unfamiliar with a publication so interesting it may be said that he divides his chart with columns for each month of the year vertically, and completes his squares horizontally with numbered lines showing the area covered by all the factors of business, above or below a gradually rising middle line across the chart representing the growing wealth of the country.

How the Stock Market Predicted

It will be observed that where these areas are shallow they tend to become broader in time consumed, and where the time to complete the area is less the depression or expansion is deeper or higher, as the case may be, the black areas above or below being assumed to balance each other, at least approximately. One of these black areas of depression shown in the Babson chart began in 1903, only developing recognizable space in the latter part of that year, and continued throughout 1904, finally emerging above the line of growing wealth in the earlier part of 1905. The stock market anticipated this area of business depression, for a primary bear swing began in September, 1902, and ran until the corresponding month of 1903. Mr. Babson's area of depression was still ruling when the market became mildly bullish, in September, 1903, and strongly bullish before the following June; while the Babson area of depression was not completed till the end of that year—1904. The Babson chart does not show any great degree of expansion until 1906, although it foreshadows it in September, 1905. But the stock market barometer foresaw all Mr. Babson's expansion, and the long bull market continued up to January, 1907, overrunning itself—a tendency of bull markets and bear markets alike.

A True Barometer

Mr. Babson's area of expansion reached its high maximum in 1907, when a bear stock market swing had already set in, continuing for eleven months until early December of that year, predicting that length of time ahead of Mr. Babson's truly calculated area of depression, which was deep, but not long in duration, and lasted till the end of 1908. His subsequent expansion area above the line did not begin to show itself in market strength until the end of July of 1908; but the stock market barometer once again foretold the coming prosperity in a bull market which had its genesis in December, 1907, and its culmination in August, 1909, beginning from that time to predict with equal accuracy, and well in advance, Mr. Babson's next period of depression.

Surely this shows that the stock market is a barometer, and that the Babson chart is more strictly a record, from which, of course, people as intelligent as its industrious compilers can draw valuable guidance for the future.   To use a much-abused word, the stock market barometer is unique.   You will remember that "unique" is a word which takes no qualifying adjective.   Our barometer is not rather unique, or almost unique, or virtually unique.   There is just one of it, and it cannot be duplicated.   It does predict, as this simple illustration has shown, the condition of business many months ahead, and no other index, or combination of indices, can assume to do that.   Our highly scientific and competent Weather Bureau often explodes the fallacy of any assumed radical change in general weather conditions.   It does not pretend to go back to the glacial age.   It tells us that there have been droughts and hard winters before, coming at uncertain and incalculable intervals.   When it attempts specific prophecy—a single particular from its immense collection of generals—it is merely guessing.   Does anybody who happened to be in Washington at the time remember the "fair and warmer" weather prophesied over the Taft inauguration?   I went over the Pennsylvania Railroad on the following day, when the storm had leveled every telegraph pole between New York and Philadelphia.   It was even said that some of the special trains had so far missed the parade that they were not in Washington then.   Even the aneroid barometer can only forecast a limited number of hours ahead, according to the atmospheric pressure.

Cycles Overestimated

There are other compilations, and that of Harvard University will be noticed in a more appropriate place.

I am inclined to think that all attach too much force to the cycle theory, very much as we have seen that Charles H. Dow did in splitting the favored ten-year cycle into an assumed but non-existent five-year bear market and a similar five-year bull market. But Mr. Babson would tell you that his areas of expansion and even of inflation, extending not five years but two years or less than three in point of time, do not necessarily blow their tops off in a final explosion and that the bottom does not drop out of his period of depression. A stock market crisis may occur in the middle of a bull market, like the Northern Pacific panic of 1901; or a near-panic, with a development more serious and radical, may occur in the course of a major bear swing in the stock market, as in 1907. Mr. Babson correctly shows that the latter was followed by a business depression that had already been foreshadowed in the downward stock market movement.

If all panics and industrial crises arose from the same causes and could be predicted with the suggested rythmical certainty, they would never happen because they would always be foreseen. This sounds something like an Irish "bull," but it may well stand as a statement of the fact. Was it not an Irishman who said that an Irish bull differed from other bulls in the respect that it was always pregnant? I do not here go deeply into this question of cycles, because it is abundantly clear that the stock market is little moved by any such consideration.

Order Is Heaven's First Law

If Wall Street is the general reservoir for the collection of the country's tiny streams of liquid capital, it is the clearing house for all the tiny contributions to the sum of truth about the facts of business. It cannot be too often repeated that the stock market movement represents the deductions from the accumulation of that truth, including the facts on building and real estate, bank clearings, business failures, money conditions, foreign trade, gold movements, commodity prices, investment markets, crop conditions, railroad earnings, political factors and social conditions, but all of these with an almost limitless number of other things, each having its tiny trickle of stock market effect.

It will be seen from this how true the postulate made in an earlier discussion was when it was said that nobody in Wall Street knows all the facts, to say nothing of the meaning of all the facts. But the impartial, passionless market barometer records them as certainly as the column of mercury records the atmospheric pressure. There is nothing fortuitous about the stock market movement, and I think I have shown that it cannot to any profitable extent be perverted to the ends of deception. There must be laws governing these things, and it is our present purpose to see if we cannot formulate them usefully. Many years ago George W. Cable said: "What we call chance may be the operation of a law so vast that we only touch its orbit once or twice in a lifetime." There

is no need to lose ourselves in the mazes of predestina-
tion and foreordination, or reduce the Westminster
Confession to absurdity by saying that life is just one
damned thing after another.   But we shall all recognize that order is Heaven's first law, and that organ-
ized society, in the Stock Exchange or elsewhere, will
tend to obey that law even if the unaided individual
intelligence is not great enough to grasp it.

Chapter VII

MANIPULATION AND PROFESSIONAL TRADING

READERS of preceding chapters may well pause here to take count of how much we have been able to infer, and how much of our inference we have been able to prove, starting on the sound basis of Dow's theory of the stock market. We have satisfied ourselves that he was right when he said that there are in progress three definite movements in the market— the major swing, upwards or downwards; its occasional suspension by a secondary rally or reaction, as the case may be; and the incalculable, and for our purposes largely negligible, daily fluctuation. We can satisfy ourselves from examples that a period of trading within a narrow range—what we have called a "line"—gaining significance as the number of trading days increases, can only mean accumulation or distribution, and that the subsequent price movement shows whether the market has become bare of stocks or saturated with an oversupply.

True to Form

But we have been able to go further than this. From the preceding article alone we see that every major swing is justified by the subsequent condition of the country's general business. It has neither needed nor received manipulation. The market consequently has often seemed to run counter to business conditions, but only for the reason which represents its greatest usefulness. It is then fulfilling its true function of prediction. It is telling us not what business is to-day but what the future course of business will be. News known is news discounted. What everybody knows has ceased to be a market factor, except in the rare instance of a panic, when the stock market is confessedly taken by surprise.

When these articles appeared in serial form in *Barron's*, the national financial weekly, I included the following inference, based upon the reading of our barometer, on September 18, 1921, the date when the quoted paragraph was written. It appeared on November 5, 1921. It was no guess, but a scientific deduction from sound premises, and correctly announced the change in the main direction of the market.

"There is a pertinent instance and test in the action of the current market. I have been challenged to offer proof of the prediction value of the stock market barometer. With the demoralized condition of European finance, the disaster to the cotton crop, the uncertainties produced by deflation, the unprincipled opportunism of our lawmakers and tax-imposers, all the aftermath of war inflation—unemployment, uneconomic wages in coal mining and railroading—with all these things overhanging the business of the country at the present moment, the stock market has acted as if there were better things in sight. It has been saying that the bear market which set in at the end of October and the beginning of November, 1919, saw its low point on June 20, 1921, at 64.90 for the twenty industrials and 65.52 for the twenty railroad stocks."

A Contemporary Example

At the beginning of the last week of August, 1921, it looked as if the bear market might be resumed by the establishment of new low points in both averages. But remembering that the averages must confirm each other, *The Wall Street Journal* said, on August 25th:

"So far as the averages are concerned, they are far from encouraging to the bull, but they do not yet jointly indicate a definite resumption of the main bear movement."

The railroad stocks were forming a "line" at that time, and after a technical break of a fraction of a point through on the lower side it was resumed, and no new low point, indicating a definite resumption of the main bear movement, was given. On September 21st, after a remarkable continuance of the line of probable accumulation in the railroad stocks and a confirmatory rally in the industrials, *The Wall Street Journal's* "Study in the Price Movement" said:

"It is beside the point to say that we are facing a hard winter. The stock market is meaningless if it does not look beyond such contingencies. It seems to be forecasting a solid foundation for better general business in the spring. It may well be that the stage for a primary bull market is being set."

By that time both the industrials and the railroads had well-developed lines of presumed accumulation, and the former had significantly made a higher point than that of the previous rally. *The Wall Street Journal's* analysis of October 4th said:

"By the well-tried methods of reading the stock market averages, only a decline of eight points in the industrial average, and nine points in the railroads, or below the low figures of the main bear movement recorded June 20th, would indicate a resumption of that movement. On the other hand, the railroad stocks alone at present figures would need to advance less than a point to record the repeated new high for both averages which would indicate a primary bull market. The industrials have already recorded that point, and both averages have shown a remarkably clear and distinct line of accumulation which is likely at any time to disclose a market bereft of its floating supply of stocks."

In the last paragraph of this closely reasoned analysis it was said:

"Prices are low because all these bearish factors our critics adduce have been discounted in the prices. When the market is taken by surprise there is a panic, and history records how seldom it is taken by surprise. To-day all the bear factors are known, serious as they admittedly are. But the stock market is not trading on what is common knowledge to-day but upon the sum of expert knowledge applied to conditions as they can be foreseen many months ahead."

Henry H. Rogers and His Critics

Here is the application of our theory, and the reader can judge from the subsequent course of the market the value of the stock market barometer. He can even make the same analysis for himself, given the same major premise and carefully tested reasoning from it.

The professional speculator might well encourage the general belief that he is invulnerable and invincible, even if an ignorant public assumes that the cards are stacked against itself and that the professional knows their backs as well as their faces. Many years ago the late Henry H. Rogers, who was not talking for publication, said to me: "The sensational newspapers, which are always attacking John D. Rockefeller and his associates for their wealth, have put millions into the treasury of the Standard Oil Company. You and I know that we are not omniscient or all-powerful. But, by editorial innuendo and suggestion in cartoons, the people who hold us up to popular envy and hate have created exactly that impression. When everybody who may have to do business with us assumes in advance that we can dictate our own terms, we have an invaluable business asset." The same agitation brought about the dissolution of the Standard Oil into its thirty-three constituent companies. That operation trebled the value of Standard Oil shares, and, incidentally, the price of gasoline. Perhaps these newspaper proprietors were holders of the stock. That was before the era of the Ford car, however, and they may have assumed that it was a public service to make the rich owner of a motor car pay more for his gasoline.

A Speculator's Reasoning

Assumption of an unfair advantage for the professional is absolutely baseless. The reasoning of a professional like Jesse Livermore is merely the reasoning presented in this and preceding articles, backed by a study of general conditions. He said on October 3, 1921, that he had been buying, and, giving him the credence of ordinary courtesy for such a voluntary statement, it is clear that he was trying to shape in his own mind what the investing and speculating public would think at a date as far ahead as he could see.

This is not manipulation. These speculators are not creating any false market or deceptive appearance of activity to lure the public into the game, like the "barker" outside a Midway show. On October 3d Jesse Livermore was quoted in the columns of *Barron's* as saying that "all market movements are based on sound reasoning. Unless a man can anticipate future events his ability to speculate successfully is limited." And he went on to add: "Speculation is a business. It is neither guesswork nor a gamble. It is hard work and plenty of it."

Dow's Clear Definition

Let us compare this with the words of Charles H. Dow in *The Wall Street Journal* twenty years before. In the editorial of July 20, 1901, he said:

"The market is not like a balloon plunging hither and thither in the wind. As a whole, it represents a serious, well-considered effort on the part of farsighted and well-informed men to adjust prices to such values as exist or which are expected to exist in the not too remote future. The thought with great operators is not whether a price can be advanced, but whether the value of property which they propose to buy will lead investors and speculators six months hence to take stock at figures from ten to twenty points above present prices."

Observe how the none too deftly expressed thought of Livermore parallels the more perfectly shaped definition of the detached and dispassionate Dow. Ber-

nard M. Baruch, after the war, gave evidence before
a Congressional committee as to a market operation
by which he had largely profited. He showed in the
simplest manner that he had merely analyzed a known
cause and foreseen clearly its probable market effect.
He showed, what nobody who knows him would question, that he had no "inside information," so called,
and that no employee in a Washington department
had sold the secrets of his office. Wall Street holds
such secrets as of little value. They may give an unfair
advantage so far as individual stocks are concerned,
but they could be entirely neglected with imperceptible
loss, even if the secret were not generally as worthless
as the seller of it.

A Good Loser—

What is there that was done by James R. Keene or
Jay Gould, by Addison Cammack or other great market figure of the past, which could not have been done,
in the fairest way, by men of equal brains and intelligence, willing to pay the price of arduous study for
the knowledge necessary to success? What is there
that Jesse Livermore or Bernard M. Baruch do which
is open to criticism? They pay the seller his price, but
they do not accept stock sold "with a string to it."
The vendor thinks his reasons for selling as good as
theirs for buying what he sells. If he were a jobber in
the woolen trade, selling his investment in American
Woolen stock, or a banker selling United States Steel
common on the devastating foreign competition which
he thinks he foresees, he would consider his own

sources of information better than those of the speculators. They take the same risks that he does. They
are often wrong, but they do not whimper about it.
I have known many operators of this kind, and I never
heard them whine when they lost, or boast greatly
when they won.

—and a Bad One

But the little gambler who takes the gutter view of
Wall Street pits his wits against trained minds, not
merely those of the speculators and the professional
traders on the floor of the Stock Exchange, but the
minds of men whose business requires them to study
business conditions. This kind of gambler is a bad
loser, and is often highly articulate. He, or those
dependent upon him, is lucky if he receives such a
lesson at his first venture that he confines his future
relation with Wall Street to denouncing it as a gambling hell. It would be all that if the stock market were
made by him or people like him. To the everlasting
credit of the country, we may confidently assume that
it is not.

Refusing a Partnership With Jay Gould

Charles H. Dow, who knew Jay Gould well and
enjoyed his confidence as much as any newspaper man
of the time, largely because of his incorruptible inde-
pendence, says in one of his editorials that Gould
based his position in the stock market primarily on
values. He tested that market with purchases of
sufficient stock to show whether there was a public

response—whether he had correctly foreseen the public appreciation of values which he thought he had recognized. If the response was not what he expected he would not hesitate to take loss after loss of a point or so, in order to reconsider his position from a detached point of view. Some years ago there was a pathetic derelict in New Street, one of the unlovely fringe of any speculative market, who could truthfully say that he had once been offered a partnership by Jay Gould. I have missed his face in recent years, but not a great many years ago he was a promising young member of the Stock Exchange. His execution of orders on the floor was remarkably good. It is a difficult and exacting task. It requires about that combination of in-- stantaneous judgment and action which would mark a star player in big-league baseball.

To this broker a number of Jay Gould's orders were entrusted. No broker, it is needless to say, saw all of them. Gould was so pleased with the way his business was done that he sent for the young man and offered him a limited partnership. To Mr. Gould's surprise, it was refused. The broker actually said: "Mr. Gould, I have executed a great many of your orders and you seem to me to make more losses than profits. That is not a business I want to share." He could not see that his vision was restricted to only one side of Gould's many-sided activities. Opportunity knocked at his door—tried to kick it in—but the young man showed that he could do only one thing well. His administrative judgment would have been worthless, as indeed it afterwards proved, for he drifted out of the Stock Exchange into New Street and from there, I suppose, into oblivion. Truly, many are called but few are chosen.

An Intelligent Trader

Rare talent of any kind commands great rewards for the reason that it is rare. The amateur who regards the market as a gamble starts wrong. He holds on when he is losing and takes small profits, to his continuing regret, when the market is going his way. The speculators he envies, those he charges with cogging the dice and marking the cards, exactly reverse his process. However strong their conviction may be they run quickly when the market does not agree with them or justify the inferences they have drawn. They may be, as Gould often was, too far ahead of the market. One of the most intelligent men I ever met in Wall Street, not long dead, was a former teacher and a fine classical scholar, whose hobby was collecting rare coins but whose business was speculation. He saved no market turns or broker's commissions by partnership in a Stock Exchange house. He was just a speculator, sitting before a customers' board or near a stock ticker. And yet that man, by judgment, study, nerve tempered by caution and, above all, a readiness to see his error quickly, never made less than $30,000 a year; dying at a good age, leaving a comfortable fortune and a collection of rare coins which brought excellent prices.

He would select his stocks on analyzed value and study the market movement. He would buy with confidence but always well within his means. He would take a two-point loss on a thousand shares of stock without hesitation if the market did not move his way. When that discouragement happened he said that he could not form a correct judgment unless he got out and took an objective view. He had originally about the capital which would have been necessary to pay for the education of a doctor or a lawyer, or to start them in business. He gave his undivided but by no means selfish attention to what he had made his business. He was always long of stocks early in a bull market, and in its last stages he generally made a trip to Europe to add to his collection of coins. He was no solitary instance. I could name others like him. But I am not advising any man to speculate, even if he has the moral stamina to comply with the same exacting requirements. If you have a business that you like, one which keeps you comfortably with a margin for the unforeseen, why speculate in stocks? I don't.

The Dial of the Boiler

Some intelligent and many irrelevant questions have been put since these discussions began, and one of them, which has something of both qualities, disputes the economic necessity for the professional speculator. I am not to be drawn into a discussion of academic economics and still less into one of abstract ethical questions. I am describing the stock market barometer as it is and the great and useful service it performs. It is necessary, therefore, to explain its by no means complicated machinery. It is neither as simple as the crude three-foot tube with its column of mercury nor so complex as the highly perfected aneroid instrument. The question whether I would be willing myself to discharge the functions of a professional speculator is beside the point. We do not need to go back to the formal logic of the Greeks twenty-four centuries ago to know that there can be no argument on matters of taste.

Every bit as important as production is distribution, and distribution of capital is the greatest function of Wall Street. The professional speculator is no more superfluous than the pressure gauge of the steam-heating plant in your cellar. Wall Street is the great financial power house of the country, and it is indispensably necessary to know when the steam pressure is becoming more than the boilers can stand. It is important here to avoid getting our metaphors mixed, but the safety valve will occur to anybody. The stock market is all that and more; and the professional speculator, however ignoble or material his motives may be, is a useful and highly dependable part of that machinery. That he may grow rich in the process is neither here nor there, unless we are to adopt the bolshevist doctrine that personal wealth is wicked. There is another doctrine, held by many who would resent the epithet of bolshevism, which is in any country much more dangerous. It holds wealth, with the power it brings, as a thing for envy and not for emulation; that if we cannot legislate everybody rich it is demonstrably possible to legislate everybody poor. One short way to that end would be to eliminate the Stock Exchange altogether. But so long as it exists it is our business to understand it. Perhaps in so doing we may develop useful suggestions for improving the barometer and extending its usefulness.

Chapter VIII

MECHANICS OF THE MARKET

IT has been shown that, for all practical purposes, manipulation has, and can have, no real effect in the main or primary movement of the stock market, as reflected in the averages. In a primary bull or bear market the actuating forces are above and beyond manipulation. But in the other movements of Dow's theory, a secondary reaction in a bull market or the corresponding secondary rally in a bear market, or in the third movement (the daily fluctuation) which goes on all the time, there is room for manipulation, but only in individual stocks, or in small groups, with a well-recognized leading issue. A raid upon the oil group, or upon the bear account in it, with special attention to Mexican Petroleum, may easily have a striking temporary effect. It shakes out some weak holders or it forces a few bears to cover, as the case may be. This sort of professional "scalping" is often in evidence in a secondary swing—for good reasons.

The Trader and the Gambler

Every primary market, bull or bear, tends to over-run itself. As the traders say, there gets to be too much company on the bull side; or conversely, the "loan crowd" shows that too many shorts are borrowing stocks. There is even a premium for lending them,

73

corresponding to what is called a "backwardation" in London. This is the professional's chance. He buys in a market which is oversold or, with testing sales, he tries out the strength of a market which has been bought not wisely but too well. The small speculator, and more particularly the small gambler, suffers at the hands of the professional. He is a follower of "tips" and "hunches." He has made no real study of the things in which he trades. He takes his information without discrimination at second hand, lacking the ability to distinguish good from bad. He has no business in the market, in the first place, and it could get along very well without him. It is a great mistake to suppose that it is he, or people like him, who keep the Stock Exchange houses in business. Every one of these will tell you that their customers are becoming better informed all the time. Of course if ignorant people will sit in a game requiring expert knowledge, against others who understand the game perfectly, they can blame their losses on no one but themselves. They do, in fact, audibly blame Wall Street. A substantial part of the time of most brokers is consumed in protecting people from themselves. It is a thankless job. A fool and his money are soon parted.

Giving a Dog a Bad Name

But it must be obvious that this is no part of the main current of speculation. It bears about the same relation to that current that the daily fluctuation does to the primary market movement. There are, of course, varying degrees of knowledge, but it is a vital mistake to suppose that speculation in stocks (for the rise at least) is a sort of gamble in which no one can win unless there is an equivalent loss by somebody else. There need be no such loss in a bull market. The weak holders who are shaken out in the secondary reactions miss a part of their profits; and, in the culmination of such a movement, a great many people who have lost sight of values and are buying on possibilities only, with the latent hope that they may unload on somebody more covetous than themselves, are apt to get hurt.

So far as blaming Wall Street is concerned, it seems to have become a case of giving a dog a bad name and hanging him. The defaulting bank employee usually pleads something of the kind. All his transactions and contracts are matters of record; but how seldom the court asks him for an exact statement of his speculative account. He says nothing about fast women and slow horses, or the many other devious ways of spending other people's money. He pleads that he was "robbed in Wall Street," and sentimental people take him back to their hearts, registering horror at the temptations of the wicked financial district, whose simplest functions they have not been at the pains to understand.

A small and unsuccessful speculator, chagrined at his inability to make money in the stock market but failing to understand the real reason, picks up a vocabulary of technical phrases which is apt to delude people who know even less of the stock market than himself.

He is fond of denouncing the "specialist" and the "floor trader." He classes them with the croupiers of a gambling house, and says that they are not even as respectable as that because their dealer's chance is extortionately larger. To take the floor trader first, it may be pointed out that his small but real advantage only stands him in good stead against the novice who is trying to snatch quick profits in an active market by the merest guessing. No competent broker encourages the outsider to do anything of the kind, and the brokers of my fairly exhaustive acquaintance in Wall Street do their best to get rid of a customer who is apt to be a liability rather than an asset, and is always a nuisance.

The Floor Trader and the Market Turn

There is no intention here to write a textbook on the practice of Wall Street and the Stock Exchange. There are excellent books covering that field. All that is necessary is to make sufficiently clear the mechanics of our barometer, and especially those things which may be assumed, rightly or wrongly, to influence it. It is sufficient to say, therefore, that a "floor trader" is necessarily a member of the Stock Exchange, and is usually a partner in a brokerage house. He unaffectedly operates for himself. He pays himself no commission, and he is at an advantage over the outside speculator in the matter of the market turn, which is, of course, the difference between the bid and asked price in the market. The more active the stock the closer this turn is, but it may be averaged at a quarter of one per cent. Assuming that the price of United States steel common is 90¼ bid and 90½ asked, the customer who gives an order to sell cannot expect to get better than 90¼, while, if he wishes to buy, he must pay 90½. The floor trader can often save this turn or part of it for himself—not, of course, against a customer. He may be able to deal at 90⅜ or even to sell at the asked price. Whatever he does has its effect in the daily fluctuation. In practice it means that the floor trader can afford to trade for a quick turn where the outsider cannot. In daily custom the trader goes home at the close with his book even, not hesitating to take an occasional loss, or glad to come out even.

"Bucketing"

It is obvious then that the floor trader, snatching a turn of a point or so, has an advantage. If the customer tried to do it he would have the broker's commissions of a legal eighth per cent each way against him, with the market turn of a quarter per cent; so that, as a mere gamble, he would be betting heavy odds on an even-money chance. A "bucket shop" would encourage him to do that, because the keeper of such an establishment works on the theory of new customers all the time, fleecing them as thoroughly as possible while he has the chance. None of his orders is really executed in the stock market; so that he himself pockets this extortionate dealer's chance. But we are considering the Stock Exchange itself, and its speculative market as a trade barometer. Bucketing is no part of the Stock Exchange's business, and the police can stop it elsewhere—if they choose.

Old and Satisfied Customers

Commission both ways and the market turn do not amount to much if the customer is buying on values, with ample margin, or with the ability to pay for his stock outright, together with the tested belief that the stock he has bought bids fair to look attractive at much higher figures. He is the sort of customer the Stock Exchange houses strive to serve. A house which was in continuous business since 1870 has recently changed its name. It had at least one customer who had been on the books for fifty years, and many for twenty years and longer. This does not look as if the outsider always lost money in Wall Street, or as if the conditions of business made losses inevitable.

A brokerage house, like any other business, works to get new clients all the time, exactly as a paper or magazine works to get new subscribers. But the experienced broker will tell you that while advertising methods will bring the customers, nothing but disinterested service will keep them. I have often noticed that the really successful man in Wall Street is curiously inarticulate. Experience has taught him to keep his tongue between his teeth, and he is not at all communicative. The unsuccessful seem to be unable to keep their losses to themselves, in most cases, and it is usually found that they are thus articulate from a radical defect in character. They habitually do too much talking and too little thinking.

No Apology Offered or Required

This is not an apology for the stock market. Our old friend, our unwilling stepfather, George III, was not renowned for his wit. But when he was offered the dedication of Bishop Watson's celebrated *Apology for the Bible* he asked if the Bible needed an apology? Let us, therefore, content ourselves with merely explaining that part of the mechanism of the stock market which should be understood for a full comprehension of the nature and usefulness of the barometer of the country's business.

"Specialists" in particular stocks, corresponding in a way to the "jobber," or more nearly the "dealer" in the London Stock Exchange, the brokers on the floor who limit their transactions to one or two active issues and are entrusted with orders in those issues by other brokerage houses, are little understood and much vilified. It is falsely assumed that they habitually, or at least occasionally, abuse their confidential position. The specialist has "stop-loss" selling orders in a number of stocks at a point or so below the market price, from brokers instructed to limit their customers' losses in the event of an unexpected decline. It is suggested that the specialist, for his own advantage, brings about that decline. The answer is that even the suspicion of such dealing would cost him his business and his reputation. It recently cost a member his seat on the Exchange, the only instance I recall.

Transactions on the floor are by word of mouth, without the passage of a written contract or even the presence of witnesses. The honor of the parties is absolute, and I can hardly recall a case where it was called in question. There must necessarily be occasional misunderstandings, but these are referred for adjustment in the usual way. The specialist could not stay in business if he did not have the interests of the brokers who employ him as much at heart as any other agent in a like position. His very living and standing in business depend upon it.

Professional Trader's Limited Influence

What is the influence of the active bear trader on the averages? It is negligible so far as the major movement is concerned, a small factor in the secondary swings and mainly influential, at times, in particular stocks in the least considerable movement, the daily fluctuation. Such operations do not affect our barometer in any degree worth serious consideration. Remember the character of the twenty railroad stocks and the twenty industrials used in the two averages. Every one of them complies with the stringent listing requirements of the New York Stock Exchange. Each company concerned publishes the fullest possible figures of its operation, at frequent intervals. There are no "inside secrets," of market value, which could by any possibility affect more than a single stock out of forty.

It may be that one of them unexpectedly passes or increases its dividend. The effect upon that particular stock, if there is any real surprise in the matter (which is highly doubtful), is negligible when spread over the other nineteen stocks of the same group. I do not recall any useful illustrative instance; but suppose unexpected dividend action produced a fluctuation of ten points. It would only make a daily difference in the average of half a point, which would be almost instantly recovered if the dividend action presaged no broad general change in business conditions. If there had been any such change we may be entirely sure that it would have already been reflected in the stock market, which would know far more about it than that, or any board of directors.

Short Selling Necessary and Useful

A discussion on the morality of short selling would be utterly out of place here. It is true that the bear cannot profit except where another loses, while the bull at the worst reaps a profit which another man might perhaps have made if he had been attending strictly to his business. But every free market for anything is helped far more than hurt by traders willing to sell short. If, indeed, there were not this liberty the result would be a most dangerous market, liable to an unsupported panic break at any stage of its progress. Voltaire said that if there had not been a God it would have been necessary to invent one. It must have been long ago, in the days when what afterward became the London Stock Exchange did its business in Jordan's Coffee House off Cornhill, that bear selling was invented.

It soon became a patent necessity; and it is curious that some of the most serious breaks in the London market have occurred, not in the wildly speculative securities, but in bank stocks, where the English law prohibits short selling. It was unsupported pressure in some bank stocks which helped to make the Baring crisis of 1890 so serious. There is no such valuable support for a falling market as the uncovered bear account. When it is absent, as in this particular instance, nothing but a bankers' combination hastily improvised can check the devastating decline. As the London Stock Exchange was reorganized in 1922 on its old basis, without further government meddling and regulation, Parliament will repeal this law and substitute (as a protection to bank stocks, that complete and constant publicity which is always the public's best safeguard.

Protection of Listing Requirements

When Charles H. Dow wrote, twenty years ago, of speculation generally, and incidentally of his theory of the market movement, some of the industrial stocks, included in the average and traded in freely on the floor of the Stock Exchange, were in what was then called the unlisted department. It would be difficult to imagine *The Wall Street Journal* speaking to-day of one of the industrials in the Dow-Jones average as a blind pool. But it did not hesitate to apply that epithet, editorially, to the American Sugar of Henry O. Havemeyer's day. The elimination of the New

York Stock Exchange's unlisted department is one of the most creditable instances of reform from within. It was bitterly opposed by some conservative members of the Stock Exchange, mainly those who profited largely by that vicious vested interest. An ex-president of that institution, now dead, took upon himself to berate me loudly, in the presence of his customers, for advocating that eminently necessary reform. He said that such agitators were driving business away from the Wall Street in which they earned their living. He threw out of his office the newspaper and the financial news service with which I was and am connected.

But his own customers made him reinstate both, with humiliating celerity. American Sugar and Amalgamated Copper and the other formerly unlisted securities are still dealt in on the floor of the Exchange. Those companies saw that they laid their management under the gravest suspicion by a refusal to comply with the terms of publicity so wholesomely exacted from reputable companies. Stock Exchange houses are naturally inclined to look askance at reforms advocated from outside. But I have never heard one of them even suggest the restoration of the unlisted department.

Federal Incorporation

It was said in an earlier discussion that something further might be done for the protection of the public, without the enactment of any of these "blue-sky" laws which only embarrass honest enterprise without seriously impeding the operations of the crook. In this discussion I can briefly set forth the sane and successful method which protects the speculator and investor in Great Britain. Under what is there called the Companies (Consolidation) Act of 1908 the London Stock Exchange is enabled to deal in any security the moment it is registered at Somerset House, London. That registration cannot be made until the fullest possible disclosure of purposes, contracts, commissions and everything else has been made. However adventurous the purposes of the company may be, the speculator knows all about them from the start. After that, under this statute, the old common-law rule of *caveat emptor* —let the buyer beware—prevails. It is properly held that the buyer can protect himself, as he should, when he can find out all about the property, its origin and its present conduct, for the fee of a shilling, at Somerset House.

There would doubtless be all sorts of ignorant opposition to Federal incorporation of this kind, with the law enforced and the public protected through limitation in the use of the mails. But I am convinced that it might well be done, and should, of course, be done in a strictly non-partisan spirit. To the utmost of its ability the New York Stock Exchange protects its members and their customers. But the New York Curb Market Association is simply an unlisted department in itself. I have no reason to believe that its government is not capable and honest, and I have not a word to say against its membership. But sooner or later it is calculated to prove a source of danger and scandal. If any of its members imagine that they have something to lose, in the setting forth of the absolute and original facts about everything in which they deal, they are making exactly the same mistake that ill-advised members of the New York Stock Exchange made when they shirked the disagreeable task of compelling a number of industrial corporations to comply with the listing requirements, on pain of being stricken from the list.

Real Reform from Within

Let me disclaim, however, the intention of crusading, or any bent toward that blatant and ignorant "reform" which has made such costly experiments in recent years. In my experience of it the standards of the Stock Exchange have steadily improved, to the permanent advantage of the investor and of the small speculator, who is, after all, only an investor in embryo. Practices were customary in Dow's day which would not be tolerated now. In any future bull market manipulation on the scale of James R. Keene, when he distributed Amalgamated Copper, would be impracticable, for the reason that the publicity now required by the Stock Exchange, in the accounts of such a company, would make it impossible to persuade the most reckless private speculator that the prospects of the new combination made it worth four times its book value, on any expert test. Even in those days "wash sales" were largely a figment of the public imagination, and "matched orders" were declined by any brokerage house of repute if their nature was suspected. The Stock Exchange rule against fictitious transactions is obeyed in spirit and in word. It was not a mere letter even in those days, whatever it might have been forty years ago, when the infant giant of American industry was only awakening to consciousness of his strength.

Chapter IX

"WATER" IN THE BAROMETER

E VERY effort has been made to simplify these discussions. They have been offered with the most stringent exclusion of extraneous matter. In serial form they aroused much criticism and comment, some of it illuminating and helpful. But old preconceptions and prejudices still survive. One critic, whose scanty knowledge of the subject appears to have been derived from the reading of perhaps two of these articles, says:

"How can we trust your barometer if we cannot trust the stocks which the Stock Exchange deals in? You have said nothing about overcapitalization. What about water?"

Watered Labor

Water is more unpopular than ever in the United States just now. But the financial center of the United States, with the business of the country in view, is far more concerned about watered labor than watered capital. There is only one way to squeeze the water out of labor—the factory or apartment house which cost a million dollars to build and represents only $500,000 of real value. That way is by bankruptcy. Of the apartment houses that were built in New York, during a period of high wages and "ca' canny" which set in long before the war, very few have not passed through a stage of financial reorganization, due to watered labor in construction, long before rents began to advance. The stock market has a short and simple method of dealing with water in stocks. It exists for the purpose of squeezing that water out. The process does not involve a receivership.

The very word "water" begs the question. You may call the capitalization of an industrial flotation "water" because you do not see the potential values of a great creative organization. But with justice, and better knowledge, the late J. Pierpont Morgan might have called that capitalization intelligently anticipated growth. Whatever it may be—and I shall give an example from the most striking instance, the capitalization of the United States Steel Corporation —the stock market is forever adjusting prices to values. The water soon evaporates.

Squeezing Out the Water

To recapitulate, we are studying the stock market barometer, having established the fact of its known and orderly movements—the long primary swing, the secondary reaction or rally, and the daily fluctuation; and to do this we are taking the averages of two groups of stocks—twenty active industrials and twenty active railroads. All adjustments of the prices of these stocks individually must primarily be based upon values. For all practical purposes the Stock Exchange is an open market, and the business of such a market is to adjust conflicting estimates to a common basis, which is expressed in the price. By manipulation, James R. Keene advanced the price of Amalgamated Copper twenty years ago to one hundred and thirty, and obviously the group of financiers which offered the stock at par originally, without success, assumed one hundred as value for it. The stock market does not make its adjustments in a day. But, over a period which seems brief in retrospect, it knocked one hundred points off the highest figure Amalgamated Copper attained in a general bull market.

This is the business of the stock market. It has to consider both basic values and prospects. At the close of a major downward movement, a primary bear market, prices will have passed below the line of values. The causes of the liquidation will have been so serious that people have been compelled to realize their holdings at less than their normal worth; less, indeed, than their book value—the worth of the company's assets, that is, irrespective of productive capacity and good will. The prices of the standard stocks will be injuriously affected by the prices of "cats and dogs" dealt in on the Curb market, many of them of such a character that any bank would refuse them as collateral in its loans. When the banks are compelled to call loans made on Stock Exchange securities, the stocks of tested worth, of properties competently and reputably managed, will be the first to suffer because it is those stocks which are pledged in bank loans. The constantly recruited Curb group is highly speculative, but trading there is always limited, and indeed safeguarded, by the large margin which is necessary to carry Curb stocks.

Stock Profits and Income Tax

Conversely, a bull market starts with stocks much below their real value, certain to be helped in anticipation by the general improvement in the country's business which the stock market foresees and discounts. In the long advance values will be gradually overtaken, and toward the close of the advance an uninformed public, incapable of recognizing the bargains which were offering when the movement started, is buying on prospects only. Experienced traders in Wall Street say that when the elevator boy and the shoeblack are asking for bull tips on the market it is time to sell and go fishing. When I sailed for Europe early in October, 1919, to report on financial conditions in Britain and Germany, the market was in the last sanguine stage of a long bull movement. The inflation bull argument then was most curious. It was that the people who had large profits would not sell, and could not sell, because in turning those paper profits into cash they would show such a large earning of income for the year that the tax-gatherer would take a prohibitive share of the profits. We analyzed this fallacy in the smoking saloon of the *Mauretania,* and at least some of the business men on board concluded to divide up with Uncle Sam. The argument was preposterous in itself, because it pictured the most vulnerable kind of bull account that it would be possible to conceive. It was glaringly up to be shot at, and the poorest marks-

man could fill it full of holes. Rough seas stove in
five of the *Mauretania's* lifeboats, and put the wire-
less apparatus out of commission for the last three
days of that voyage. When we arrived at Cher-
bourg we learned that the stock market itself had
begun to free the bulls of stocks from the embar-
rassment of paying excessive income tax. They had
not much to worry about in that respect by the end
of the year, for the paper profits had been rapidly
extinguished.

Well-Distributed Holdings

There is no way of permanently holding up artificial
prices created by an overbought market. One great
protection to the public is in widely distributed stock
ownership. When a single group in Wall Street owns
practically all of the stock in a property like Stutz
Motor, that group can call the market price anything
it chooses. It will not be the "market" price because
there will be no real market. Abraham Lincoln pointed
out long ago that you could not talk five legs onto a
dog by renaming its tail. All the stocks in the average
have shared in the wide and healthy distribution of
securities. The average holding of Pennsylvania
(which has the greatest capitalization of any of the
railroads in our average) or of the five and a half
million shares of United States Steel common is nothing near one hundred shares for each holder. So far
as the public is concerned, there is, indeed, safety in
numbers.

"Valuation" and Market Prices

To the inquirer quoted at the beginning of this article, who asks, "What about water?" we may answer, well, what about it? He cannot show us any water in the averages. We may go further and tell him that he cannot show us any water, at prices and not at the nominal par, in the whole Stock Exchange list. For the railroads, no valuation which could be instituted by Congress and carried out by a committee of the Interstate Commerce Commission could begin to compare with the market prices of the securities themselves, taken in a normal month of a normal year, with the prices not inflated on overestimated prospects or deflated by forced liquidation, brought about largely to protect unsalable securities and warehouse receipts not associated with the railroads or the standard industrial companies in any way.

Every scrap of intelligence and knowledge available, uninfluenced in any real degree by manipulation, has been brought to bear in the adjustment of the stock market prices. Reproduction value, real estate value, franchises, right of way, good will—everything else— have been brought into the free-market estimate in a way which no valuation committee appointed by Congress could ever attain. The Interstate Commerce Commission's valuation of a railroad has merely historical worth—if it has any. As a true estimate of the property, if the method of fixing it were commonly just, it is out of date the moment it is printed, or, indeed, months before it is printed. But the Stock

Exchange price records the value from day to day, from month to month, from year to year, from bull market to bear market, from one of Jevons's cycle dates to another; and the bankers of America and any other civilized country accept that valuation and advance real money on it, without reference to the arbitrary estimate of the Interstate Commerce Commission.

The Fetish of Watered Stock

It is astonishing to what depths of foolishness the fetish of watered stock has carried this country. The capitalization in stocks and bonds of its railroads, alleged to represent water, is not one-fifth that of the railroads of the British Islands, mile for mile. It is less per mile than that of any European country or of any government or privately owned railroad in Britain's self-governing colonies. I am not afraid to go on record with the statement that the American railroads are uneconomically undercapitalized, on their real value. The charge of watered stock made against the listed industrial corporations is equally absurd. The stock market had far more than squeezed out the water in that capitalization at the Stock Exchange prices current in 1921. It had squeezed blood.

As this is written, United States Steel common is selling under $80 a share. But stringent analysis of an industrial corporation offering the most exhaustive figures of any like company in the world gives a book value to the common stock of $261 a share. In the twenty years of its history it has put upwards of a billion dollars into the property in new construction, and so little is this watered in the capital that this new investment out of earnings is represented in property account by only $275,000,000. The quick assets, largely cash, are over $600,000,000 alone, something like $120 a share with the whole concern scrapped. Where is the water? A common stock capital of $550,000,000 looks large, but it is only relatively large. Was not Morgan right if he called this intelligently anticipated growth? If his spirit could revisit the pale glimpses of the moon, surely he would be astonished at his own moderation.

And yet the distribution of the United States Steel common and preferred stocks, made in the major swing of a great bull market, was brought about largely by the most stupendous manipulation the market ever saw, under the direction of the late James R. Keene. And what was the end of that manipulation? It was to sell the common stock at fifty and the preferred stock at par. If the people who bought at those prices put the stock away after paying for it, would they have anything to regret even at the low market prices of August, 1921, attained after a major bear swing of unusually long duration?

Buying on Values

Probably some one will charge me with writing a bull argument about Steel common, because I set this simple illustration before the public. There again we have the inveterate prejudice against Wall Street.

The facts I have stated are of record, accessible to anybody, perfectly well known to some of the people at least who were selling Steel common in 1921. But they were selling the stock because they needed the money, at a time when most of us needed money. When the Rothschild of the days of Waterloo, a week before the result of that battle was known, was buying British consols at fifty-four, a friend asked him how he could buy with such confidence on an outlook so uncertain. He said that if the outlook were certain consols would not be selling at fifty-four. He knew that with that uncertainty they must necessarily be selling below their value. Everybody needed money at the same time, and he was one of the few people who had any. I suppose no one will ever know how Russell Sage did it, but he could lay his hands upon more real money in a panic than anybody in Wall Street. He believed in quick and liquid assets, short-time paper maturing all the time, call loans and deposits—everything which could be turned into cash, not to hoard but to buy freely when people who had lost sight of values were selling.

A Story of Russell Sage

All sorts of stories are told of Russell Sage and his extraordinary frugality. That is not exactly the word I would use; nor would I call it miserliness, for he was anything but a miser. I remember the last time I ever saw him, when I was a young reporter, or at least a younger reporter. I was trying to find out something about a railroad property in which he was

dominant with another financier of nation wide noto-
riety, or reputation. Lying is a word which is seldom
used (or needed) in Wall Street, and it would be better to say that the other financier had given me information calculated to let me deceive myself if I was
not exceptionally wide-awake. With the idea, therefore, of seeing if Mr. Sage's terminological inexacti-
tude would differ from his comrade's, with enough
significance to enable me to deduce something from
the points upon which the two fairy tales did not agree,
I went over to see Sage, who was always accessible to
the newspaper men.

He greeted me in the most friendly way, as indeed
he did anybody whose visit had nothing to do with
money. I put my question and he rapidly changed
the subject. He said: "Do you know anything about
suspenders?" I was exasperated, but I replied modestly that I did not know any more about them than
any other wearer. "What do you think of these?"
said Uncle Russell, handing me over a pair certainly
inferior to those worn by reporters, who are not, or
certainly were not at that time, given to undue extrav-
agance in such an article of attire. "What about
them?" I asked. "Well, what do you think of them?"
said Sage; "I gave thirty-five cents for those." Perhaps I was a little vindictive, having failed to secure
even the poor information I had come to seek. I
said: "You were robbed. You can get better in Hester
Street for a quarter." Sage looked at me doubtfully.
"I don't believe it," he said. But he was really trou-
bled. It was not the difference of ten cents, and I

would not have sworn to the Hester Street quotation. It was the principle of the thing. His judgment of values had been impugned.

Values and Averages

And there you have it. The things in which Russell Sage dealt had value. He had to know those values, and it was by knowing them when they had ceased to be apparent to other people that he died worth more than $70,000,000. The stock market barometer shows present and prospective values. It is necessary in reading it to judge whether a long movement has carried the average prices below that line or above it. In looking back over the various analyses of the stock market as a guide to general business, published in *The Wall Street Journal* since Charles H. Dow died, at the end of 1902, I find a typical instance of the application of the averages which may seem remarkable to the reader, although I regard it as the merest common sense. There is no one so unpopular as the man who is always telling you that he "told you so," but the illustration is impersonal.

A Cautious but Correct Forecast

No severer test could be taken than the interpretation of the averages in what might almost be called the transition period between a bear and a bull market. The bear market which developed from September, 1902, saw its low points in the September of the following year, and it is weeks or even months afterwards before the change in the major swing can be definitely asserted. But on December 5, 1903, *The Wall Street Journal,* after a review of the fundamentally sound tendency of business in then recent years, said:

"Considering the extraordinary advance in wealth of the United States during that period, considering that railroad mileage has not increased in anything like the ratio of increase in surplus earnings, and finally considering that the ratio of increase in surplus earnings available for dividends has been at all times in excess of the rise in market prices and at the present time shows a larger percentage on market price than at any time since the former boom started, the question may well be asked whether the decline in stocks has not culminated. There is at least some evidence in favor of an affirmative answer to that question."

A Bull Market Confirmed

It would be easy to say that such an opinion could have been given without the help of the averages, but it was given with the price movement clearly in view and at a time when there was an easy possibility that the main bear movement might be resumed. It correctly foresaw the bull market, allowing for the caution necessary in such a prediction and, indeed, for the fact that analysis of the market movement was still in its infancy. The bull market then foreseen ran throughout 1904, and can be said to have terminated only in January, 1907. But some nine months after this editorial analysis of the business situation, judged by the averages, was written, *The Wall Street Journal* tackled the almost equally difficult question of whether the bull market then getting into full swing might be expected to continue. Remember that the advance had been running with moderate but increasing strength for twelve months, which would allow for at least some discounting in values. On September 17, 1904, *The Wall Street Journal* said:

"There is apparently nothing in sight to lead one to believe that railroad values are not on the whole maintaining their high position, and that as time goes on this will bring a further appreciation of prices. Much will depend on the coming winter, which will at all events bring a clear indication of the general trend of values. In the long run values make prices. It is safe to say that if present values are maintained, present prices are not on an average high enough.

"It must further be remembered that the continued increase in the production of gold is a most powerful factor, which cannot fail to be felt in the future as making for higher prices of securities other than those of fixed yield."

A Vindication of the Theory

Note carefully that last line. We have satisfied ourselves that bonds held for fixed income decline when the cost of living rises, and more gold means that the gold dollar will buy less because gold is the world's accepted standard of value. But it stimulates speculation, and the stock market had seen this in 1904, when this was written, even if the houses with bonds to sell thought it rather "unclubby" to say anything which would disturb their business. Of course, these quotations are far from dogmatic, because Dow's Theory was only beginning to be understood. We shall see as the years went on that the theory allowed for much more explicit statements of the market's condition and its prospects. It is sufficient to record how soon the stock market barometer proved its usefulness when Dow's sound method of reading it had been set forth.

Chapter X

"A LITTLE CLOUD OUT OF THE SEA, LIKE A MAN'S HAND"—1906

IN discussions such as these it is necessary to anticipate objections and explain apparent discrepancies.
There is nothing more deceptively fascinating than a
hypothesis which holds together too well. Out of
that sort of theory much obstinate dogma arises, which
seems able to continue its existence after time has
proved the theory unsound or inadequate. We have
established what is called Dow's theory of the price
movement—the major swing, the secondary reaction
or rally, and the daily fluctuation—and out of it have
been able to evolve a working method of reading the
stock market barometer so constituted. But we are
to guard ourselves against being too cocksure, and to
recognize that while there is no rule without an exception, any exception should prove the rule.

The San Francisco Earthquake

The year 1906 presents an interesting problem in
this way. It is the problem of an arrested main bull
movement or an accentuated secondary reaction, according to the way you look at it. It has been said
that major bull markets and bear markets alike tend
to overrun themselves. If the stock market were
omniscient it would protect itself against this over-

inflation or over-liquidation, as it automatically protects itself against everything which it can possibly
foresee.   But we must concede that, even when we
have allowed for the further established fact that the
stock market represents the sum of all available knowledge about the conditions of business and the influences
which affect business, it cannot protect itself against
what it cannot foresee.   It could not foresee the San
Francisco earthquake of April 18, 1906, or the subsequent devastating fire.

Tactful to Call it a Fire

If you want to make yourself popular with that
somewhat strident individual, the California "native
son," you will not even allude to the San Francisco
earthquake.   In California it is considered bad man-
ners to do anything of the sort.   All that is conceded
there is the fire.   For our purpose the earthquake
admits of no argument.   Chronic California boosters,
however, cannot permit a general impression that
there might be, for instance, another earthquake in
San Francisco as bad as the last.   A fire, on the other
hand, might occur to any city, anywhere, without de-
tracting from those natural advantages of climate
and other things of which California is so proud.
There is nothing more charming than the naivete
of the Los Angeles native, who says "It is a fine day,
if I say so myself."   But earthquakes are different.
They put the Pacific coast in a class by itself, and a
class not at all to the taste of the inhabitants.   As

Beau Brummell, the great English dandy of the early years of last century, said: "A hole may be the result of an accident which could happen to any gentleman, but a darn is premeditated poverty."

Effect on the Stock Market

But the San Francisco earthquake came up in a clear sky, and took an already reactionary stock market by surprise. You will remember the clause in the Lloyds ship insurance policies which excepts "the act of God and the King's enemies." This aberration of Nature was an exception, and it went far to explain an exceptional year in the record of the stock-market barometer. There was an undoubted bull market from September, 1903, reaching a high point in January, 1906. It did not hold that point without recession; and it may be said that as a general rule there is often no marked warning line of distribution at the top of a major bull swing, especially when that bull swing has overrun itself, as, for instance, it did in 1919. The market in the spring of 1906 was declining, but with no such precipitancy as to indicate the bull market would not be resumed, or had even been much overbought when the earthquake occurred. We must remember how serious the losses were. The convulsion set up a fire in the ruins of the immense number of collapsed houses or those shaken to their foundations, and this fire rapidly assumed the proportions of what the insurance companies call a conflagration. The American companies, without exception of consequence, and the English companies, paid up promptly, to help the sufferers, although they had an excellent fighting case over the earthquake itself. We might have learned a little of German methods from the action of Hamburg companies, who adopted the opposite policy and repudiated their liability. It might have taught us something of the German methods in the conduct of war and diplomacy, of the German conceptions of the spirit of a contract and of sportsmanship. At least after that time the fire insurance companies of Hamburg wrote little insurance in America.

Sound Prediction Under Difficulties

When the stock market is taken by such a surprise there is a violent break closely akin to that of a panic. The basis of a panic, when analyzed, is essentially surprise. It cannot be said that the stock market of 1906, in the last days of April, got out of hand. But the decline had been sufficiently serious. The twenty railroad stocks which sold at 138.36 on January 22, 1906, on May 3d had declined over eighteen points; the twelve industrials then used had reacted from one hundred and three on January 19th to 86.45 on the later date. There seems to be some sort of uniformity which obtains in breaks like this. Experience records a recovery of part of the panic break, with a subsequent and much slower decline which really tests the strength of the stock market. In fact, *The Wall Street Journal* of July 6, 1906, called attention to this

fact, in predicting a general recovery from the showing of the averages.   It said:

"It is a uniform experience, over the years when such averages
have been kept, that a panic decline is followed by a sharp rally
of from 40 per cent to 60 per cent of the movement, and then by
an irregular sag ultimately carrying the price to about the old
low point.   It seems to need this to bale out the weak holders
who were helped over the panic.   It could hardly be said that
the break on the San Francisco disaster was exactly of the panic
class, and the market in rallying recovered to 131.05 in the case
of the railroad stocks, which is only 1.61 below the price at which
the earthquake decline started.   The rally, however, does represent about 60 per cent of the decline since January 22d, and the
course of the market since has been curiously parallel to the
movement observed after a panic rally.   It seems fair to infer
that liquidation of very much the same kind as that following a
panic has been necessary."

Seriousness of the Disaster

At this distance of time we may easily forget how
serious the San Francisco disaster was. The loss direct
has been estimated at $600,000,000. The Aetna Fire
Insurance Company admitted that the conflagration
had cost it the savings of forty years. If that was the
effect on the strongest fire insurance company in the
United States, and one of the strongest in the world,
how severe must have been the consequences elsewhere. It was all very well for the shallow, half-
taught optimist to say that broken windows made work
for glaziers and manufacturers of glass. But it cost
you something to put in a new pane, and the money
you spent on it would have been spent on something

else, while, as Bastiat said, you would still have your window. If that sort of reasoning were good, the quick road to prosperity would be to burn down all the cities in the United States.

We see that the railroad stocks suffered more than the industrials, and we should remember that they were in a higher class, both relatively and positively. But in a sudden and demoralizing break people sell the things for which there is some market in order to protect those for which there is no market. As *The Wall Street Journal* put it at that time: "The first decline in a panic is scare, and the second and slower decline is the demonstration of the general shock to confidence;" going on to say, in speaking of the market on July 2d, that the line of prices was well below the line of values and that the indications were bullish.

Rally From a Break in a Bull Market

This inference proved correct, and it has been the custom, which is followed in these discussions, to consider the bull market which began in September, 1903, as actually terminating and turning to the bear side, not in January, 1906, but in December of the same year. At the time the bullish inference quoted was published the market was making a line which proved, as the analyst correctly surmised, to be one of accumulation. The forecast was soon verified, and on August 21st *The Wall Street Journal* again discussed the market from the point of view of the averages. There was a greatly active market at that time, and it remarked how absurd it was to suppose that within two hours of trading on a Saturday one single interest could possibly manipulate one million six hundred thousand shares. This is a useful confirmation, coming out of the past of fifteen years ago, of what we have already seen for ourselves in demonstrating the relative unimportance of manipulation. In that discussion *The Wall Street Journal* went on to say: "We can only suppose that the long decline between January 22d and July 2d represented a somewhat extended bear swing in a bull market."

Average Deductions Uniformly Correct

Remember that this correct inference was drawn at the time, and not after the event. I could easily go back and show how trustworthy these deductions have been over the twenty-odd years since Dow formulated his theory. It would be absurd to say that it was possible to call the exact turn in the major swings, much less anticipate the unexpected. But these studies in the price movement did what was much more useful from the point of view of those using the barometer from day to day: they were continually right when they said of a major movement that it was still in progress, even when a deceptive secondary movement had made superficial observers bearish in a bull market or bullish in a bear market.

There is a story, probably apocryphal, of James R. Keene saying that he would be well content to be right 51 per cent of the time. I don't believe he ever said it. He must have found a much larger percentage necessary. The balance in his favor would not have paid operating costs, to say nothing of keeping a racing stable. But the deductions from the evidence of the price movement have been right, as the printed record proves, much the most of the time. After searching both the record and my conscience I can find no instance of a radical misinterpretation of the meaning of the barometer. The studies based upon its use were uniformly able to anticipate what the public was thinking about business before the public knew its own thoughts. The errors, where any occurred, were mainly due to the almost impossibility of forecasting the secondary movement of the market. This is really much more difficult than the interpreting of the major swing, just as it is easier for the Weather Bureau to forecast weather for a large area than it is to say whether it will rain in New York to-morrow morning.

Initiation of a Bear Market

Near the top of this bull market *The Wall Street Journal* uttered a caution. It pointed out, on December 15, 1906, that there had been a "line," especially in the twenty active railroad stocks, and that the possibility of a break through the lower level of the line should be considered as indicating the warning of a coming decline. This forecast did not commit itself to anything more than a possible bear swing in what had been for three years a primary bull market. It was altogether too early to call the actual turn. In the beginning of 1907, large railroad earnings, materialized in the case of the spectacular dividend policy announced for the Harriman roads during 1906, were set off against high money rates, which, as we soon saw, were already beginning to warn the market, and business generally, of that severe crisis brought about later in the year; when the reserve of the old national banking system virtually went to pieces, call money became practically unobtainable at unparalleled rates, and the banks resorted to clearing-house certificates for the first time since the panic of 1893.

In the month of January, 1907, the active professional traders were selling stocks. Political meddling was beginning to scare investors, and before the year was out there was what amounted to a strike of capital. The decline in stocks had already started, and it is interesting to trace the elapsed time taken to decide that a major bear swing had replaced the preceding long-continued bull movement. A decline of prices in January is always disturbing to the stock market because that is a time of year when, other things being equal, the tendency is oftenest bullish. It is a time for cheap money, and the reinvestment of the profits of the preceding year. It is a time, moreover, when it is peculiarly unpopular to talk bearish in Wall Street. The prophet of evil, as I have already frequently demonstrated, is totally without honor in that part of the country.

Boom Times and a Falling Barometer

In the long bull market there had been an unusually large emission of new issues, and it was then that the late J. Pierpont Morgan originated the phrase about undigested securities. America loves a good phrase, and that one caught hold. Industrial earnings, and especially those of the United States Steel Corporation, continued remarkably good. The railroads were making an excellent showing of both gross and net. But the sharp decline in the averages in January made our commentator most cautious, particularly in declining to predict a rally, much less assume that nothing more than a secondary reaction had been established. It was altogether too soon to be positive about the major movement. In fact the severe decline kept everybody guessing; but it appears from the records that early in March the existence of a primary bear market was conceded and *The Wall Street Journal,* very like any other newspaper, was doing all it could to cheer up the dispirited investor with a statement of the genuinely satisfactory features.

Some Bearish Influences

But the market was looking at all the facts, and the far-reaching consequences of some of them were reflected in stocks. These bear arguments were given on March 15, 1907, and they read curiously now. They were:

"1. Excessive prosperity.

"2. High cost of living, due largely to the effect upon prices of a great gold production.

"3. Readjustment of values to the higher rates of interest.

"4. Speculation in land absorbing liquid capital that might otherwise be available for commercial enterprises.

"5. Roosevelt and his policy of government regulation of the corporations.

"6. Anti-railroad agitation in the various states.

"7. Progress of socialistic sentiment and demagogic attacks on wealth.

"8. Harriman investigation of exposure of bad practices in high finance.

"9. War between big financial interests.

"10. Over-production of securities.

"11. Effect of San Francisco earthquake."

There were other causes quoted of only momentary consequence, in which possible bear manipulation was put last. It has been said already that there never was a bear market which was not justified by the facts subsequently disclosed. Are we not entitled to say that some of these influences became permanent, to an extent which even the stock market could not possibly foresee, conceding that it is, at least theoretically, of longer and larger vision than any of us? As after events proved, the over-regulation of the railroads alone was sufficient to justify investors in protecting themselves, whatever the consequences to the stock market might be.

An Abnormal Money Market

In retrospect, the year 1907 seems to me the most interesting I have ever spent in Wall Street, and perhaps the most instructive. It is full of lessons and warnings. I wish that the scope of these discussions permitted a treatment of it in greater detail. There is no better story of it for the student than that of Alexander Dana Noyes in his *Forty Years of American Finance*. He was financial editor of the *Evening Post* at that time. I remember that at the beginning of the year, when industry was booming, when railroad gross and net earnings were making about the best showing on record, when the stock market was only receding a little from three years of advance, where prices, moreover, at least on paper, had not overtaken values, he was struck, as I was, by the abnormal money market. That is the time of year when money should be cheap, and it was almost painfully tight in February. The stock market foresaw the meaning of it long before we did, as the major bear swing of 1907 showed.

No Bigger Than a Man's Hand

There was a broker of that time, since dead, whose face comes up before me as I write. He talked in terms of Wall Street, but his illustrations were vivid and his intelligence was well above the average. He was an educated lover of music, and much more reverent than he sounded. He was speaking to me one day about a performance of Mendelssohn's "Elijah" that he had once heard, with the title role taken by the greatest oratorio artist of all time, the late Charles Santley. The dramatic story had appealed to my friend. He talked of the priests of Baal being "cornered bears of the stock Elijah controlled," and of "their frantic efforts to cover their shorts." He was impressed with the way Elijah had, as he expressed it, "joshed" them in their extremity, suggesting that their god was taking a nap or was, peradventure, "on a journey." There was a phrase that had stuck in his mind which describes the condition at the beginning of 1907: "Behold, there ariseth a little cloud out of the sea, like a man's hand." The "great rain" followed in the autumn of the year 1907.

Not only was the collapse in business tremendous. It developed with a suddenness which simply took our breath away. At the close of the year I was traveling on the Pennsylvania railroad with Mr. Samuel Rea, now the president and then the first vice-president of the road. The Pennsylvania carries— and carried then—a tenth of the railroad freight of the United States. Mr. Rea said that at a time when they were only a month away from the peak of their load, apparently able to count upon the crop movement and the industrial traffic, both ways, of the Pittsburgh district, business seemed to shut up like a jackknife, almost overnight. We could see the empty cars in the stub-end sidings and yards all along the system between Philadelphia and Pittsburgh, at a time of year when railroads are normally using everything but the cripples in the repair shops.

The Deadly Hand of Politics

There had been nothing like it since the collapse of 1893, when that Congressional monument of economic ignorance and sectional folly, the Sherman Silver Pur-

chase Act, reaped its grisly harvest in the most demoralizing and far-reaching panic we ever saw.   That
seemed to have been a lesson to our lawgivers.   The
lean years which followed that panic, with the almost
universal bankruptcy of the railroads and those who
served them, finally put the fear of the Lord into the
politicians.   For ten prosperous years previous to 1907
they had quit kicking the business dog around.   But
in that year they had fully resumed that highly expensive sport, and before the end of the year there
was a strike of capital.   Every man who had anything to lose was terrified.   Every man who knew
anything foresaw what bureaucratic meddling and unintelligent regulation would do for the business of
the country.   It seems to me, if I am not wandering
from my text, that this is largely what is the matter
with the country now, war or no war, and that the
stock market for two years past has been foreseeing
some of the further consequences of fool politics.   It
may also be that in the impending improvement in
business, already foreshadowed by the averages and
the underlying investment demand shown in bonds,
the market foresees some return to sanity, even if the
indications in Congress at present are anything but
encouraging.

Chapter XI

THE UNPUNCTURED CYCLE

WE have been considering in some necessary detail the record of the stock market barometer, and we shall have some further historical study to make in that interesting and little understood period between the bear market which culminated in 1910 and the outbreak of the World War. We have hitherto paid small attention to the tempting "cycle theory" of human affairs, and especially of business affairs. In an early discussion I set forth the panic dates for the eighteenth and nineteenth centuries as recorded by Jevons, together with Dow's brief account of our panics of last century. But it was essential to establish something of an irregular stock market cycle of our own, not necessarily, and hardly more than incidentally, involving a panic—for, indeed, the panic has more than once proved to be merely an interruption in the main movement of the barometer.

Our Own Modest Cycle

We can see that we have established some sort of irregular rotation through Dow's theory of the stock market price movement—its major swing up or down; its secondary reaction or rally, as the case may be; and the daily fluctuation in prices on the Stock Exchange as reflected in the records of the averages.

But the theory of the longer rhythmical cycle will not down. It seems to be almost an obsession with many of my readers and critics. None of them seems to have analyzed his belief in it in any searching way. The general impression is that there is "something in" the idea; that if it is not proved true it should be true; that the world's panic dates themselves indicate a striking degree of periodicity; that, given such periodicity in the past, we may anticipate something like it in the future; that men will always be as stupid in the conduct of their own business as they seem to have been when judged by the records of history.

Basis of the Cycle Theory

Probably this unwillingness to analyze the panic theory arises from the fact that in the eighteenth century, according to Jevons, there were exactly ten noteworthy crises at an average of ten years apart. I am content to waive the one Jevons omitted—that of 1715, when the Scots invaded England—because there were not enough spots on the sun in that year to establish his daring theory of the relation between the two phenomena. We may note that Jevons gave 1793 and 1804–5 as crisis years, while it is of record that our own first panic of the nineteenth century was consequent upon the British capture of the city of Washington in 1814—an event which no cycle could have predicted, unless we are to assume that the cycle theory could have predicted the late war. But, counting 1814, and what Dow calls the "near approach to a crisis" in 1819, there were ten American crises in the nineteenth century.

Let us see how the cyclist—if that is the correct word—approaches the subject. The ten-year interval between the British crisis of 1804–5 and our own of 1814 might stimulate him at first. And the really serious and nation wide crises of 1837 and 1857 would give him a great deal of confidence. He would recall the ten-year intervals of Jevons, and that we had up to 1837 recorded four crises of sorts, in four decades of the new century. We did not greatly share the panic in Europe in 1847, although it was sufficiently serious there to impress itself upon American memory. But when the cycle enthusiast found a real panic in 1857, he cried "Aha! We have now discovered the secret. There is a twenty-year cycle, with a big crisis at each end, and a little crisis in the middle. We may now confidently set about humoring the facts to fit this beautiful theory."

Misfitting Dates

On that showing there should have been another first-class panic, with nation wide consequences, in 1877. But apparently the machinery slipped a cog, for the panic came in 1873. From the devastating folly of overtrading on a greenback basis, it would have come in 1872 but for the accident that we had in that year an enormous wheat crop, which brought splendid prices in the world market because of the almost total crop failure in Russia. Here, then, was a contraction of the interval between great crises. The twenty-year theory was deflated to sixteen, and it is hard to derive much consolation from the fact that the Overend-Gurney failure in London in 1866 had marked a date conveniently between the two great crises. The London panic of 1866 was accompanied by a heavy fall in prices in our Stock Exchange. In April of that year there was a corner in Michigan Southern and rampant speculation. The truthful but cautious Dow says that the relapse from this "was rather more than normal."

But the three panic years 1873, 1884 and 1893 did something to revive the confidence of the ten and twenty-year theorists. The first and the last were crises of almost world wide magnitude and equally far-reaching consequences. Our cyclists said: "That slip-up in the reduction to sixteen years for the interval between crises occurring in 1857 and 1873 was merely fortuitous, or at least we shall be able to explain it satisfactorily when we have deduced only a little more about the laws which govern these things." And the twenty-year cyclists prophesied, saying: "There are twenty years between 1873 and 1893. Our barometer is getting into shape. There will be a minor crisis round about 1903 and a major panic in 1913, or not later than 1914."

Lost in Transit

What is the use of the theory, indeed, unless it can be made the basis for at least as much prophecy as that? But between 1893 and 1907 we have an interval

of fourteen years. Has the twenty-year period contracted, or the ten-year period expanded, to fourteen
years? Is there any dependable periodicity about the
thing? We see that there was not the slightest reason
for any crisis in the years presumably anticipated by
the cycle theorist—1903 or 1913. Indeed, the volume of the world's speculative business was not large
enough to make a crisis in those years. It is reasonably certain that a smash cannot be brought about
unless an edifice of speculation has been constructed
sufficiently high to make a noise when it topples over.

What is the value of all this as a forecast for business? I cannot see that it has any. The theory has
to make so many concessions—takes so much humoring, in fact—that it ceases to have more than a value
for record. We see that the sweeping conclusions
based upon the cycle assumption had to be changed
again and again. Does much that is really useful
remain? I am anything but a sceptic; but this whole
method of playing the cycles looks to me absurdly
like cheating yourself at solitaire. I can understand
stringent rules, arbitrary rules, unreasonable rules,
in any game. But my mind fails to grasp a game
where you change the rules as you go along.

Are They Equal?

And what becomes of that imposing premise that
"action and reaction are equal?" Are they? There
is little real evidence to prove the assumption, in
recorded human affairs. Of course the holders of that

theory may respond, "Well, if they are not equal they ought to be." I cannot even see why they ought to be. Certainly, holding a Christian faith in the perfectibility of human nature, I do not see why crises should not be eliminated altogether. It is easy to see how the periods between them at least seem to have grown longer. The interval between 1893 and 1907 was fourteen years, and 1920 was no panic year.

Unless we are to force the construction of what constitutes a panic until we actually distort it, we can hardly regard the deflation liquidation of 1920 as a typical crisis. It could not begin to compare with the damaging effects of 1893, 1873, 1857, or 1837. It had none of the earmarks of a panic year. I dare say I shall believe, in five years' time, that the drastic contraction and deflation were about the best thing that could have happened to us. They should certainly discount all sorts of trouble in the future.

A Business Pathology Needed

There must be some sort of scientific pathology of business affairs, or perhaps it might be better to call it morbid psychology. I have suggested in another chapter how utterly inadequate the records of history are in the vital matter of commerce and all that contributes to it. But we are beginning to acquire a scientific knowledge of the symptoms of the diseases which afflict it. In this respect we have probably made more advance in the past quarter of a century than in all the years since Carthage sold the purple weaves of Tyre to Rome. We may well hope that we are developing a scientific method of diagnosing the symptoms of business disease. There was no such method in 1893, bcause there were no such records as we have today.

But why need we assume that once every ten years or twenty years, or any other period, the most intelligent part of mankind loses its head and forgets all the lessons of the past? One thing is certain about a panic. It could never occur if it were foreseen. Are we not working toward a sum of knowledge and an accuracy of analysis which will, in a sufficiently safe measure, foresee all but the non-insurable risks—"the act of God and the King's enemies?"

The Federal Reserve Safeguard

I can see a great deal too much politics, and many defects, in the Federal Reserve banking system. But under that system it is hard to imagine a set of conditions which would force the country to resort once more to clearing-house certificates, as it did in 1907 and 1893. It would pass the wit of man to devise a perfect banking system; and what would seem perfect to one would appear utterly inadequate to another. But the progress from the old national banking system to the Federal Reserve system represents the most tremendous stride in business practice which the country has ever seen. Is not the Reserve system itself an entirely new factor for the cycle theorist to consider?

It must not be assumed for a moment that possible crises in the future may be dismissed from consideration. On the contrary, they are certain to come. But may we not hope that, with fuller knowledge, they will be at least in part anticipated and, in their most dangerous effects, radically mitigated?

Teaching the Teacher

If these studies have shown the man who takes an intelligent, even if not a financial interest in Wall Street, that knowledge will protect him there as it will anywhere else, the educational design has been largely accomplished. Certainly one of the desirable educative services of this series has been to show the writer how much there was about the stock market movement which he had never before formulated to himself in any useful fashion. The way to get at the essence of such a proposition is pragmatic—to live with it from day to day. The stock market problem, considered in the light of Dow's Theory, is essentially simple. It can be set forth in a thoroughly useful way, provided only that the teacher is neither a crank nor a quack, a gambler or a crook. Harvard University is performing a greatly needed service in putting out tabulations and index charts on general business conditions which are above suspicion. The compilers have not tied themselves down to dangerous assumptions. They are not lashed to an assumed "medial line" of national wealth with a constant upward tendency at the same rate of speed in good times or bad, which loses its certainty in face of the grim facts of war, and hysterically changes its course.

Does the Physical Law Apply?

Such a system as that of Harvard University is not committed to the proposition that in human affairs action and reaction are equal. That is a fine-sounding phrase, but it should require incalculably more evidence than has yet been adduced to persuade us to adapt a law of physics to something so unstable and elusive as human nature itself. Among the many things which our stock market averages prove, one stands out clearly. It is that so far as the price movement is concerned action and reaction are not equal. We do not have an instance of a bull market offset in the extent of its advance by an exactly corresponding decline in a bear market. And if this is true, as it demonstrably is, about the extent of the price movement in any given major swing, it is still more true about the time consumed. We have seen that bull markets are, as a rule, of materially longer duration than bear markets. There is no automatically balancing equation there. I do not believe there is such an equation in human affairs anywhere. Certainly there is none recorded in history. I am compelled to rely upon others for tabular figure compilations of all kinds, and do not profess to have used my modest razor for the cutting of any of these tables of stone. But in all the study of figures prepared for use in my profession, I have been unable to find a balance of action and reaction.

Extent and Duration Incalculable

Certainly the stock market barometer shows nothing of the kind. There is no approximation to the regularity of the pendulum, either in the arc of the swing or its velocity. We see a bear market declining forty points, a bull market advancing fifty points over more than twice the period, a bear market declining nearly sixty points, a bull market recovering forty-five points, a bear market declining less than thirty points, a major swing upward of not much more than twenty points, a bull market advancing nearly sixty points in the industrials with a simultaneous advance of less than thirty in the railroads, and a different period for each successive swing. This, in approximate figures, is the record for a quarter of a century. There is, obviously, a rough periodicity about such movements. But if we begin to twist them into some mathematically calculable, regularly recurring "cycle," the next main movement, up or down, will leave us all adrift, with nothing to hold on to but an empty theory and an empty purse.

Sham Mysteries

I do not want to dogmatize about this, although I am trying to make what is essentially a scientifically treated subject popularly interesting, if, indeed, sermons are ever popular. One trouble of all teaching, and a moral danger to every teacher, is that the authority necessarily accorded to the instructor leads him to make something of a mystery of his trade. His

unconscious desire to eliminate embarrassing competition leads him to exaggeration of the difficulties to be
encountered in acquiring a sound knowledge of the
subject. In a brief time, as human affairs run, there
will be a sort of cult amplifying and complicating an
otherwise simple thesis. Every religion breeds a
priesthood, where sacerdotal succession becomes more
important, or at least much more jealously defended,
than mere salvation. Both in the English common
law and the canon law handicrafts were sometimes
referred to as mysteries. The plumber who comes
into your house likes you to believe that his elaborate
preparations, and the general mess he makes, are evidence of the difficulty of the task he has accomplished
—a difficulty you as a layman are entirely unable to
measure—and a sufficient pretext for the extortionate
bill he renders.

Tipsters and Insiders

I have known some likable people connected with
what are frankly stock-tipping agencies. There is a
market for what they supply, and they are necessarily
excellent judges of human nature. They are never
bearish on the stock market. They are often successful and prosperous in a bull market, and I suppose that
the savings of the fat years support them in the lean
ones. They tell the unscientific speculator what he
wants to know, but not what he needs to know. Sometimes the guessing is good, and always there is the suggestion that there is a mystery about reading the stock

market movement. If this is true of what they teach on the general market, it is still more true about individual stocks. With them "insiders" are always buying. In my experience I have known many insiders, and for every purpose of the small speculator they were far oftener wrong than right.

As a matter of fact these so-called insiders, the real men who conduct the real business of a corporation, are too busy to spend their time over the stock ticker. They are far too limited, too restricted to their particular trade, to be good judges of the turn of the market. They are normally bullish on their own property, in the respect that they believe it to be a growing concern with great possibilities. But of the fluctuations of business which will affect their stock, together with the rest in the same group or all the other railroad and industrial stocks in the same market, their view is singularly limited. It is not mere cynicism but truth to say that sufficient inside information can ruin anybody in Wall Street.

That is not only true, but it is an excellent thing that it is true. Of course the executive officers of large corporations should have a sound general knowledge of conditions outside their own sphere. They should be well instructed. They might read this book with advantage, if it only taught them to take a more objective view. But even with the basis of a general education, such as is required in a good university of the man who intends afterwards to specialize in law or surgery, their very occupation unduly affects their sense of proportion.

Our Trustworthy Guide

This is why the stock market barometer is so valuable. It makes little of cycles or systems, interesting and even well-grounded inferences or common fads. It uses them all so far as they are useful, together with every other scrap of information it is possible to collect. The market movement reflects all the real knowledge available, and every day's trading sifts the wheat from the chaff. If the resultant showing of grain is poor, the market reflects the estimate of its value in lower prices. If the winnowing is good, prices advance long before the most industrious and up-to-date student of general business conditions can bushel up the residue and set it forth in his pictorial chart. Few of us can be Keplers or Newtons. But it is possible to formulate working rules which will help and protect any man in that forecast of the future which he must necessarily make every day of his life. This is what the stock market barometer does. It makes no false claims. It admits highly human and obvious limitations. But such as it is, it can honestly claim that it has a quality of forecast which no other business record yet devised has even closely approached.

Chapter XII

CONTINUING the important and, indeed, vital subject of the prediction value of the stock market barometer, if we are to prove the validity of Dow's theory of the price movement, the analyses of the stock market averages published at irregular periods in *The Wall Street Journal* in 1907–8 may be here submitted. These are of record, and there is a personal reason why they should have impressed themselves upon my memory. At the end of the year 1907 the late Sereno S. Pratt, a man of sound economic knowledge, sterling character and exceptional ability as a newspaper man, relinquished the editorial chair of *The Wall Street Journal* for the dignified and less exacting post of secretary to the New York Chamber of Commerce.

Impersonal Editorials

Apart from the fact that they are not signed, newspaper editorials have far less of any personal quality than the public supposes or politicians assume. The editor is, of course, personally responsible for them, not only to the proprietors of the paper but civilly and criminally under the law. His own editorials are checked, when necessary, by the experts of the paper who "cover" particular subjects, and what they write editorially is in turn subject to the editor's revision. Several competent persons have seen and criticized an editorial before it appears, in any well-conducted paper. I succeeded Pratt at the beginning of 1908, but it is impossible for me to say, even if the matter were not in some degree confidential, to what extent the editorial discussions of the averages were a matter of individual thought, although the methods of an editor unconsciously impress themselves upon his staff. At any rate Pratt and I were of one mind in the method of reading the averages which the paper had inherited from Charles H. Dow, its founder.

Detecting the End of a Bear Swing

It will be remembered, from the preceding article, that there was a short but severe major bear swing lasting throughout 1907, really culminating on November 21st of that year. In the last week of November the industrial stocks rallied sharply, as they might equally have done in a secondary upward swing in a bear market; and the most difficult of all barometer problems, that of calling the turn of the market, presented itself. On December 5th *The Wall Street Journal* said:

"Since November 21st, when the average price of twenty railroad stocks touched 81.41, its lowest point, there has been an advance of 7.70 to 89.11, which was the record at the close of yesterday's strong market. During these ten days there have been only two days of decline. This is a very substantial rally, and perhaps it is too rapid, all things considered, although it still leaves prices on a basis which would seem to discount in large part the reasonable trade contraction of the future."

On December 23d there was an incidental reference to the averages in the discussion of the general developments of the week. The writer seems to have felt rather than asserted the change, which it would have been rash to predict, and said:

"It will be noticed that there has been quite a typical movement of the average price of railroad stocks. It declined twenty-six points from July 20th to November 21st. It rallied nine points in the following fortnight, reacted four points in the next ten days, and has rallied two points in the past week. This is really the shortened swing of the pendulum, as it approaches equilibrium."

A Self-Correcting Barometer

Before we go further it is necessary to say something about the secondary movement of which this paragraph gives a simple, concrete instance, sufficient for our present purposes. It will be observed that the reaction following the rally from the low points of the bear market was checked before it reached the old low, and for purposes of record it may be said that the movement of the twelve industrial stocks then used in the average was roughly parallel and confirmatory. Perhaps the last sentence in the paragraph quoted is the most illuminating if it were intended to develop in this article the meaning and function of the secondary swing. It may be said that in that way our barometer tends to adjust itself. At the turn of a bear market there is a chaos of knowledge of all kinds, and an almost inextricable confusion of opinion, which is gradually resolving itself into order. It follows that speculators and investors tend to anticipate the market movement and often look too far ahead.

Right Too Soon

It would be possible to offer endless instances of people who lost money in Wall Street because they were right too soon. One illuminating instance occurs to me as far back as the bull market which developed in the summer preceding the re-election of McKinley in 1900. One of the most conspicuous traders on the floor then was a partner in an active arbitrage house which has long since gone out of existence. For the sake of the layman it may be explained that an arbitrage house is (or was) one of those which did business by cable exchange with the London market, taking advantage of the fluctuating differences between the prices in the forenoon on the New York Stock Exchange and those in what at that time of our day would be the afternoon in the London Exchange. But in those dull summer days there was not enough business for the arbitrage houses, or anybody else. The total recorded transactions, which have in their time exceeded three million shares a day, dwindled down to considerably less than a hundred thousand.

Louis Wormser, however, was as active as a trader could be on the floor in such circumstances. He was bullish all through the summer. Other traders complained that he went about spoiling what little market there was in any stock which was momentarily active. It is fair to say that he was entirely within his rights as a floor trader and a member of the Exchange. The market did not begin to gain strength or volume until the last few weeks of the presidential campaign. Wormser was then on the right side and followed the market up. I suspect he even fancied he was leading it. For three days after the election stocks were very strong. They were so strong that he was convinced the bull movement had sufficiently discounted the re-election of McKinley. He turned bearish, and probably lost in a few days all he may have made on the bull side in the preceding five months. That bull market, as we have shown, did not culminate until September, 1902, in spite of the serious interruption of the Northern Pacific corner and panic. This is an excellent example of a speculator who saw only one of the many factors where the market saw all of them, and who was not content to trust the barometer. It may, indeed, have been that Wormser's prominence in a restricted market, a relatively large frog in a small puddle, had given him the impression, by no means singular, that he alone constituted the market, as he sometimes had in the dull days preceding the rise.

A Courageous Prediction

Returning to the bull market of 1908 and 1909, which *The Wall Street Journal* was evidently beginning to foresee, on December 25, 1907, that newspaper said, "We have seen the low price for the year in all probability." On January 10, 1908, when the country was still quivering from the shock of the developments of 1907, when the clearing-house certificates were a vivid reality, *The Wall Street Journal*, manifestly judging by the barometer alone, was able to record a significant rally. Speaking of this preliminary movement, it says that it gives "the impression that it is one of those sharp fluctuations which follow an extreme low point and precede, at greater or less distance, a permanent turn in the tide." That seems fairly courageous and clear as a prediction, and one of exactly the conservative kind business men were being led to expect from the general consideration of the stock market barometer. Let us keep in mind that Dow's theory is not a system devised for beating the speculative game, an infallible method of playing the market. The averages, indeed, must be read with a single heart. They become deceptive if and when the wish is father to the thought. We have all heard that when the neophyte meddles with the magician's wand he is apt to raise the devil.

Reviewing the Collapse

Prediction was anything but a comfortable task in the beginning of a bull market which nobody at that time would concede, much less forecast with any degree of certainty. In an earlier chapter of this series great stress was laid on the suddenness with which business collapsed in 1907. *The Wall Street Journal* recalls the conditions, and the startling change, in its editorial of January 24, 1908:

"Consider, for instance, the rapidity with which the pendulum of business has swung in this country from extreme prosperity to great prostration. Almost in a single night the situation changed from one extreme to another. Even after the panic had swept through Wall Street with terrific force a high official of a leading railroad commented upon the fact that the traffic of his line had the day before touched high-water mark. Three weeks later the same official reported that the business of the line had fallen off abruptly. Anecdotes of this kind could be multiplied indefinitely.

"It is only three months since the panic started in Wall Street, and yet that time has been sufficient to produce what amounts to a revolution in the economic conditions of the country. Three months ago there were not cars enough to move the freight. Now there are several tens of thousands of empty freight cars on the sidings and in the terminals. Three months ago the iron and steel trade was at the very height of its activity. It took only five or six weeks to cut off the demand and to close mills. If a chart were drawn to describe the reduction in iron and steel production in the past ten weeks, it would make almost a perpendicular line, so sudden and extreme has been the contraction."

A Bull Market Recognized

These extracts could be supplemented by and contrasted with the uniformly bullish inferences drawn from the stock market barometer during the winter and spring of 1908, when the business of the country was, apparently, in the deepest stage of depression. The depression was recognized; but the fact that the stock market was acting not upon the things of the moment but upon all the facts, as far ahead as it could see them, was never allowed to become obscure. It will be seen that *The Wall Street Journal* set forth

the known facts in the paragraphs quoted above. A
well-known chart showed its lowest point of depression at that time and did not cross its medial line, to
begin its ensuing area of expansion, until the following
November. But the stock market anticipated that
record by a clear twelve months, and the faithful
barometer predicted the recovery when there was apparently not a patch of clear sky on the horizon.

Reprobating the "Frivolous" Recovery

Looking back on those days of early responsibility,
it is matter of thankfulness to me to have had Dow's
sound theory to back me in the face of unbelievably
virulent criticism. In the mind of the demagogue
Wall Street can never be forgiven for being right when
he is wrong. The country at that time was full of all
kinds of agitation for the curbing, controlling, regulating and general bedeviling of business. Discontent
was general, and it was a winter of unemployment.
Some of the letters received, in which this bullish attitude of the stock market was denounced in the most
unmeasured terms, would sound funny now, although
they were anything but funny then. We seemed to be
in the position of the "coon" at the country fair who
puts his head through a hole in a sheet as a target
for those willing to pay their nickels for the privilege
of a shot at him. The lightest accusation was that
Wall Street was "fiddling while Rome was burning."
The general charge took the form that guilty manipulation by gamblers was in progress.

If you will refer back to the twenty-five-year chart published with an earlier discussion you will note that the recorded sales at that time were the lowest since 1904, indicating a market so narrow that manipulation would have been wasted even if it had been possible. But that charge is always made in a bear market and in the transition period between a major decline and its succeeding upward movement. If I had not already advanced so many arguments to prove what an inconsiderable factor manipulation really is, the volume of sales itself would be sufficient to make my point. But these sturdy protestants thought otherwise, and continued to fill my wastebasket with revilings for many months to come. For a time at least, a bull market was positively unpopular.

Relevance of the Volume of Trading

It is worth while to note here that the volume of trading is always larger in a bull market than in a bear market. It expands as prices go up and contracts as they decline. A moment's thought will reveal the reason. When the market has been under long depression many people have lost money, actually and on paper, and the fund for speculation or speculative investment is correspondingly contracted. On the advance, however, many people are making money, actually and on paper, and the wellnigh universal experience has been that in the last stages of a bull market they trade in stocks beyond their real resources. This is uniformly true of major bull swings, but is subject

to great modification in the secondary movements. A
sharp reaction in a bull market will often stimulate
the volume of business. There is a picturesque example
of this in the most spectacular reaction of the kind.
The average monthly sales in May, 1901, have not
been closely approached since. They were more than
one million eight hundred thousand shares a day, including Saturdays, when there is only two hours of
trading, and it was on the 9th of May that the Northern Pacific panic took place. There will be an opportunity to take up the secondary swing in some detail
in a future discussion, and it is not necessary for our
purpose to expand upon the subject now.

An Unbiased Mind

Not to be tedious, but to counter the charge of
saying "I told you so," on ex post facto evidence, it
has been necessary to offer these examples of the practical use of the stock market barometer. There is,
indeed, little in these predictions to excite boasting.
Any intelligent student of the averages who has once
grasped the principle of the stock market barometer
can draw such deductions for himself, provided he
brings to the task a really unbiased mind. An interest
in the stock market would be almost certain to weaken
his judgment. It is only human to foresee what you
hope and, indeed, what you expected when you bought
stocks for the rise or sold them short. But the analyst
of the price movement, writing for the guidance of
others, must be absolutely disinterested. There are all

sorts of traps to catch him if he is not, particularly if he has previously committed himself to inferences not clearly justified by the premises. Sheer pride of opinion has ruined more speculators in the stock market than all other causes put together.

An Unfortunate Guess

One of the shortest ways of going wrong is to accept an indication by one average which has not been clearly confirmed by the other. On May 10, 1921, the New York *American* ventured into prophecy on its financial page. To reinforce its prediction its forecaster published a reproduction of the Dow-Jones chart. As the chart and the accompanying figures were taken without acknowledgment, altruists who believe that ill-gotten gains do not prosper will hear with satisfaction that the author of the Hearst *American* article did not even understand the meaning of what he had appropriated. He announced a bull movement for the industrial stocks, even prescribing its limits, a degree of prophecy hitherto unsuspected in the barometer; while the railroad stocks, as he expressed it, "marked time." It was a most unfortunate guess, for the industrials declined a further thirteen points, making their new low in June; while the railroads, so far from marking time, also showed a substantial reaction.

Averages Must Confirm Each Other

This was a case where the observer was misled by a bullish indication given in the industrial average which was not confirmed by the railroads. The former had been making what we have learned to call a line, and after a secondary rally in a bear market showed some strength, at a figure above the line and calculated to suggest accumulation if there had been any evidence of the same thing in the railroad stocks. But there was nothing of the kind, and it is to be hoped that the readers of the Hearst *American* article did not follow the tip; for the industrials, as shown by the averages, did not cross the closing figure of the day on which the bullish advice was given until the second trading day of December, seven months after.

It is possible, however, for us to assume charitably that this expounder of the barometer was not quite so superficial as he sounds. There may have been in his mind a recollection of the bull market of 1919, which the industrials made entirely off their own bat. If you will study the chart published with a later chapter, headed "An Exception to Prove the Rule," you will see that such an experience could not be repeated unless our railroad stocks returned to government ownership and guaranty—a condition which at that time took them entirely out of the speculative class and left them moving downward with bonds and other securities held for fixed income. These, as we know, inevitably decline in price with an advance in the cost of living, which was then in full flood.

This illustration serves to emphasize the fact that while the two averages may vary in strength they will not materially vary in direction, especially in a major movement. Throughout all the years in which both averages have been kept this rule has proved entirely dependable. It is not only true of the major swings of the market but it is approximately true of the secondary reactions and rallies. It would not be true of the daily fluctuation, and it might be utterly misleading so far as individual stocks are concerned. The indications of a single average can, and do, look seductively like the real thing, as I have discovered to my cost; for in that way I find, upon analysis of articles written long ago, that I more than once went wrong. It says much for the value of our barometer that error came from trusting it too little rather than too much.

Sticking to Our Text

It has been suggested that I should discuss the causes which were related to the major movements of the stock market—the depressions in business, the recoveries and the alleged or real overexpansion. I have my own opinion about the causes of the panic of 1907. I do not agree with writers rated as competent as myself, who ascribe it to E. H. Harriman and the "overexpansion" of the American railroads from 1901 to 1906; who choose to think that the advance in the Bank of England rate to the sufficiently startling figure of 7 per cent at the end of 1906 was a direct result of gambling in railroad stocks by Mr. Roosevelt's "malefactors of great wealth." And by no stretch of faith can I believe that Harriman produced a panic in Alexandria, Egypt, in April, 1907; another in Japan within a month; what the London

Economist called "the biggest financial disaster that had overtaken the city since 1857" in Hamburg in October; and still another in Chile—all preceding our own crisis at the end of October. It has seemed to me that the subsequent paralysis of railroad development, which should have gone on at the billion-dollar-a-year rate James J. Hill suggested in 1906, but was suspended almost entirely, was a much more serious matter for the country than the reciprocal ownership of railroad stocks of E. H. Harriman's plans. There could be no menace to the public there, with the Interstate Commerce Commission to protect us through the freight rates.

But all this is beside the point. I am writing about the barometer, not about the weather. History reads queerly fourteen years after the event to those who were in a position to know the facts, who might even have been, to at least a modest extent, part of that history. But where it is necessary to review history here these discussions will still stick to the text.

Chapter XIII

NATURE AND USES OF SECONDARY SWINGS

BEFORE resuming the historical demonstration of the effectiveness of the stock market barometer which has been the subject of our most recent discussions, there is a good opportunity here for some consideration of the secondary swing. Previous discussions have shown how it was possible successfully to diagnose a major swing in its incipient stages. But the secondary movement postulated in Dow's Theory is a different matter. We have proved by analysis the correctness of the theory of the market as containing three distinct and, in a way, simultaneous movements —the great primary swing up or down; the secondary movement, represented by reactions in a bull market and corresponding rallies in a bear market; and the daily fluctuation. It may be that this discussion will seem to be addressed more to the speculator or embryo investor than to those who consider using the stock market barometer as a guide and warning to business.

How to Call the Turn

It may be conceded at once that if it is hard to call the turn of a great bear or bull market it is still harder to say when a secondary movement is due, although there are no insuperable difficulties in the way of showing the termination of the secondary movement and the resumption of the main market trend. We cannot dogmatize about the depth of such movements, in duration or extent. We have seen, from a study of what was really a secondary reaction in a bull market aggravated by the San Francisco calamity in 1906, that such a reaction can look deceptively like the real thing—the development of a new major swing. It can look so vigorous and convincing, as in the case of the Northern Pacific panic of 1901, that even experienced traders will rashly assume that the bull market is over.

Dow estimated the length of a counter movement at from forty to sixty days, but subsequent experience has shown that this longer range is exceedingly rare and that the duration may be appreciably less than forty days. The daily fluctuation might be so considerable as to constitute almost a secondary reaction in itself, if the extent of it were all we were considering. When it was known that the government would take over the railroads, at the end of December, 1917, there was an advance in a single day in the railroad average of over six points. There have been true secondary movements which did not carry even so far as this. It is a tried rule, which will help to guide us in studying the secondary movement, that the change in the broad general direction of the market is abrupt, while the resumption of the major movement is appreciably slower. The latter is frequently foretold by a line of accumulation in a bull market or a line of dis tribution in a bear market.

More Meteors Than Stars

Who is to foresee the sharp break? It seems to depend upon a set of causes altogether different from the adjustment of prices to values, which is the main function and intent of the major swing. It represents a technical market condition more than a summing up and reflection of general knowledge. It means, as the professionals say, that there is too much company on the bull side; or, conversely, that people are selling a bear market short, regardless of the diminishing floating supply of stocks. I have declined in more than one place to advise any man to speculate. That virtuous attitude is easy and cheap, but it will acquire more significance if I do not presume to advise against speculating where a free American citizen feels he has the qualities necessary for success and, more particularly, if he is the kind of man who can stand success. That is the severest of all tests, in other places than Wall Street. There have been many meteors in the financial sky, but few fixed stars.

In the secondary movement of the market the professional has a real and abiding advantage over the amateur. It is an emergency in which his technical experience tells. "Tape reading" is a sort of sixth sense, and the man on the floor can feel a change coming even better than the most accomplished tape reader if he has real aptitude for his work. There are some games in which the amateur is better than the professional. There are many in which he seems at least as good. But in the long run, in nearly all games, the professional will win oftener than the amateur. He will win more when there is anything considerable at stake and he will lose less when losses are inevitable.

Advantage of the Expert

Some authorities on auction bridge estimate that good cards constitute 80 per cent of the advantage in the game. An indifferent or unsound player can win, and even continue to win over an extended period, if he holds good hands, enjoys rather more than average luck and is blessed with good partners. But the remaining 20 per cent makes the vital difference between the incurably mediocre player and the expert. Playing constantly over a sufficient period of time to average the element of chance, the first-class player must win. He will win, moreover, without any unfair advantage. If, indeed, he depended upon collusive information from his partner, for instance, he would be merely a sharper and never a really first-class player. The advantage of the crook has always been overestimated. His mentality is at some point defective, or he would not be a crook. I have fallen in with a few—surprisingly few—crooks in Wall Street, in both the professional and the amateur class. They are soon detected, and with their sole advantage eliminated they find their level at the very bottom of the heap. *Nemo repente fit turpissimus;* and, in practice, they amount to little.

Graduating Professionals

Of the many successful speculators who fight for their own hand, like Hal o' the Wynd, those who, not being members of the Stock Exchange or partners in any brokerage house, are therefore obliged to concede the broker's commission and the market turn, all sooner or later become, in every intent, professionals. They devote to the business of speculation exactly the jealously exclusive attention which a successful man gives to any kind of business. The outsider who takes only "an occasional flutter" in the stock market, however shrewd and well informed he may be, will lose money in the secondary swings, where he is pitted against the professional. He cannot recognize the change in movement quickly enough to adapt his attitude; he is usually constitutionally averse from taking a loss where he has previously been right. The professional acts upon the shortest notice, and reactions or rallies give little notice.

Wall Street Normally Bullish

But the intelligent amateur is on all fours with the professional when a bull market has reacted and become dull. In the old days Wall Street formulated a number of maxims for itself, and one of these was, "Never sell a dull market." It is bad advice in a major bear swing, for the market then will become dull after a sharp rally, and experienced traders will accordingly put out their shorts again. But Wall

Street is inherently bullish. One reason for this is that the financial district does not make money in a bear market, contrary to the ideas of people who think that then is the time when the Street reaps its harvest, and wickedly turns disaster to its own advantage. Wall Street lives on commissions, and not on what it might make by selling short the securities it originates. Large trading and large commissions go together. They are a feature of a bull market, but never one of a bear market. So true is it that Wall Street is normally and healthily bullish, by experience, that I have never known a great trader, with his first reputation established as a bear operator, who did not either turn bull or drop out of the market altogether.

When we studied the major swings we saw that bull markets last longer than bear markets, and we might have seen that over a period of years long enough to average both bull and bear swings the tendency seems upward, or at least has heretofore advanced, with the growing wealth of the country. Personally, I do not believe that the war has changed this fundamental fact, at least for the inexhaustible United States, if a special movement of the railroads, to be treated later, for a time at least, modifies the assumption.

James R. Keene

So far as the bear trader is concerned, I am entirely certain that James R. Keene lost as much money as he ever made on the bear side, and that he made all the money he left and spent on his racing stable by his purchases of securities which subsequently appreciated in value. I never enjoyed his intimate acquaintance. It is not unfair, at this distance of time, to say that newspaper men with responsibilities do not cultivate intimacy with large professional speculators. Such intimacy can be misconstrued, however innocent the personal relations may be, and easily results (for Wall Street is reeking with gossip and scandal) in giving the reporter an undesirable reputation for being the interested mouthpiece of that particular operator. This, of course, is a condition which no clean newspaper could or should tolerate.

This is not to say that the newspaper men, or even most of those who had the entree to Keene's highly inaccessible suite at his son-in-law, Talbot J. Taylor's office in Broad Street, were not men of honor. There were good reasons for liking Keene, who was by no means the cold and bloodless bandit some people, with ideas of financiers gathered from the scarehead newspapers or the moving-picture screen, have supposed. He had attractive qualities, and he was a man of his word, even if he was merciless to those who dealt with him and failed to keep theirs. All of us liked his admiring affection for his son Foxall, and his sportsman's love of a fine horse. Little that his enemies ever did to him in the stock market—and that was plenty—hurt him like the death of his favorite Sysonby, a horse he bred himself and one of the greatest three-year-olds that ever looked through a bridle. Among the newspaper men who could afford to know Keene was Edwin Lefevre, then on the New York

Globe. But it is no more than just to say that Lefevre was less a friend than a connoisseur of Keene. He studied him, in a highly amusing way, for use in his cynical but effective *Wall Street Stories,* in *Samson Rock of Wall Street, The Golden Flood* and other tales of a like character, now somewhat out of date but interesting reading for those who knew the different Wall Street of twenty years ago.

Addison Cammack

There is another reason why bear operators are credited with more short selling and market "wrecking" than they ever performed or even conceived. Such an operator can bull stocks and keep himself in the background, while a campaign on the bear side is usually dramatic, with the principal figure very much in the spotlight. Addison Cammack's era was rather before my time, but people who knew him well say that his bear campaigns were short, sometimes successful and sometimes not, and that he would have been soon ruined or driven into other environment if he had not been an excellent judge of values, and much more interested financially in the growth and prosperity of the country than in efforts to check it. He made his big money buying Northern Pacific, on reconstruction, at $7 a share. He probably had more real belief in the greatness of the United States than some of those critics who are so ready to impugn Wall Street's patriotism. Keene was right, if premature, in his abortive bull campaign in Southern Pacific.

Selling Commodities Short

A bear has few friends, because obviously he cannot make money unless other people lose it. It is curiously illogical that this feeling against him extends even to the cases where he forsakes stocks for operations on the short side in commodities like wheat or cotton. But there is nothing incompatible with a bull position in stocks and a bear position in wheat. There is nothing antagonistic to the greater prosperity of the country in believing that such prosperity will be enhanced if the humble consuming worker can get more flour or bread at lower prices. It would be utterly impossible to synchronize the movements of wheat or cotton with those of stocks. These commodities often decline when securities are advancing. It is not the general opinion, but it seems to me that a bear of wheat who breaks a corner in that commodity, even if his end is selfish, is performing something in the nature of a public service.

Such an opinion as this, of course, will be unpopular with the farmer and still more unpopular with the farmer's political friends, to whom wheat at $5 a bushel looks like prosperity, with wealth beyond the dreams of avarice. It might well mean famine and widespread destitution. The farmer and his friends have become sensitive since their own wheat pool (not different morally from any other attempted corner in the staff of life), formed in 1919 to carry the price of wheat above $3 a bushel, collapsed under the futile leadership of the Non-Partisan League and the moral support of some of the members of what now constitutes the agricultural "bloc" in the United States Senate. That corner failed, and it is no unkindness to the farmer to say that it deserved to fail. The stock market of 1920 was warning him that such a pool could not succeed, in ample time for him to have realized all his wheat at prices well over $2 a bushel.

How the Barometer Adjusts Itself

We are not wandering from our text. Weakness in the cotton or grain markets may have much to do with secondary reactions in the stock market, if only for the financial commitments involved. Secondary movements, indeed, are influenced by much more transitory conditions than any of those which govern the major swing. The question is pertinently asked, "Do the averages predict a secondary reaction in any dependable way?" There would be such a prediction, naturally, if, in the course of a major bull swing, the market made a line in both averages, and then a price below the line to indicate that saturation point had been reached; and the converse would be true in a bear market. But experience tells us that when the line occurs it is, generally, not before but after a secondary break or rally. This line, then, is most useful to the speculator who has previously sold and wants to get into the market again, because a bull indication after a line of accumulation would point the way to a new figure higher than that from which the secondary decline took its origin. Such a new top would be conclusive evidence, on all our records, that the bull movement had been resumed.

But these discussions are designed less for speculators than for those who wish to study the stock
market barometer as a guide to the general business
of the country. These students may well ask what is
the real purpose and usefulness of the secondary
movement. If we are allowed to mix our metaphor,
it may be said that the secondary movement is not
unlike a device sometimes used for adjusting com-
passes. Many of you have seen a ship's launch describing circles in the harbor, and wondered what it
meant. I am well aware that the metaphor is anything
but perfect, but it is clear that the secondary movement serves the valuable purpose of correcting our
barometer. Our guide is, to that extent at least, self-
adjusting. Remember that we are dealing with no
such certain element as the mercury in the tube, whose
properties we know all about. The stock market
barometer is taking every conceivable thing into account, including that most fluid, inconstant and incalculable element, human nature itself. We cannot,
therefore, expect the mechanical exactness of physical
science.

Not Too Good to Be True

We might well be disposed to suspect our barometer if it were too exact. Our attitude would be that
of a city magistrate toward police evidence, when
every police witness tells exactly the same story in the
same words. Such evidence is altogether too good to
be true. I am repeatedly asked if I am quite sure
about the low or high point of a given turning date;

whether, for instance, the low of the bear market from which we are now emerging was really June, 1921, or should not be considered in relation to the new low point, scored by the industrials alone, in the following August. It has been said that the averages must confirm each other, but if you like to take it that way and it suits your habit of mind, by all means allow yourself that much latitude. I cannot see that it makes any material difference. I have been shown figure charts where bear and bull movements, from the course of a single constantly active stock like United States Steel common, were professedly predicted with mathematical exactness. They have not inspired me, and I do not believe that they could stand the long years of test to which our barometer has been subjected.

There are other critics, far less kindly and with no real desire to help, who find no difficulty in picking holes in our theory because they do not wish to be convinced. They are merely contentious. They can, of course, find plenty of movements, especially secondary ones, which they think the barometer failed to forecast. What of it? An instrument of any such accuracy as they demand would be a human impossibility, and indeed, I do not think that any of us, in the present stage of man's moral development, could be trusted with such a certainty. One way to bring about a world smash would be for some thoroughly well-intentioned altruist to take the management of the planet out of the hands of its Creator.

Chapter XIV

1909, AND SOME DEFECTS OF HISTORY

SINCE we have set the understanding of the stock market barometer as our goal, we are not to be discouraged by the real and fancied obstacles still remaining. We can always hearten ourselves by looking back and seeing how much we have already overcome. Perhaps the reward is in the race we run, not in the prize. This is not to say that the mere reading of this series of studies is any achievement if the reader has not, thereby, added to his mental bank balance. But if we look back we can see that we have not only established Dow's theory of the price movement, but constructed or deduced a workable barometer from it—a barometer with the invaluable quality of long distance forecast. We should know our theory by heart. It is that the stock market has three movements—its broad swing upward or downward, extending from a year to three years; its secondary reactions or rallies, as the case may be, lasting from a few days to many weeks; and the daily fluctuation. These movements are simultaneous, much as the advancing tide shows wave recessions, although each succeeding roller comes further up the beach. Perhaps it might be permissible to say that the secondary movement suspends for a time the great primary swing, although a natural law is still in force even

when we counteract it.   My pen would fall from my
fingers to the ground or the desk, by the attraction of
gravitation, and that law continues operative, if not
active.   In a like way of putting it, the secondary
movement can be regarded as simultaneous with the
major swing, which still continues to govern.

That Unbalanced Equation

It has been necessary to refer in previous articles to
business charts and records, and I would be the last
to seek a quarrel with the compilers of such useful
data.   All I contend is that these charts and records
are hardly, in a useful sense, barometers.   They are
hazy about the future, even where they make the
assumption that they are based upon a great law of
physics—that action and reaction are equal.   They
have still to show me that they have included all the
factors of their equation.   Certainly these business
charts did not include the possibility of Germany win-
ning the war in 1918.   The bear market in stocks in
1917 took count of all that these tabulations ever
formulated, and this overwhelming possibility besides.
It is true that we can form little conception of what
may happen in the future unless we are familiar with
what has happened in the past, where like causes
have produced like effects.   But forecast may be mistaken or premature long enough to ruin any business
man, with no other guide than that.   One of these
business-chart authorities not long ago advocated the
purchase of a certain stock, on the basis of the earn-

ings and dividends for a period of ten years past. There was a fundamental change in conditions, aggravated by an ill-judged change in policy, and the people who bought that stock suffered severe losses. How would a present holder of such a stock as American Sugar, for instance, have fared if he had bought the common stock in 1920 on its dividend record?

Insufficient Premises

Reasoning of that kind has too narrow a base. It lacks foresight. It is like saying that a patient will recover, irrespective of his symptoms, because he has enjoyed good health for ten years past. This is an example of reasoning from insufficient premises. No doubt the possibilities of changes in management and other things, which sometimes wreck concerns with a previously good dividend record, are averaged in the total of a recording agency's tables. But even when these things are averaged they are a record and not a barometer. The data of the Weather Bureau are of the highest value, but they do not pretend to predict a dry summer or a mild winter. You and I know from personal experience that the weather in New York is likely to be cold in January and hot in July. We could infer that much without assistance from the Weather Bureau. That bureau can give us only an inadequately short view. It cannot tell us that there will be fine weather for our picnic the day after to-morrow. Still less can it tell the farmer that the temperature and humidity of the coming summer will be such that he should plant potatoes instead of corn. It can show the records and probabilities; but the farmer must use his own judgment; while we take chances on the kind of weather that will make or mar our picnic.

How Little the Best Man Knows

We have seen that the stock market barometer does predict. It shows us what will happen to the general volume of business many months ahead. It even goes further and warns us of the danger of international events which could upset all ordinary calculations based on the course of business as inferred from the records. It cannot be too often repeated that the stock market barometer is acting upon all the knowledge available. I recently asked one of the greatest financiers in Wall Street, often credited, by sensation-loving journals, with the most searching knowledge of financial conditions and their influence upon coming events, what sort of percentage of the available knowledge he supposed he had. He said, "I have never worked that out. But if I had 50 per cent of all the knowledge which is reflected in the movement of stocks I am confident that I would be far better equipped than any other man in Wall Street." This was from a banker who handles the financing of great railroads and industrial corporations, whose foreign connections are of the very highest class. When he could confess this without false modesty to one he would not be foolish enough to deceive, how absurd must be the

assumed omniscience of the "financial octopus" the
politician is so fond of parading!

A Needless Accuracy

We have come a long way in the reading of the
barometer based upon Dow's Theory. We have seen
that a "line" in the average—a succession of closing
prices, over a sufficient number of days for a fair
volume of trading within a narrow range—must indicate either accumulation or distribution; and that
a movement of the average price out of that line,
downward or upward, will confidently indicate a
change in the general market direction of at least a
secondary and even a primary character, which we can
depend upon where either average is confirmed by the
other.

We have also satisfied ourselves that the averages
must confirm each other, although they may not break
out of their respective lines on the same day or in the
same week. It is sufficient if they take the same direction. It is by no means necessary, as experience shows,
that the low or the high point of a primary movement should be made in both averages on the same
day. All we assume is that the market has turned,
with the two averages confirming, even although one
of the averages subsequently makes a new low point
or a new high point, but is not confirmed by the other.
The previous lows or highs made by both averages
may best be taken as representing the turn of the
market.

This seems to be a difficulty which is still puzzling a number of people who expect an absolute mathematical accuracy from the averages, such as I would be the last to claim, if only for the reason that it is not needed. One critic believes that I am wrong in assuming that the low point of the last bear movement was in June, 1921, because the industrials made a lower point in the following August. But that lower point was not confirmed by the railroad average. Consequently, it is negligible from our point of view, although if it adds to the sum of that gentleman's certainty he will not go far wrong if he dates his upward movement from August and not from June.

A Double Top in 1909

In the present discussion it will be useful to show the turn of the market to the bear side in 1909. This is likely to be confusing to our meticulous critics, because the railroad stocks made their high for the preceding bull movement at 134.46 in August, 1909; while the industrials made a high of 100.12 at the end of the following September, 100.50 early in October, and 100.53, the highest of the year, at the beginning of November. The last high, taken with that preceding, is an example of what is called a double top. It is by no means infallible, but is often useful; and experience has shown that when the market makes a double top or a double bottom in the averages there is strong reason for suspecting that the rise or decline is over. If, however, I say that a bull market saw its top in August, 1909, and that the bear market set in from that date, somebody will tell me that the bear movement cannot be said to have set in until the beginning of November. What does it matter? If we combine the condition exhibited then with what we have learned from a study of the line of distribution or accumulation, we shall see that distribution preceding an important downward turn, possibly secondary but proving to be primary in this case, had been in progress and had established its inevitable consequences, at any rate before the completion of the first week's trading of November, 1909.

Bulls of Stocks Well Warned

That seems to me about as adequate a barometrical indication as we dare expect from a gauge which has to take into consideration all the fallibility of human nature itself. Never was the bull of stocks given such repeated chances as in 1909 to take profits at the top, or a few points below it. In a previous discussion I have said that the bull market which originated in December, 1907, was actually almost unpopular. The previous bear market had predicted an era of corporation baiting, originated by President Roosevelt, who could never have foreseen the absurd lengths to which his animadversions upon "malefactors of great wealth" would be carried, or the devastating implications which would be drawn by people much more ignorant and far less sincere than himself.

The bull market of 1908–9 did not please a number

To Criticize a Critic

of highly respectable and competent critics.   I have appreciated and recommended elsewhere *Forty Years of American Finance,* by Alexander D. Noyes.   His review appears to have been carried only to the beginning of 1909, to judge by his concluding paragraph. He seems to reprehend the bull market then in progress.   He certainly failed to see that it would continue in force up to August, so far as the railroads were concerned, up to November as shown by the industrial average, and that, at the end of the year 1909, the railroads would be no lower than one hundred and thirty on December 31st, as against one hundred and thirty-four in the middle of August, and the industrials a bare point away from the top.   Mr. Noyes says, in speaking of the bull market, with what can fairly be called a somewhat unsuccessful essay in prophecy:

"The end of this singular demonstration came with the opening of 1909, when facts were suddenly recognized, when prices for steel and other commodities came down, and when the Stock Exchange demonstrations ended.   With the closing of the year 1908, this history may properly close; for it marked the ending of a chapter."

But we have seen, from the record of the averages, that the chapter was not closed so summarily as Mr. Noyes assumed.   We may say, for convenience, that the bull market had spent its force in August, 1909— or in November, as we choose to look at it.   But the bear market which foresaw the next period of depression did not begin to "hit on all cylinders" until January, 1910. Here again we see a profound and able observer influenced by accepting a record for a barometer.

A Record Too Brief

To a student of history—and the writer modestly claims to be something of the kind himself—it is source of unceasing regret that there is relatively so little real history to study. Our table of averages is only truly effective for rather over a quarter of a century. When we say that the twenty active railroad stocks must confirm the twenty industrials it seems to me that this implies, at least in part, that less than forty stocks do not give a sufficiently inclusive picture of the market. I might, in some subsequent discussion, offer a partial and incomplete record of the years from 1860 to 1880, with an average high and low, month by month, of fifteen miscellaneous stocks. I may as well say now that I do not think that it has any conclusive teaching value; or that if it had been kept contemporaneously with the events of that time, and not compiled years after, it would have given business anything like the thoroughly trustworthy indications which we can read in the more perfect double-average barometer of to-day.

How History Records the Wrong Things

But my criticism of history goes much further than the mere records of which we are treating. It is that

all available history, as far back as we can trace—
from Egypt and the supposed cradle of the race in
Asia Minor—records the wrong things. It tells us
all about the dynasties of the Pharaohs, and nothing
about those productive middle-class brains of management which made those dynasties rich—gave them a
real people to rule over. We know that there were
rulers and wars, slaves and industrial workers enjoy-
ing different degrees of freedom. We know now that,
so far from labor creating everything—the preposterous major premise of Karl Marx—labor creates
only a fraction of the sum of human wealth compared
with the product of brains. Of the "people" of the
past, in the sense that the Bolshevist demagogue uses
the word, we know a good deal. Professor Thorold
Rogers, of Oxford, many years ago compiled a tabulation of wages in England, from the time of the
Tudors. But history seems to give something of the
bottom and a great deal too much of the top. It tells
us nothing, or next to nothing, of the middle class
which must be the directing brain force of a nation
with any commerce whatever.

Where Are the Business Records?

What do we really know about the Carthaginians?
They were the greatest trading nation of their time.
We might well afford to sacrifice the detailed accounts
of the campaigns of Hannibal, to throw away most
of what we know about the second Punic War, to
scrap nearly all that part of history, in exchange for

only one year's accounting of a typical Carthaginian merchant engaged in foreign trade. We would have more practical knowledge, applicable to the problems of to-day, from that single merchant's books of the year 250 B.C. than we can get from the *Decline and Fall of the Roman Empire,* and all it incidentally says about Carthage, to say nothing of the practical conduct of commerce in those days.

How did that merchant do his business? He dealt in tin from Cornwall and dyestuffs from Tyre. He had correspondents all over the known world, which then extended from Britain in the west to India in the east. Did he, or could he, for the tin or dyestuffs he received, pay exclusively in coined gold or silver? He may well have exchanged one of his commodities for another, or something else for both. How did he pay? How did he settle his balances? Did he have bills of exchange? I am inclined to think that he did, whatever form they may have taken, although no papyrus or parchment has survived. But history does not tell us the one thing we want to know. How did the Carthaginians adjust their international trade balances? They necessarily had them. The merchants of Joppa or Sidon or Alexandria kept books, or their equivalent. They had a record of what they imported from Carthage and what they exported there and elsewhere. Rome owed Carthage balances in account, in triangular transactions which must have required some knowledge of double entry, with more or less regular exchange quotations to balance one national coinage against another. What does history tell us about all this? Absolutely nothing. And yet that knowledge would be of infinitely greater value to us, would save us more mistakes, than Xenophon's deathless story of the retreat of the ten thousand.

Who Financed Xerxes?

Heaven forbid that we should lose the inspiring lesson of Thermopylae. We have seen, in the Great War, that men are still capable of rising to the heroism of the fated three hundred. But what of the contractors who fed and clothed and armed the "five million men" in the army of the victorious Xerxes? "The mountains look on Marathon—and Marathon looks on the sea," and they may continue looking at each other, until the crack of doom, without telling us the cost of the ship's stores consumed in the fleet which transported the defeated Persians. "You have the Pyrrhic dance as yet, where is the Pyrrhic phalanx gone?" We could dispense with the dance if we knew how the Pyrrhic phalanx got its necessary three square meals a day, and from whence its food was imported. I am far from endorsing the Henry Ford criticism of history—it is not "bunk"; but what would we not give for a trustworthy analysis of the economic consequences of Diocletian's price-fixing edicts, in the year 301?

Where did the Greeks buy their naval stores? How were they assembled? How was the account settled? Was it in coined money, or in a draft written on parchment, transferring one merchant's debt to another in order to balance the books of a third? All this is left out of classical history, and is sadly lacking in modern history. It was not until the middle of the nineteenth century that Green wrote, not a history of the kings of England, but *A Short History of The English People*. It was all too short; and the most important part of the English people was loftily minimized—that respectable but inarticulate element which goes about attending to its own business and manages to "keep out of the papers." No one would belittle the record of the events which led up to·the signing of Magna Charta. But if I am not greatly interested in King John, I want to know much more than history records about those useful mercantile and financial figures personified by Walter Scott in Isaac of York. The tortured Jew's extracted tooth outweighs, in real historical value, the sceptre of the Plantagenet king.

What of the Banking in the Middle Ages?

The more we search the work of the earlier historians, the more we are astonished at their inability to see a thing so self-evident, for they were almost invariably drawn from the class they failed to chronicle, except where it touched politics. Froude devotes chapters of a volume of his history to the divorce of Catherine of Aragon. He tells us nothing of value about the financial transactions involved in such a simple matter as the collection and payment of Queen

Catherine's dowry to Henry VIII. I have heard experienced newspaper men say, "The most interesting news never gets into the papers." There is a good deal of cynical truth in that remark, and certainly the most instructive historical facts seldom get into the histories.

That is why the diary of Samuel Pepys, not written for publication, tells us more of the real things we want to know than anything which has ever been written, contemporaneously and since, about the period of the Restoration. It is almost from that date that we begin to get some familiar idea of what banking was like, and how it was conducted in the great city of London two and a half centuries ago. Our knowledge, so far as available records are concerned, hardly, in any real sense, antedates the incorporation of the Bank of England, at the end of the seventeenth century. The records of commerce and banking of the earlier financiers are almost hopelessly wanting. There must have been such records arising out of the colonial expansion of Holland, Spain and Portugal or, working back through the years, in the trade of the Genoese and the Venetians. But these highly respectable historians seemed to think that the birth of a king's bastard was more important than the opening of an avenue of trade, with the creation of the financial machinery necessary for its development.

How New Is Credit?

I am credibly informed that banking, and even branch banking, has been in use in China for at least two thousand years, with drafts, credits and the usual banking machinery, if in a much simplified form. It must also be admitted that the great structure of to-day's credit is essentially modern. But it would be absurd to assume that it is all modern, merely because we know so little about history. The trading of Carthage, Genoa and Venice was largely barter. But we may be sure that it was not all barter. Not only the Church canon law but the Bible itself and like works have many allusions to the sin of usury. But usury meant interest, and interest meant credit, just as coinage meant exchange. It was not all pawn-broking; nor was the banking of the Middle Ages. There is some evidence that the same people both received and paid interest. The merchant, then as now, probably had a good deal more practical sense than the theologian, and certainly a clearer idea of the line between legitimate interest and usury. The trouble is that historians, up to a late date, have been influenced by the ecclesiastical attitude toward money lending. They are exasperatingly dogmatic on the things they admit they don't know. I am inclined to suspect that it was not the early Middle Ages that were "dark" but only the historians. I am even disposed to agree with my friend Dr. James J. Walsh that, in point of real civilization and attainment, both artistic and literary, the thirteenth century in Europe compares favorably with our own. And even he has been unable to elicit anything of real usefulness about the mechanics of commerce.

And if this is the sum of our knowledge of the his-

Socialism's False Assumption

tory of the most vital part of human affairs, the history of the men who paid the taxes and the men who made the taxes possible; the history of those who took the bare product of labor and fructified it tenfold—how difficult is it for us to gather together enough particulars to frame a trustworthy generalization from the wholly modern tabulation of the records of trade, industry and finance! There has recently been published a book by H. G. Wells, *The Outline of History,* which at least has had the excellent effect of persuading a number of people to read history who have done little serious reading in the course of their lives. But that "outline" is devoted to proving a fallacious assumption—that men are groping their way, rather blindly, in the direction of international socialism. Is there one single record in all the inadequate volumes of history, upon which Mr. Wells and we ourselves necessarily depend, which indicates anything of the kind? Everything points to the development of the efficient individual. There is nothing in the Wells inference which does not ignore the factor of management in production, dominant now and dominant always, from the time when man learned to save something out of his harvest, to keep himself and others through the coming winter, and exchange for what he could not produce.

A Sound and Conservative Forecast

With regard to the use of the barometer in the turn of the market in 1909, *The Wall Street Journal* on

September 11th, a month after the railroads had recorded their high, said:

"The movement of the average on Thursday's break was one which has often marked the commencement of a downward swing. The indication as yet is not very authoritative, but whatever we may think about a resumption of the bull movement, 'now that all the bad news is out,' the averages undoubtedly look more bearish than they have done in a long period.

"Pessimism has never been the policy of this paper, but it published an earnest plea for conservatism when the market was at the top. Nothing has occurred since which has not emphasized the position taken."

From that time forward, although the market, as we have seen, was remarkably firm, showing only modified secondary downward swings practically up to the end of the year, *The Wall Street Journal* continued to draw lessons of warning from the averages. On October 28th it said, after pointing out the extent of the rally necessary to re-establish the old bull market:

"There is no pretense here to pass an opinion upon the market from any other point of view than a purely technical one, based upon the experience of the price movements as shown in the average record of many years, but the depression in the barometer, here evidenced, is well worthy of the consideration of thoughtful traders."

Growing Effectiveness of the Barometer

Remarking how widely the idea of a bull market in 1910 was then held *The Wall Street Journal* was unpopularly bearish on December 18, 1909, although both averages were within a very few points of the top. It is interesting to note that one of the bear arguments (other than that of the averages) discussed at that time was the high cost of living! On December 28th, any idea of a January boom—a movement always talked of at the beginning of the year—was rather cruelly discouraged. It would be easy to multiply examples. It is sufficient here to show, before taking up the discussion of the four years of somewhat indecisive market movements which preceded the war, how faithfully the stock market barometer, twelve years ago, was already serving its purpose.

Chapter XV

A "LINE" AND AN EXAMPLE—1914

IN past discussions of the stock market barometer—
the record by daily averages of the closing "bid"
prices of a number of selected industrial and railroad
stocks, taken in two separate groups to check and confirm each other—emphasis has been laid upon what
is called a "line." It is needless to say that no inference of value can be drawn from a single day's trading. However large the transactions may be, they
cannot show the general trend. This daily fluctuation
is merely the third and least important movement
defined in Dow's theory of the averages. If we could
imagine such a thing as an irregular daily tidal movement it is just that. The general level of the sea is
not changed by an abnormally high tide in the Bay of
Fundy or a tidal bore in the mouth of some Chinese
river. The ocean's real encroachments and recessions
take time.

A Definition

The line, therefore, may be considered as often
preceding an appreciable recovery in a primary bear
market or a well-defined reaction in a primary bull
market, and, rarely, as the possible turning of a major
movement. It can almost be set down as axiomatic
for all our purposes that a line is and must necessarily

be either one of accumulation or one of distribution. For a time the buying and selling power are in equilibrium. There are some most significant lines in the history of the averages to which reference has already been made.

Predicting the War

To show the special value of the averages as a barometer forecasting what even Wall Street itself does not know in any general sense or at any rate does not realize, the extraordinary line made by both averages, industrials and railroads, in the months of May, June and July, 1914, preceding the outbreak of the Great War, is here submitted. No severer test of the averages could be chosen. The war came as a surprise to the whole world. Did the stock market foresee it? It may be fairly claimed that it did, and had predicted it, or trouble of the most momentous character, before the end of July, while the German army crossed into Belgium on August 3d–4th.

Let it be remembered that a primary bear movement had then been in progress in the stock market since October, 1912. In May, 1914, both averages started to make a line of unusual length. The fluctuations in the railroads were between one hundred and three and one hundred and one, and in the industrials between eighty-one and seventy-nine. Only once, on June 25th, did the railroads give a warning at one hundred. This was taken back the following day with a continuance of the line in both averages up to July

18th in the case of the railroads and July 27th in the case of the industrials. At the latter date, eight days before the German army invaded Belgium, the industrials confirmed the warning the railroads had given.

Definition of a "Line"

The accompanying figure chart, taken from May 1, 1914, to July 30th, answers many questions. The line, like others recorded in the averages, was presumably one of accumulation or distribution. At the end of April the bear market had continued for nineteen months, and there is fair conjecture that had there been no war this would have proved a line of accumulation, followed by the bull market which actually started in the ensuing December, soon after the Stock Exchange reopened for business.

This chart answers also the questions as to the dimensions or breadth of a line, which, of course, in theory may be prolonged indefinitely and in this instance had actually extended over sixty-six trading days in the industrials and seventy-one in the railroads. It will be seen that three points was the extreme range in the industrials and four points that in the more stable railroad stocks. The line proved to have been one of distribution, and indeed the market had become so saturated with stocks that the Stock Exchange closed its doors for the first time since the gold panic of 1873.

AVERAGES FROM MAY 1, 1914
TO CLOSING OF THE STOCK EXCHANGE

ach figure represents the average closing bid price of **twenty railroad stocks and twelve industrial stocks, and a complete trading day.**

RAILROADS

```
————————————————————————————MAY————————————————————————————
                         103 103 103 103 103 103 103 103 103 103
2 102 102 102 102 102 102 102 102 102     102 102                 102
                 101 101 101
```
```
——————————————————————————JUNE——————————————————————————
        103 103 103 103 103 103 103         103 103
2 102 102 102                       102 102 102 102 102             102
I                                               101 101 101 101
                                                100
```
```
——————————————————————————JULY——————————————————————————
            103
2 102 102 102 102 102
            101 101 101 101
                    100 100 100 100
                            ..
                            98  98  98
                                    97  97  97
                                            96
                                            ..
                                            ..  94
                                            93
```

INDUSTRIALS

```
——————————————————————————MAY——————————————————————————
                     81 81   81   81   81   81   81 81   81 81   81
              80 80 80 80             80 80                      80
79 79 79 79 79 79
```
```
——————————————————————————JUNE——————————————————————————
   81 81 81 81 81 81 81 81 81 81 81 81 81 81 81 81 81
80                                          80 80 80 80 80
                                            79
```
```
——————————————————————————JULY——————————————————————————
      81 81 81 81 81 81 81 81
80                    80 80 80 80 80 80 80 80 80
                                           79 79 79
                                           ..
                                           76  76
```

What Had Happened?

What had happened? German holders of American stocks and the best informed European bankers had sold in this market. If there had been no war all this would have been absorbed by the American investor at the unrepresentative low prices prevailing in a bear market which in July, 1914, had been operative for twenty-two months. All of it was absorbed by the American investor in the following year. The supply from Europe then, and subsequently, as the war forced foreign holders to realize, and war loans compelled the liquidation of other investments, took the place of the normal supply of new investment securities which it is the duty of Wall Street to create through concentration of opportunity and of savings and the bringing of the two things together. Over-regulation of the railroads, now recognized to have been an economic crime, had paralyzed their power to create new capital long before the war. The public attention had been diverted for five years before that calamity to industrial opportunity, some of it, like the shady oil promotions of our inflation period, of a dangerously speculative character. Without the foreign sales of American securities and the war, turning us in effect from a debtor to a creditor nation, there would have been a dearth of capital opportunity; and this is why after the all-revealing break late in July the market made only a relatively small decline on the reopening of the Stock Exchange, in December, immediately swinging into one of its great bull periods.

Relation to Volume

Knowledge is valuable not merely for telling us what to do but for telling us what to avoid.   Inside information, so called, is a dangerous commodity in Wall Street, especially if you trade upon it, but at least it guards you against the rumors which cannot possibly be so.   Diligent study of the averages will sufficiently show where a "line," having proved to be one of accumulation, has given definite information, not merely useful to the trader but valuable to those who look upon the stock market as a means of forecasting the trend of the country's general business.

Here is an appropriate opportunity for adding something about volume of sales.   This volume is much less significant than is generally supposed.   It is purely relative, and what would be a large volume in one state of the market supply might well be negligible in a greatly active market.   If the line means absorption, this absorption sums up the market supply, whether it be three hundred thousand shares or three million.   Showers of rain vary in intensity, area and duration.   But they all result from the moisture in the air reaching saturation point.   Rain is rain whether it covers a county or a state, in five hours or five days.

How to Know a Bull Market

It might well be asked, how are we to tell when a secondary swing, upward for instance, has developed into a primary bull market?   The result is seen in the averages in a succession of zig-zag steps. If the secondary swing reacts a little after what would ordinarily be its culmination in a primary bear market but does not decline to the old low figures, and subsequently recovers to points better than the new high established on the earlier rally, we may assume with confidence that a primary bull market of indefinite length has been established. It is, of course, impossible for the barometer to predict the duration of the movement, any more than the aneroid can tell us on October 30th what the weather will be on Election Day.

Barometrical Limitations

There is no need to expect omniscience from an aneroid barometer, which, as we know, frequently takes back its predictions and would be a most untrustworthy guide for the mariner if it did not. This is true of the stock market barometer, which must be intelligently read. Surgeons and physicians in our time have been greatly helped, to the lasting advantage of human life and comfort, by the X-ray photograph. But these medical men will tell you that the photograph itself must be read by an expert; that to the mere general practitioner not accustomed to its frequent use it may be unintelligible or misleading. The results of an X-ray to disclose, for instance, pyorrhea "pockets" at the roots of the teeth would be meaningless to the layman and perhaps even to some dentists. But any dentist could qualify himself to read those indications, and it is here submitted that any intelligent layman with a sympathetic interest in the stock market movement, by no means necessarily speculative, can read the stock market barometer.

Speculation's Necessity and Function

Wall Street is a mystery to many men who have unsuccessfully tried to speculate there without knowledge, only to become convinced that they have in some way been cheated in what is no better than a gambling game. It has not been the purpose of these chapters to discuss ethical questions; as, for instance, the morality of speculation or the line which divides speculation from gambling, or the place of gambling in the Ten Commandments, or the supposed special sinfulness of short selling. The personal opinion of the writer is that speculation within a man's means is unaffected by any question of morality. Perhaps this is only another way of saying that its morality is taken for granted, just as the lawful conduct of a man's business is assumed. If the man chooses to make speculation his business, or part of his business, the ethical question becomes purely academic. Speculation is one of the greatest essentials in the development of a nation. The spirit which inspires it can be called by prettier names, like adventure and enterprise. Certainly if no one had been willing to take a speculative risk for a larger profit than mere investment provided the railroads of the United States would have stopped at the eastern foothills of the Alleghenies, and what the maps of our childhood called "the great American desert," now our great wheat and corn-producing states, would have remained a desert for all we knew to the contrary.

Rudyard Kipling once said that if the British army had always waited for supports the British Empire would have stopped at Margate beach. The speculator in the stock market, or any free market, is a fact and not a theory. He is the embryo investor who does not wait for supports. It will be a bad day for this country, and a sign that having ceased to grow it has begun to dwindle, when it abandons free markets and the free speculation which they necessarily entail.

Difficult But Not Unfair

It is not true to say that the outside speculator always loses money in Wall Street if he continues speculating long enough, as the present writer (who does not trade on margin himself) can testify from numerous instances to the contrary. But the man who means to hold his own in an encounter requiring capital, courage, judgment, caution, and arduously acquired information from study must devote the same attention to that business that he would to any other business. So far as Wall Street is concerned, the simile of a game of chance is always a bad and misleading one. But it may be said that to those who will not or cannot comply with the conditions of the game when playing against expert exponents of it, trading in Wall Street is a sheer gamble, with a deadly percentage in favor of the dealer (who does not need to be dishonest) and against such a player. No one would play auction bridge against scientific players without learning how to bid and how to draw correct inferences in the play. He would refrain, if only out of mercy for his prospective partner. But the man who will not risk his own and his partner's money in that way will not hesitate to speculate in Wall Street. Is it surprising that he loses his money?

Who Makes the Market?

This seems an appropriate place to answer a question which may be said to go to the root of the matter. "Who makes the market?" The manipulators? The great banking houses of issue with new securities to float? The professional traders on the floor of the Stock Exchange? The large individual "operators" who talk to newspaper reporters of their profits and tell Congressional committees how they made them, but never say a word about their losses? Certainly not. The market is made by the saving, investing public of the whole United States, first, last and all the time. There is no possible financial combination which can manipulate a bull market, by propaganda or in any other way, when the combined intelligence of the investing public sees that it is time to curtail their commitments in view of a coming decline in prices, earnings and the volume of trade. The most an expert manipulator can do is to stimulate activity in a particular stock, or a small group in a market which is already rising on its merits, with the approval of public sentiment. We hear about the successful manipulation of the market, in United States Steel or Amalgamated Copper, by the late James R. Keene in 1901 and 1902; but we hear nothing of almost innumerable attempts to manipulate for distribution abandoned because the general trend of the market made the operation profitless and dangerous. The great private financing houses are normally sellers of securities because it is their business to manufacture them, in the promotion of new enterprises, and the direction of the great reservoir of public capital into such channels. Individual Wall Street capitalists buy for private investment, and I could tell, from the wills filed for probate, of the unbelievable minor errors of judgment of this kind made by men so well informed as the late J. Pierpont Morgan or the late E. H. Harriman, to name only two of many.

Speculation's Sound Basis

It has been said before that the stock market represents, in a crystallized form, the aggregate of all America knows about its own business, and, incidentally, about the business of its neighbors. When a man finds his jobbing trade or his factory showing a surplus he tends to invest that surplus in easily negotiable securities. If this improvement is general it is all reflected and anticipated in the market, for he can buy in July and carry on ample margin what he knows he can pay for outright when he divides profits at the end of the year. He does not wait till the end of the year, because he realizes that the knowledge he possesses in July will by that time have become common property, and will have been discounted in the price. He buys ahead just as he buys the raw materials for his factory ahead, at a time when the securities or the raw materials look cheap. It is important to note that this is, in the very best sense, sentiment, which comes from the Latin verb *sentire*—"to perceive by the senses and the mind, to feel, to think." This is anything but sentimentalism, which is not encouraged in Wall Street.

Sentiment

Wall Street knows what sentiment is. It is a thing of high emprise, of adventure, of noble effort to a worthy end. It carried Boone across the Appalachians, and the Argonauts of 1849 through the passes of the Rocky Mountains. It is something we inherit from our forefathers of Shakespeare's time. It is what they brought with them when they put out upon the trackless sea, defying the galleons of Spain, and named a plantation on an unknown continent after their Virgin Queen. Virginia is still here but, as Austin Dobson sings, and Admiral Dewey might have asked, where are the galleons of Spain? This sentiment is a life-giving principle in national growth, not to be confused with sentimental statutes for "an official state flower," with "smile weeks" and slop-over "mothers' days." In the English-speaking race it is a perception which greatly survives for great occasions.   It was sentiment which first gave a kingly funeral, and a memorial stone in Westminster Abbey, to the Unknown Soldier who had saved the race.   It was sentiment which made all London still its voice and hold its breath, one year, to the minute, after the declaration of the armistice.   I spent those exalted two minutes at the Mansion House Corner, in the City of London, in November, 1919.   It was a moving sight, indeed, when it could bring tears to the eyes of the hardened newspaper reporter.

A great price movement is not the ordained outcome of enlightened individual choice, or even of individual leadership.   It is a thing far greater and more impressive, at least to one who has learned, from personal contact, in Wall Street and out,

> "How very weak the very wise,
> How very small the very great are."

Chapter XVI

AN EXCEPTION TO PROVE THE RULE

A PROVERB has been called the wisdom of many and the wit of one. Sometimes, when the controversialist finds the proverb inconvenient, he calls it a glittering generality or a truism. A French philosopher told us that all generalizations are fallacious, "including this one." But a truism is presumably true, even if it is trite. It is said that there is no rule without an exception, but as a sufficient number of exceptions would make it necessary to formulate a new rule, especially in economics, the proverb which best suits our purpose is that which says that the exception proves the rule, although Coke's *"Exceptio probat regulam de rebus exceptis"* is not what we want. But the proverb is even startlingly true about what may be called the great exception in the stock market averages.

Our two averages of railroad and industrial stocks must confirm each other to give weight to any inference drawn from the price movement. The history of the stock market as shown by these averages, going back many years, proves conclusively that the two averages move together. But there was one exception to this rule, and it is the more valuable for our purpose in that it is the exception which proves the rule we have set up.

Some Necessary History

It adds to the interest of the study of this subject that it is necessary to make excursions into contemporary history to explain the meaning of the price movement, often only fully apparent after the movement has been under way for many months. In 1918, for some nine months after we had entered the Great War, both averages showed a primary bull market with a strong secondary reaction over the end of that year. During that year the railroad stocks fully shared that upward swing but subsequently sold off, making almost a bear market of their own in 1919, when the industrials were strongest. Letters were written during the serial publication of these discussions, in which this well-known fact was adduced as a reason for rejecting the entire theory based upon the averages. But if ever an exception proved the rule this one does.

Remember that the industrial and railroad stocks used in the averages are essentially speculative. Only to a limited extent are they held for fixed income by people to whom safety of the principal should be the main consideration, and their holders are constantly changing. If they were not speculative they would be useless for a stock market barometer. The reason why railroad stocks during 1919 did not share the bull market in the industrials was that, through government ownership and government guaranty, they had in a real sense ceased, for the time at least, to be speculative. They could not advance in any market,

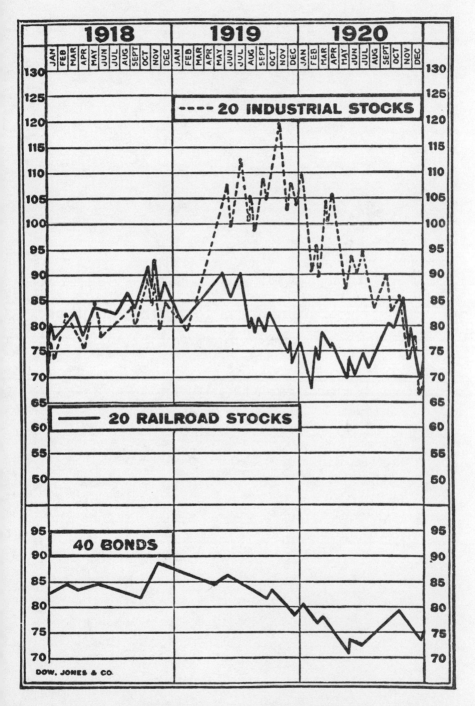

MOVEMENT OF STOCK-MARKET AVERAGES

bull or bear, more than enough to discount the estimated value of that guaranty.

An Impaired Barometer

Thus for a year or more the averages had half
their usual value as a barometer, or indeed less than
half, for the movement in the industrials lacked the
essential confirmation of a corresponding movement
in the speculative railroad stocks. It is made clear
by the accompanying chart that during that period the
railroads followed not the speculative market but the
market for bonds. They had nothing to expect beyond the government guaranty, unless, indeed, far-
sighted holders of them could have foreseen the
destruction of earning capacity resulting from the
colossal waste of government ownership and its subsequent collapse. It will be shown that the railroad
stocks during the period of that ownership paralleled
the speculative industrials accidentally and for different reasons, only so far as to discount the supposed
value of a government guaranty; relapsed, and recovered with an ensuing price movement governed essentially by the totally different conditions which are
compelling in the case of bonds.

An Important Distinction

There is some need to point out here the essential
difference between a bond and a stock. The stock is a
partnership obligation, while the bond is a debt, a

mortgage, a liability ranking ahead of the stock. The stockholder is a partner in the business, while the bondholder is a creditor of the company. The bondholder has lent the concern his money on the fixed assets, such as the railroad's real estate or the manufacturer's mills. But the essence of the bond is that its speculative feature to the holder is subordinate, or even non-existent. It is held for its income return. The price fluctuates strictly according to the purchasing power of the income. The price of the bond will be high when the necessaries of life are low, and the investment bond will decline in price as the cost of necessaries advances. It would be easy, but constantly misleading, to say that the price of bonds is regulated by the value of money. The interest rate fluctuates from day to day, and only by the issue terms of long-time bonds can we get any idea of the quotation for money over a long period of years, which is at the best an estimate, and often wrong.

A Definition for the Layman

It is simplest to say that the price of securities held for fixed income is in inverse ratio to the cost of living. If the latter is high the price of bonds or other securities held for fixed income will be low and their apparent yield, measured in dollars, will be large. If the cost of living is low the price of securities held for fixed income will be high and the apparent income, represented by the yield in dollars, will be correspondingly less.

Effects of Government Guaranty

It is plain, then, that with a government guaranty of a minimum return, based upon the average earnings of three years ended June 30, 1917, the railroads entered the fixed income class. If they had continued speculative, with no government guaranty and no government ownership, their fluctuations would not have been governed by the cost of living but by their earning capacity, and chiefly by their prospective earning capacity; for it cannot be too often repeated that the stock market is not reflecting conditions as they are to-day but conditions as far ahead as the combined intelligence of the country there concentrated can foresee them.

Let us consider the history of the war period as it affected the railroad stocks. When we entered the war, in the spring of 1917, the arrangement between the government and the railroads was purely tentative. So far as the stockholders knew, their investments were still speculative, and these followed the speculative trend. It was not until late on the day after Christmas, 1917, that the announcement that the railroads would be definitely taken over by the government was made. The stock market had not time to discount the new ownership on that day, but on the following day, December 27th, the average price of the twenty active railroad stocks closed at 78.08—an advance of no less than 6.41 points from the closing prices of the day before. For not more than two days previously was the idea that the roads would be per-

manently taken over considered seriously in the Street,
although it had been expected for some time past that
the government would advance the money for maturing
obligations and capital improvements.   On the morning of the day of the announcement one of the New
York newspapers, in the confidence of the Wilson Administration, had a story to the effect that the plan
was to take the roads over for a compensation based
on the average of five years' net earnings.   It is impossible to plumb the depths of Mr. Wilson's mind,
but this new ownership was assumed, then and for
long afterwards, to be permanent government ownership for all intents and purposes.

How the Averages Diverged

From the accompanying chart it will be seen that
in the rally throughout 1918 from the bear swing
which had followed the first bull market of the Great
War—that culminating in October, 1916—the railroad averages had accompanied the industrials in a
steady advance.   But from the time when the fate
of the stockholders became dominated by government
management and guaranty the two averages parted
company.   The high point of the movement in railroads was made in October, 1918, while the bull
market in the industrial stocks did not culminate until
November, 1919.   Toward midsummer of the latter
year the railroads had made some recovery, after a
break following the first impetuous buying on government guaranty.   But from that point they steadily

declined while the principal advance in the industrials was made, continuing to do so while the preliminary movement of the great decline of 1920 was in progress. In 1920 they ran counter to the falling industrials, on the way up actually crossing the industrials on the way down, in the autumn of 1920. There was simultaneously a confirmatory recovery in bonds.

The Esch-Cummins Act

It will be seen that the decline in the railroads in 1919 and the recovery in 1920 virtually paralleled the movement of the average daily prices of forty representative bonds in those years. It will be noticed how closely this corresponded to the inflation and subsequent deflation of the cost of living. During the spring and summer of 1919, while Mr. Wilson was absent in Europe, it was frequently reported that he was disappointed with the unexpected costliness and inefficiency of government ownership, and that he would seek an early opportunity for a return of the railroads to their private owners. There is reason to believe that he did expect, or at least hope, to return them about August 1, 1919, anticipating that Congress would have passed appropriate legislation by that time. Congress was working on the Esch-Cummins bill, now called the Transportation Act, which dragged through the summer and autumn until, on November 16th, the House of Representatives passed the measure. It was at that time, or early in December, that the President positively declared that he would return the roads on January 1st.   But the Senate did not pass the Esch-Cummins bill until late in February, 1920; so that the President was compelled to extend the limit he had fixed by two months.

Selling "Ex-Control"

But more than nine months before, in May, 1919, when the railroad average was making the first figure of a "double top," completed in July, *The Wall Street Journal* said that the strength of these stocks in the face of discouraging reports of earnings might be due to the fact that they were beginning to sell "ex-control."   There is no question that the decline from the point of the further (July) rally to the early low of 1920 was due to the appalling damage inflicted by government ownership, which actually, in most cases, had raised the operating cost above the operating revenue. The principal item, wages, had been advanced beyond all reason, by a management which was political rather than financial, and the cost of everything the railroads consumed had been multiplied.   The war administration had actually bid up railroad ties in Maine against itself, the only buyer, from thirty-seven cents each to $1.40.   It is noteworthy also that at that time the large but absolutely necessary increase in rates to render the railroads self-supporting under private operation was only being discussed.   It was in fact not granted by the Interstate Commerce Commission until the time of its usefulness had passed.

A Difference of Kind

Federal control actually ended on February 28, 1920, two days after the signing of the Esch-Cummins act, which, however, extended federal compensation for another six months, created the Labor Board and gave the Interstate Commerce Commission the 6 per cent net return as a rule of rate-making. Rates were not advanced until the following August, but Wall Street knew that they must necessarily be advanced, and, as usual, discounted that advantage as far ahead as it could see it—in this case nearly six months.

In considering the effect of the war upon business and production it is well to assure ourselves as to what extent the conditions it created are different, in kind or only in degree, from those following other wars. This was a difference in kind. Without help from other quarters the industrial stocks made a bull market off their own bat—a thing they had never done before. Stress is laid upon this fundamental difference here, and the causes which created it, because unless it is thoroughly explained and grasped it is inevitable that teachers and students of the future, to whom these discussions are intended to appeal quite as much as to the readers of the present, will become confused and discouraged, in the face of what might well be considered irreconcilable difficulties and discrepancies. Still another instance will be furnished of a like searching test.

A Sense of Proportion—and of Humor

There is no need for us to fall in love with our theory or to regard it in the false perspective of the enthusiast for any fad. If you hold a silver dollar at arm's length you can see it in its correct relation to surrounding objects. If you bring it too close to the eye its relation to those objects will become distorted and exaggerated, and you can hold it so close that you can see nothing else. Heaven forbid that I should attempt to found a school of economists prepared to die for the thesis that the world wabbles along on a theory of averages. There is no cry here for disciples. We can forgive a great deal to the founder of a school, but we can seldom forgive the school. Let us, therefore, hold the stock market barometer at such a readable distance from the eye that we shall not consider the barometer more important than the weather it predicts. We have sound theory to go upon, or this and the preceding chapters have been written in vain. Don't let us overwork it, as so many statisticians do. Scientists, even the greatest, are inclined to worship their hypotheses, with humiliating results. Herbert Spencer, the great synthetic philosopher, once said to the late Professor Huxley: "You may hardly believe it, but I, myself, wrote the beginning and at least the framework of a tragedy." "I can quite believe it," said Huxley. "I know the plot. It was how a perfectly beautiful theory was murdered by an ugly little fact."

Our Material Is Mostly Modern

Some disappointment has been expressed that Charles H. Dow said so little that was definite upon his own theory of the market movement, or was able to draw so few of the inferences which were implicit in that theory, to say nothing of the practical and useful truths developed from its application. The wonder is that he got so far with the scanty materials then available. In the latter part of 1902, when Dow died, but six of the twenty industrial stocks now in the average were in the average then, and the number of such stocks used was only twelve. Ten years before, it would have been impossible to find a sufficient number of representative and consistently active industrial stocks to make an average at all. The old averages, and I wish I were able to show examples of the market movement back as far as 1860, with at least a single average for fifteen stocks, had not the advantage of their present double form. We see how vitally important it is to have two averages correcting and confirming each other. But when McKinley was re-elected it was necessary to include Western Union even in the railroad averages, for lack of a consistent degree of activity in a sufficient number of stocks. We need not belittle the pioneers, or overpraise them. They necessarily had to break ground for themselves and improvise their own tools, while we, with all the benefit of their experience, only too often turn out work which is certainly less creative and often less sincere.

Chapter XVII

IF there had not been a bear market in stocks in the year 1917 it is probable that this series of discussions would never have been prepared. I should have felt that inferences from the sum of knowledge and intelligence represented by the market movement were empiric, or based upon insufficient premises. I should have said that the market was, for some incomprehensible reason, unable to look beyond the borders of the United States. It would have seemed plain that it was incapable of taking a sane and self-protective view of international affairs. Its findings might have been worth little more than the fluctuations in turnips at the crossroads grocery, for our chain of reasoning is as strong as its weakest link. But there was a major bear swing from October–November, 1916, until December of the following year which may justly be called the barometer's greatest vindication.

Uncertainty of the War Outlook

One of those precipitate critics who has failed to grasp the principle so constantly repeated in these discussions—that of the analyzed triple movement of the stock market and its bearing upon future events—asked why the market in the year 1917 made a warning major bear movement although business charts continued to show a large volume of practical prosperity, then and in the following year; while Babson's familiar black area of good business was never once below his amended line of growth, from the latter part of 1915 to near the end of 1920? But what constituted the excess volume of American business during the earlier war years? Was it not making supplies for the combatants? Were we not feeding them and arming them, and taking payment in I O U's? Have we not many billions of the I O U's outstanding, some of them never likely to be paid?

These things are important to remember, but there was a specific reason why there was a bear market in 1917, apart from the fact that the stock market kept its head, and did not treat war profits as a complete offset to the destruction of our past and future foreign customers. For the whole of that year the issue of the war was in doubt. The sum of market knowledge did not preclude a final German victory. Not until the end of 1917 did the stock market barometer begin to predict that the allies would win. The bull market which was born in December of that year anticipated the armistice by eleven months, and the failure of Germany's last tremendous drive by six months. However bravely we believe right must triumph, the wish, in 1917, was father to the thought. The bear market which then concluded had been a measure of insurance. It can teach little to those who cannot distinguish one kind of "prosperity" from another. It was the sanest of all stock market movements. It offers a demonstration of the market's vision higher than anything we have previously analyzed.

If Germany Had Won

Many readers must have asked themselves what would have happened to the world if Germany and her allies had won. Many more must have dismissed the possibility as too dreadful to contemplate. Conditions are bad enough now, in all conscience. But what would they have been with France crushed, Belgium enslaved, Italy in a state of anarchy, Great Britain ruined, bankrupt and unable to feed herself, with her merchant marine destroyed? What would have been the burden of the hundreds of billions of ransom Germany would have laid upon the world? How should we have liked her for a neighbor in the Caribbean? There has been a disintegration of nations, or perhaps a rebirth of nationalities (some possibly spurious), which has produced sufficiently grave consequences. But what would have happened to the world if the British Empire had been brought to irrecoverable wreck?

Such a possibility might well daunt the staunchest heart, but the stock market faced it, in 1917. It asked itself exactly these questions. Admiral Sims has told us since how desperate was the condition which the allies at that time confidentially admitted. It was not until the end of that year that our assistance became effective, although we had gone to war, largely unprepared, in the spring. The stock market did not know then (for no man knew) whether we should not be too late. There was little question that we might save our own skins, but it was the business of the market to insure against the consequences if we failed to save the allies. It has been said, in an earlier discussion, that the stock market takes into account many other things in addition to those chosen for tabulation and analysis by the most complete information bureau. Honest compilers of such records would be the last to contend that the warning movement of the stock market is limited in its application to a mere reflection of the coming business of the United States only.

Britain's National Debt

It will be highly instructive to treat in another discussion of the quiet years of contracted business which followed the bull market of 1908–9 and preceded the great war boom. There is a manifest connection between the bear market before the war and an event which, nevertheless, upset all calculations. It was a thing so vast that even now we are at a loss to find precedents in history, although there are incomplete ones following the long quarter of a century of war which culminated with the battle of Waterloo in 1815. We can probably get a better parallel there than some observers have supposed, if we accept length as to some degree offsetting intensity, and take the relative size of the conflicts compared with population and national wealth. There is one significant illustration which has not been offered elsewhere, so far as I know. It is that of the British national debt after the immense losses of the Napoleonic wars. Great Britain's debt at that time (1815–16) represented 31½ per cent of her estimated national wealth. Throughout the greater part of the century, and during the long reign of Queen Victoria, the debt was gradually paid off, until, previous to the Boer War (1899–1902) it amounted to not much more than 4 per cent of the estimated wealth.

In round figures, the Boer War cost Great Britain about a billion dollars, and raised the proportion of debt to national wealth to over 6 per cent. In the years between 1902 and 1914, in spite of the steady increase in the cost of living and the growth of taxation, the British national debt was again declining, although it did not reach the low proportion to national wealth of 1899. The British debt now is estimated at 33 per cent of the national wealth, or a proportion of about 1½ per cent more than that at the conclusion of the Napoleonic wars, which had lasted, with a three-year interregnum, from 1793 to 1815. No doubt it is a formidably high proportion. But it is far from a hopeless proportion; and this is a basic reason why, of all the money units depreciated in the conflict, the British pound sterling approximates respectably in exchange credit to the American dollar.

One of Our Own Liabilities

In 1917 the stock market was asking itself what would happen to the pound sterling, and everything

else, if Germany won. If the German printing presses
are working overtime to turn out paper marks, what
sort of currencies would the allies be circulating now
had the German drive in the spring of 1918 succeeded?
We have satisfied ourselves by analysis that the essential quality of the stock market barometer is its foresight. Could there have been a more striking instance
of the clarity of its vision than that salutary bear market, when we were deceiving ourselves with paper
profits, inflation wages and inflation prices? In 1916
we had placed in the hands of the labor unions, through
the Adamson Act, the power to inflate wages without
guaranty of any corresponding productive return.
Congress, with a presidential election in sight, had
tried to buy votes, lulling the American consumer and
taxpayer, who were to pay the bill, with professions of
a philanthropic desire to inaugurate shorter hours with
consequent greater safety for the railroad traveler.
Of course the Adamson Act did not mean shorter
hours but only earlier, and more, overtime. The
hours of railroad labor were actually lengthened; for
it was made strictly to the interest of the men, up to
sixteen hours, to stretch their day to the legal limit.
We know now what the demoralizing effect upon other
labor was, in every department of industry. With
such a precedent no wage demand was too preposterous
after our own entry into the war, early in 1917, had
tied our hands. There was hardly a single manufacturer in the country, and certainly not a consumer, who
did not reap the deadly consequences of that humiliating Congressional surrender.

What Watered Labor Means

In an earlier chapter, that on "Water in the Barometer," I have alluded to watered labor as being incomparably more deadly than watered capital. How many billions of our national debt might not have been deducted, as never incurred, if there had been no such dilution? Mr. Piez, director-general of the Emergency Fleet Corporation during the war, estimated that the efficiency of labor had been dangerously reduced through smaller individual output and larger wages, the latter only excused by the higher prices for commodities of which those wages themselves had been the automatic cause. He said:

"Labor had been deliberately slack during the war. In the Atlantic Coast shipyards workmen received $2 for the same time that a year ago (1916) brought only $1, but that the individual output was only two-thirds of what it had been a year before."

Guy Morrison Walker, in *The Things That Are Caesar's,* quoting Director-General Piez, says that the unit of cost production during our share in the war was only one-third what it was at the beginning of hostilities. Estimating our national debt at $24,000,000,000 and deducting from it all, up to $11,000,000,000, owed by the allied nations who borrowed from us, there remains $13,000,000,000, of which a large part, possibly half, constitutes watered labor. But we are to remember that in the advances to the allies, which were made not in cash but in the necessaries of war, of which labor was the costliest

item, the water was also present in the same proportions. It was less the cash wages than the slacking,
shirking and bad work. If we took all the water
which has ever been squeezed out of corporation capitalization, by the remorseless stock market, we should
not have a sum anything nearly approaching the shame-
lessly watered labor upon which we and our children
and our children's children must continue to pay interest for half a century to come.

Paying for Bad Work

It has not been difficult to show the largely nominal
character of "water" in capitalization. How relatively
seldom has it represented any real loss, to anybody,
compared with the irreparable losses from watered
labor! How unsatisfying must seem the industrial
and commercial activity, recorded of the five years of
the war in graphic statistical tabulation, when we have
deducted from it the triple price for that prosperity
for which from henceforth we have to pay. Everyone
of those sham dollars must be met in real dollars.
Every wasted hour of bad work or shirked work has
to be paid for in an hour of good work.

Secondary Inflation—And After

If I had to forecast the coming major bull swing
in stocks, and the area of a possible secondary inflation, likely to be much less than that of the war but
sufficiently obvious, I would compare it with the six
years which followed the battle of Waterloo in Great

Britain. It was in 1821 that the Bank of England went back upon a gold basis, and the premium upon gold disappeared. A self-deluded House of Commons admitted in 1819 that the famous *Bullion Report* was right, and that fiat money was wrong. And then followed the years in which the deflation of the war levels was taken in hand by a nation in which every sixth person was a registered pauper. Dare we suppose that we shall not pay our relatively lighter bill in some such way as this, sooner or later? It is less than four years since the armistice. The bull market in progress while this is written may or may not carry us to a date corresponding to that of 1821 in Europe. We are in no such desperate condition as Great Britain was then. But our foreign customers have an almost incalculably greater reckoning to meet. It is not a problem which can be solved by quack remedies. It can, indeed, be settled only by throwing the quack remedies out of the window, for the patient has been doped to the danger point.

Unsuspected Qualities of the Barometer

But sufficient unto the day is the evil thereof. The stock market barometer is enough for our purpose in that it records, well in advance, the periods of depression and prosperity alike, giving, as we have seen, the signal for a clear track ahead and the warning of danger. The averages are saying now that general business will be more active and more cheerful in the summer of 1922. The barometer does not profess to predict the duration of such prosperity, although on close scrutiny it seems to give tolerably clear indications of the character of the boom or depression which it forecasts. The business depression of 1908–9, predicted by the bear market of 1907, was deep rather than long. The period of prosperity of the latter part of 1909 and 1910 was more extended but much shallower; and the market bull movement which preceded it was also slower and longer than the bear market, while its range was correspondingly less. This is strikingly true of the narrower later fluctuations, both in business and in the stock market, with the latter characteristically preceding the former. It was only in the war years that the preceding major swings of the stock market became as vigorous as the developments in our trade.

It is also noteworthy that during those quiet years of narrow fluctuations before the war the volume of transactions in stocks, as shown in our twenty-five-year chart, contracted also. The average monthly transactions compare in volume, upon the whole, rather unfavorably with those preceding the re-election of McKinley in 1900. The years 1911, 1912, 1913, and 1914 show a volume of trading below that recorded in the years 1897, 1898, 1899, and 1900; and the year 1899 made a better showing in the average transactions than any one of the later years here taken for comparison.

Forecasting the War

We may say, therefore, that the stock market does in a measure foresee, although probably in a way not sufficiently definite to be of much practical usefulness, the character, and even the dimensions, of the thing it predicts.   One thing it foresaw, so far as human knowledge could, was the war itself.   Somebody knew that it was a lively possibility, and the bear market which preceded the war was no accident or mere coincidence.   It will be remembered that in the latter part of 1912 a bear movement set in, of decidedly mild intensity compared with most of the bear movements of the past and especially those to which we have given particular consideration.   There was an area of business depression of no great depth in 1914 which could be offered as partly convincing justification of the preceding major bear swing.   But there can be little doubt that the decline was also influenced by liquidation of stock held by those who realized the dangerous possibilities in the German attitude toward other nations. This must have started somewhere about the opening of the Kiel Canal, strategically connecting the Baltic with the North Sea through German territory.

It may be justly claimed that the bear market, quite apart from predicting a contraction in business, was also discounting the possibilities of war.   In a previous study, referring to the line of distribution made in 1914, before the outbreak of hostilities, it was shown that foreign liquidation was responsible for turning what would normally have been a line of accumulation into a line of distribution, during the period of almost three months of equilibrium so represented.   To those who profess themselves dissatisfied that the major stock market movements are not always immediately

adjustable to the various current business charts, it
may be said that the fault is not in our barometer.
That is universal, and takes note of international facts
where those tabulations do not. If, therefore, they
inadequately confirm our deductions, so much the worse
for them. We have found that the more severe the
test we apply to our barometer the more triumphantly
does it vindicate its usefulness. It would be difficult
to overestimate the value of its prescience both before
the war and in the course of the conflict. What if
the war had come at the top of a bull market?

Chapter XVIII

A SWEEPING assertion requiring no qualification would probably be one of two things. It would be an axiom, self-evident and containing its own proof; as, for instance, "the sum of the angles of any triangle is equal to two right angles." Or it would be a truism not greatly worth stating. I have said in previous necessary criticism that tabulated business records, however presented, are at best records, and only in a minor degree forecasts. But that is a statement which requires at least some qualification, because the youngest but most scientific of our business records embodies a quality of forecast. This is the service of Harvard University's Committee on Economic Research. Its index chart does offer a method of forecasting business, for the good reason that it adapts the idea of the stock market barometer, which has been in successful use by *The Wall Street Journal* and its allied publications for the past twenty years.

A Chart With a Forecast

Those familiar with the Harvard economic service will recollect that it uses three lines in its business chart —a line of speculation, a line of banking and a line of business. It commits itself to no floundering attempt to show that "action and reaction are equal." Its service dates from after the war; but it publishes a chart from 1903 to 1914 inclusive, which is a most valuable confirmation of what has been here laid down in the discussion of the stock market barometer. Its line of speculation, during those twelve years, uniformly precedes the lines of business and banking. In other words speculation anticipates the developments of business, which is exactly what these chapters have been directed to prove.

The Harvard Committee on Economic Research takes the average stock market prices for its line of speculation. It recognizes how completely the war threw many such calculations out of gear by breaking up the very foundations upon which they were based. Harvard, therefore, does not publish any chart of the years of the war. I find, in looking back over my records and newspaper comments, that conclusions upon the stock market movement and its prophetic relation to the business of the country were dropped almost entirely for the same reason. We have seen that when the government took over the railroads on a guaranty we had remaining merely the speculative movement of the industrial stocks, without any corresponding movement of the railroads to check and confirm it. We have seen also, in analyzing the war period which the Harvard service not unwisely ignores, that the stock market did, in a most valuable way, act as best it could in holding before the public mind the possibilities of the war itself, notably in the bear market of 1917, and that it also foreshadowed the war in the line of distribution for the three months preceding its outbreak.

A Movement Greater Than the Major Swing

But there is another indication given by the averages which, while of the greatest importance to-day, has been largely unrecognized. We have seen that the railroad stocks, where there was a free market for them, in the years under private ownership, shared the major swings; and that we had a bull market culminating in 1909, a bear market determined in the following year, a greatly restricted and hesitating bull market, especially in the railroad stocks, carrying into the latter part of 1912, and another bear market culminating immediately after the reopening of the Stock Exchange in December, 1914, following eighteen weeks of war.

There is a historical significance—a lesson and warning of the very first importance—in the general trend downward of the prices of railroad stocks from 1906 to June, 1921. This is a movement not only wider than the major swings but even more considerable than any of these assumed cycle periods with which a previous discussion dealt. It has extended nearly sixteen years. It is not only likely but as nearly certain as anything merely human can be, that the railroad stocks on the average will improve in the coming year 1922. But there is a radical reason why they will not, in any near period of time, attain the old freedom and buoyancy which they enjoyed in the later lifetime of great railroad builders like James J. Hill and Edward H. Harriman. A condition for railroad enterprise has been established which has not only taken much of the speculative value out of the stocks but much of the permanent value as well. It is a condition which has left the railroads themselves emasculated and weak, with their virile creative power removed.

Roosevelt and the Railroads

If Theodore Roosevelt could have foreseen the deadly consequences of the agitation against railroad corporations which he inaugurated; if he could have realized that he was not applying temporary checks to temporary evils, that his policies, so called, carried to their logical conclusion, would cripple railroad enterprise for incalculable years to come, and perhaps forever, in order to punish a few who had abused the power which necessarily accrues to successful enterprise—we may be sure he would have acted far otherwise. The public power to reform has been construed, in the past fourteen years, as the power to destroy. Railroad development, which in the past has not only accompanied the increase in population but, on this continent at least, has preceded it, is now moribund or dead. No new capital has been forthcoming for the greatly needed extension of railroad facilities to parts of the country that do not enjoy them, to say nothing of greater terminal facilities. Lines of communication are the very arteries of civilization. But the adaptation of the Roosevelt theories—or rather the misconception of those theories, the ascription to Theodore Roosevelt of ideas he never held—has resulted in a hardening of those arteries, in a weakening of the great central heart which pumps the lifeblood through them.

An Arrested Development

We can see the fact for ourselves in the mileage of the United States taken contemporaneously with each ten-year census. If we had two hundred and forty thousand eight hundred and thirty miles of railroad in 1910—an increase of nearly 25 per cent since 1900 and more than double the railroad mileage in 1880— we should have had a continuing increase, shown in the census of 1920, of as much as ninety thousand miles. We have not had one-sixth of it. The increase has been less than fifteen thousand miles, the irreducible minimum, just enough to keep the railroads alive. A "craven fear of being great" has possessed our politicians. They have paralyzed the growth of our most important industry rather than permit a few conspicuous individuals to grow rich by the turning of great ideas to great needs. Harriman and Hill were rich when they died. I knew them both, and I know that their wealth was almost fortuitous. They were rich because they could have done nothing creative without the necessary financial strength to make them independent. But Harriman never controlled the stock of one of the railroads he directed. He was

implicitly and deservedly trusted by the stockholders.
He never had a voting majority in Southern Pacific,
Union Pacific or even Chicago & Alton. He and
Hill, incidentally to their own wealth, brought comfort, competence, affluence, to millions of Americans
they never saw. The period of railroad development
so clearly set forth in the record and chart of our
barometer from 1897, the end of the reconstruction
era, to 1907, the beginning of the destruction era, was
upon the whole the greatest, most deservedly successful and most creative period in American history.

A Cycle of Human Folly

We have seen and proved the correctness of Dow's
theory of the price movement. We know that the
stock market has simultaneously a major swing upward or downward, a secondary reaction or rally, and
a daily fluctuation. But might we not almost go
further and establish a sort of cycle of our own, not
related in the least to those cycles which we have previously considered, with their imposing and instructive
lists of panic dates? The Harvard University chart
ventures as far as is wise and profitable. Its series is
"Depression," "Revival," "Prosperity," "Strain,"
"Crisis," without assuming absolute length for any of
these states, and even taking "Strain" and "Crisis,"
or "Crisis" and "Panic," or "Strain" and "Panic," as
in some cases coincident. But there is another cycle
which we can deduce from our records of the averages,
which could almost be called a cycle of human folly.

It could only occur in a democracy such as ours, where a people with the power to govern themselves too rashly assume and misconstrue the greatest privilege of such a democracy—the power to make their own mistakes.

Coxey's Army

It will not be difficult to show what I mean. In the year 1890, with a Republican President and a Republican Congress, the air was full of uncertainty and sectionalism; and legislation, which is always in some degree a compromise, had become an immoral compromise. A true statesman can compromise successfully on non-essentials with no real sacrifice of vital principles. But the Sherman Silver Purchase Act was a sacrifice of principle which brought about the gravest consequences, because it adulterated the very lifeblood of our financial system. The great and inevitable panic, due to consequent inflation and overspeculation, might well have come in 1892 had it not been that, in that year, we had an extraordinarily large wheat harvest coincidentally with a complete failure of the crop of Russia, our only considerable international competitor. The panic came, therefore, in 1893.

For four years after the country was full of very much the same kind of Populism which is so rife at present. Coxey's Army started from Masillon, Ohio, to march on Washington in 1894. Coxey's main postulate—that prosperity could be restored with the unlimited issue of fiat money—was marching all over the United States. The Middle West was rotten with it. The turn of the tide was marked by William Allen White's celebrated editorial, "What's the Matter With Kansas?" Railroad managers, during those dreadful years, were in the last depths of despair. All but a few strong and sound roads went into bankruptcy. As much as 87 per cent of the country's railroad mileage in 1896 was in receivership. Only with the first election of McKinley did the country emerge into a state of sanity and light.

Ten Prosperous Years

It had tried out the Populist follies—free silver and all the rest of them—and found that they pointed in the direction of national bankruptcy. Politicians were terrified at the results of their rash enactments. For ten years, between 1897 and 1907, the paralyzing hand of politics was removed from the business of the United States. We never had such a period of prosperity, before or since. The railroad development in that time was greater than it had ever been before. It was a decade which saw the broadest and most beneficent industrial amalgamations, of which the United States Steel Corporation is the outstanding example. It was a time when the cost of living was upon the whole low, although it was rising in the latter part of the ten-year period. It was a time when wages were good, not merely in their amount as expressed in dollars and cents, but in their purchasing power.

"And Jesurun Waxed Fat, and Kicked"

But "Jesurun waxed fat, and kicked." Can it be that democracies cannot stand prosperity? Or is there still no need to make so wide an assumption? We have seen that labor agitation reaches its maximum, not in the lean years, when unions are impotent or non-existent, but in the fat years, when labor is at a premium and the leaders have at their disposal more union funds than they can wisely spend. Agitation is not, as so many of us have assumed, the result of trade depression. It is, indeed, the kicking of the national Jesurun when he waxes fat. The dangerous foundation of the Populism which ineffaceably marked the nineties had been laid in the years before. We seem to be running into such an era of Populism once more. The war has, of course, thrown any possible "cycle" out of kilter, but the evil fertilization of the impressionable public mind, implanted by the agitation against personal property, is bound to bear its noxious fruit in the years to come.

Public Opinion's Second Thoughts

It would be extending the purpose of the stock market barometer, and the design of these discussions beyond their proper field, if I ventured upon a forecast based upon this cycle of popular folly. We can see how far behind us the golden ten-year period of true prosperity is. We can name the peak of it. We saw its sudden and dramatic collapse in 1907. The feverish productive activity growing out of the war is no fair test, just as it is no sound basis. Before another ten years like those between 1897 and 1907 can be inaugurated, must the country go through a period at the end of which it will ask itself, not "What's the matter with Kansas?" but "What's the matter with America?" I would be a poor American indeed if I did not believe that the good sense of the American people can find the right answer when that day comes. There is no weaker fallacy of democracy than the one which assumes that public opinion is always right. It depends on what you call "public opinion." Such opinion, as represented by the voice of the noisiest, in its first expression is generally wrong, or right for the wrong reason. But the second thought of the great American people, as history shows, is usually right.

Recalling Lincoln

Annually we repeat to each other the great words of the Gettysburg Address. Lincoln declared that what was said there—and be it remembered that he was not at the time considered the principal orator of that great occasion—would bear little place in men's memories compared with what was done there. He underrated, with characteristic modesty, the imperishable quality of a great thought greatly expressed. Lincoln's words in 1863 at Gettysburg will be remembered by millions who will hardly know the conditions of that battle or which side won it, except to assume that the imperishable Union was there sustained. But if, at that time, there had been in operation a federal law to "recall" officers federally elected, it is well within the bounds of probability that Lincoln might have been recalled and not re-elected. It was not until the following year that his re-election to the presidency was a certainty, and there are readers of these discussions old enough to remember the moral depression of 1863 and its effect upon the public mind.

Paying for Government Meddling

It can be seen, from this instance of many, that the second thought of the American mind was right, where its first impression may well have been wrong. Look at the enthusiasm recently created in the Middle West by the Non-Partisan League, with its half grain of truth and its bushel of quackery or fraud. Dare we assume that we have extruded that poison from our system? Hardly a week passes that a bill for the creation of billions of fiat money, under one pretext or another, is not introduced into the Congress of the United States.

If there is one lesson which should have been burned in upon the public mind in the past decade, it is that when government interferes with private enterprise, even where that enterprise is directed to the development of a public utility, it can do incalculable harm and very little good. The people who develop the railroads and the natural resources of the country are only ourselves. Railroad ownership is, in a way, more representative than ever Congress can be. It includes every depositor in the saving banks, every holder of an insurance policy, and, indirectly, every holder of a United States bond, so long as the interest on that bond is dependent on taxation largely derived from railroad enterprise.

Legislating Everybody Poor

It must be admitted that this chapter is less about the averages as a barometer than as a record. But our discussions would be incomplete if the most important lesson of that record were overlooked for the easily understood psychological reason that it is written in such large letters across the sky. Look at the course of the railroad averages on the twenty-five-year chart. More than sixteen years ago the twenty active railroad stocks made the highest point on record, at 138.36, on January 22, 1906. They never saw that figure again, but came within less than four points of it in August, 1909, at 134.46. The next high point was in October, 1912, at 124.35—more than fourteen points below the record. On the next advance the net recession was still further, while the railroad average reached only 109.43 on January 31, 1914, the top of a half-hearted rally. Even the next recovery, in the first bull market of the war, only carried the railroad stocks to 112.28, on October 4, 1916. They did not share the bull market of 1919, as we know, for we have devoted an earlier chapter to the study of the reason.

To-day the price is fifty points below the record, and

less than fourteen points above the low figure of July 25, 1898—more than twenty-three years ago. Analyze this steady decline over a period of sixteen years, sufficient to include the simple cycle of the Harvard University Committee on Economic Research at least twice over—more than long enough to exceed the period between two of our greatest panics—those of 1857 and 1873—covering a time 60 per cent longer than the Jevons ten-year cycle. See how the steadily declining line of values mocks and belittles the assumed medial line of growing national wealth postulated in some of the better-known business charts. Can the richest nation in the world afford to allow its politicians to run its greatest investment and its greatest industry into the ground as steadily and stupidly as this? Are we throwing away the thing our fathers built, or allowing politicians to squander it, from some idea that the ruin of the railroad stockholders will make other people richer and happier? We know, or ought to know, that we cannot legislate everybody rich. But here is one more example added to that of Russia, of how it is possible to legislate everybody poor.

Chapter XIX

IT has been shown in previous discussions how relatively unimportant stock market manipulation is. But history presents some striking instances of manipulation, and much was possible in the Wall Street of two decades back which would not be feasible or tolerated to-day. It would not, for instance, be within the bounds of possibility to manipulate either the Steel stocks or Amalgamated Copper for distribution to-day as they were undoubtedly manipulated by James R. Keene twenty-one years ago. These two stocks are merely offered for example, and it is not to be assumed that I am placing them on a parity. There was an arrogant impudence about the distribution of Amalgamated Copper which makes me hot all over, even now. I remember that I criticized it, with all the freedom the law (and Charles H. Dow) allowed, at the time it was in progress.

Conceived in Sin

The Amalgamated Copper Company was conceived in sin and born under similar auspices. It was offered for subscription with a capital of $75,000,000 early in 1899, and the subscription books closed on May 4th of that year. A number of "newspapers," of a kind now happily defunct, reported that the stock had been "five times oversubscribed!" It did not sound probable, with the stock selling at a heavy discount in less than a month. The general stock market was on the down grade then. It did not turn until the summer of the following year. Of all the contemporary comments on that disreputable exploit those of the *Boston News Bureau,* which flatly refused to be humbugged, were about the most vitriolic. Here is one of them, published less than a month after the fivefold "oversubscription." On June 1, 1899, the *Boston News Bureau* said:

"The drop in Amalgamated Copper stock which was the feature of the trading in outside securities yesterday, was particularly appropriate at this time when the general railway list is on the down grade. Many shrewd observers in Wall Street contend that the formation of the Amalgamated Copper Company was the red flag which warned conservative investors and speculators away from the security market; that a blind pool calling for a capital of $75,000,000 should be oversubscribed five times was an indication to the better element of speculators that the public lost its head and the crash would not be far distant.

"One of the worst features of the whole case is that the National City Bank, which is the largest institution of its kind in this country, should have stood sponsor for such a transaction," etc., etc.

Amalgamated Copper

It will be seen that, in spite of all the flubdub circulated about "oversubscription," the flotation had been a failure. The *Boston News Bureau* continued to comment upon "'The Amalgamated Fiasco," "Promises and Predictions Against Realities," "The Humor and Pathos of Copper Promises," in an acridly humorous vein. In the same month of June there were rumors that control of the Anaconda company had been purchased by the organizers of Amalgamated Copper, for something like $45 a share, though it was quoted at $70 a share by the time Amalgamated was floated, and was said to be going into the new Amalgamated company at $100 a share. The same Boston article points out that the $75,000,000 capital of Amalgamated Copper should have been sufficient to pay for the entire capital of the constituent companies, although only a control, presumably 51 per cent, was declared to have been acquired. The whole transaction was so raw that in the better Wall Street of to-day it seems almost unbelievable.

Keene's Part in Distribution

In the latter part of 1904, three years after the manipulated distribution of the stock by James R. Keene had taken place, that eminent operator wrote a letter, which became public, in which he admitted that he distributed, "for the account of Henry H. Rogers and associates," $22,000,000 of Amalgamated Copper (two hundred and twenty thousand shares) at prices ranging from ninety to ninety-six. In that letter he indicated the period of distribution with sufficient clearness. In the following January I published, in *The Wall Street Journal*, an analysis of what he had done, as shown by the recorded sales, under the title

of "A Study in Manipulation."   That analysis did not
deal with the ethical question.   You cannot say much
about the ethics of people who seem to have none.   By
taking the sales of Amalgamated Copper stock, as
recorded on the ticker, together with the names of the
brokers executing orders as reported from the Stock
Exchange, and by comparing periods of activity it
seemed possible to dot Mr. Keene's "i's" and cross
his "t's."

It had the result of making me some enemies in
Wall Street, although, to do James R. Keene justice,
I do not think he was one of them.   I have said before
that we were never intimate.   But he made oppor-
tunities to see me at various times after that analysis
was published, and nothing I could say seemed to convince him that I had not had some illicit access to his
books.   As he put it, "Somebody must have leaked."
The Wall Street of that time, and the nature of his
own business, made Keene habitually suspicious.   His
mentality was incomplete in the respect that he found
it hard to believe a simple truth where it depended
upon the unsupported word of anybody.   Really great
men, and some children, know when to believe—and
whom.   Keene was not a great man.

A Difference Between Steel and Copper

Leaving all questions of ethics apart, there was
probably nothing more ably done in its day than the
distribution of Amalgamated Copper in the stock
market.   Keene's handling of United States Steel com-

mon and preferred will remain an example of consummate generalship. But in that instance he had the enormous advantage of a public which wanted the stock he had to sell. It is not true that there was much real "water" in the capitalization of Steel. What was called watered capital was only intelligently anticipated growth. United States Steel was floated in 1901, and three years afterwards was showing a well-established surplus of 4.9 per cent on the common stock sold to the public at fifty, which surplus had been more than doubled by 1905. In an earlier article I have pointed out the genuine book value of the stock now.

But Amalgamated Copper was an utterly different proposition. As a work of art the distribution, compared with that of Steel, bears about the relation of a Meissonier to one of the heroic battle pictures of De Neuville. Keene, in his subsequent statement, said that he was reluctant to take the matter in hand. It was not that he had to create a market, as in the case of United States Steel common and preferred; he had to begin his distribution in a market which others had done their stupid best to spoil.

Earlier Manipulation

On analysis of the sales, the first significant period seems to be that between December 3, 1900, and about the middle of January, 1901. Taking advantage of the general bull movement which set in shortly before the second election of McKinley, such members of the public as had really subscribed for Amalgamated Copper originally were unloading on the promoters of the enterprise. Certain "court circulars" of the time were talking boldly of "inside buying." They were right for once. Insiders were buying because they could not help themselves. They were "accumulating," much against their will, to judge from the downward movement of the stock. With a knowledge of the backs of the cards as well as the faces, the "Standard Oil crowd" which hatched the company could not conceal their crude and clumsy methods. We may here recapitulate the movements and total sales during this period:

The opening price December 3, 1900, was   96
Sales from December 3d to December
    13th were   160,000
The fluctuation in that period was from 96 to 90¼
Sales from December 14, 1900, to January 11, 1901, were..............   295,000
The fluctuation in that period was from 89¾ to 96

With all this stimulation the closing price on January 11, 1901, was only 91⅛.

Keene's First Appearance

Keene's first appearance seems to have been made then, and he was much too clever not to see that it would be necessary to break the market for the stock before he put it to a level which would attract the speculative public. The next record is:

Opening price January 12, 1901....   91
Sales from January 12th to January
    19th   70,000

Fluctuation in that period from..... 92¼ to 90¼
Closing price January 19th.........   90½
Sales from January 20th to January
  26th   88,000
Fluctuation in that period from..... 92 to 83¾
Closing price January 26th.........   89

This closing price of January 26th is a tribute to
Keene's ability. It was a much more real price than
the ninety-six momentarily established by the fatuous
"insiders" in the previous December. The beginning
of Keene's operations is characteristic. There were
transactions averaging from twenty thousand to thirty
thousand shares daily in the third week of January,
1901, when, on the 20th of the month, the price was
hammered to eighty-six, fluctuated between 83¾ and
89 on the following day, and tended to settle down
stolidly at 88¼ on the day after. The gossip obtain-
able at the time was beneath contempt from a news
point of view, but was well calculated to stimulate the
avarice of the public. Everything tended to show
that, if Keene was in the market at all, he was raiding
the stock for a turn on the bear side. It is not ven-
turing too far to say that he had previously taken no
trouble to cover up his tracks, in order to create exactly
that impression.

What a Major Bull Swing Made Possible

But the McKinley boom in the broadening market
was well under way. Stocks were in that great swing,
so violently interrupted, but not terminated, by the

Northern Pacific corner and panic of the following May. Nothing could have suited Keene better than to have it believed that he was short of a "Standard Oil stock." He admits to having sold all the stock of the Rogers pool, at prices from ninety to ninety-six, shortly before the advance to one hundred and twenty-eight. That advance did not take place until the middle of the following April, but early in March the stock was already selling well above par. I assumed, when writing in 1905, that Keene meant that the $22,000,000 of stock was not credited to Rogers and his friends at one average price, but perhaps in a series of large blocks of stock averaging from ninety to ninety-six, after allowing for the cost of manipulation. Some of it was, of course, sold much higher, but we have already seen that some of it was sold below eighty-four.

Keene's Second Stage

Keene was not the man to press the market when it was going his way, and there followed a period where the stock was judiciously allowed to take care of itself, with occasional stimulus to cultivate bullish sentiment. Transactions were in relatively light volume. In the next period the extreme fluctuation was less than five points, but it is noteworthy that the higher figure was the prevailing price when we see Keene's hand again:

Sales January 26th to February 23d..   110,000
Fluctuation in that period.......... 92⅜ to 87¾

In this quiet period of a month he may have sold some real stock but certainly never forced it on the market. It is difficult to say how many shares he actually dealt in that he might distribute so large a quantity. It was possibly ultimately three times the stock he had to sell. In the early stages he was employing brokers on both sides of the market, even if they did not know that they were executing matched orders. That was, and is, against the Stock Exchange rules, and we can afford, at this distance of time, to give them the benefit of the doubt. As the market improved, manipulation of that kind probably grew less, and of course as the public took hold it disappeared altogether.

Keene's Final Distribution

What may be called the third movement shows the final distribution of the stock:

Opening price February 28th........   92⅜
Sales February 28th to April 3d......   780,000
Fluctuation in that period from...... 92 to 103¾
Closing price April 3d............   100⅜

It is in this period that Keene probably distributed the bulk of his two hundred and twenty thousand shares. He admitted that much to me, and was never satisfied with my answer to his question as to how I knew.

It is one of the discreditable facts of that period that throughout this trading Amalgamated Copper was practically on an 8 per cent basis. It was declaring 1½ per cent quarterly, with a half per cent extra; and its directors, with that extraordinary fatuity for which the public ultimately paid, were convinced that they could hold up the world price of the metal indefinitely. One of the items of gossip in the early part of the Keene movement was to the effect that the decline of the metal in London, then and now the world's free market for copper, had at last been checked effectually. It was not so. But it was as near the truth as any of the rumors of that curious time. It was some years before the competing copper magnate, Augustus Heinze, reached a settlement with the Amalgamated Copper people, but such a settlement was among the rumors then exploited, and one of the principal bull arguments.

The Public's Own Boom

As a net result of the manipulation here detailed Keene had, in the first fortnight of April, 1901, created a market for the stock which may well have surprised himself. It was at least twice as broad as it had been in February or March, with daily transactions amounting to two hundred and fourteen thousand shares in one case, and to almost as much on several other days during that month. It should be compared with the record, during Keene's activities, of seventy-seven thousand shares on March 6th, with an extreme fluctuation of nearly three points.

It may be taken that the subsequent trading showed all obstacles removed from the stock's pathway to the top:

Sales from April 4th to April 16th. .   1,275,000
Advance in price from . . . . 101⅛ to 128⅜

The stock of the Rogers pool had been marketed and, indeed, greedily eaten up in the enthusiasm of a general bull market.

Their Own Gold Brick

It is a humiliating exhibit in the indictment of human nature that the "insiders" who had called in Keene seem actually to have begun to believe in their own gold brick. It is of record that Henry H. Rogers, quite in the manner of the man who has "heard something from a friend of his who knows an insider," informed Keene that "the stock was going to advance; that he had received letters from parties who were going to buy, and that he suggested Mr. Keene should join in the movement." It is needless to say that the net was vainly spread in the sight of that wary old bird. But the stock certainly advanced some twenty points beyond the price at which it was selling when Keene had finished his distribution.

It is also significant, in the study of an incident which is not at all likely to recur, that, in the later trading, houses which felt flattered in those days to be called "Keene brokers" were much more conspicuous than in the earlier time when the real Keene trading was in progress. Mr. Keene's name, to judge by the gossip current at the time, was only mentioned when he had safely completed his selling. What happened subsequently would be interesting to know, but there is not the same evidence to go upon.

Petroleum and Swelled Head

There is no "Standard Oil crowd" now. The millionaires who comprised that group were new to the possession of great wealth. They believed themselves invincible, up to the time of the issue of Amalgamated Copper. They made many mistakes, then and after, but as time went on they learned sense and got out of the stock market. They were so overwhelmingly right about petroleum, and particularly Standard Oil, that they could afford to risk enormous losses in other directions. Some day some one will unkindly tell the story of young Mr. John D. Rockefeller, and his venture in "Little Leather." Only a young man with a really well-to-do father could afford to spend so much on his education. There is good reason to suppose that his expensive post-graduate course in the school of experience had permanent and even admirable effect.

I have told, in earlier discussions, how heartily wrong Henry H. Rogers could be, and how his pride of opinion laid all the blame upon the ignorant stock market, which, in the last showdown, is always right. When he died in 1908 he was worth $50,000,000, and it is possible that his estate would have shown twice that amount had he lived another two years. Some of his work was good, and calculated to endure. The Virginian Railroad was the best built road, in its original construction, ever undertaken and completed in the United States. It almost broke the heart of its godfather that, with his financial backing and personal wealth, he was compelled to borrow money in

1907 for his pet railroad, on terms equal to 7 per cent with his personal guaranty. Even there he miscalculated the meaning of the stock market. It was saying, in the most explicit way, that H. H. Rogers was lucky to get money on any terms whatever. Money of that kind during the panic year may be said to have commanded anything the lender chose to ask.

Lessons from the Incident

In this detailed examination of a notorious essay in manipulation there are some important lessons on the nature and quality of our barometer. Remember that Amalgamated Copper was in the Unlisted Department of the Stock Exchange, which is now abolished. It was, as the *Boston News Bureau* said at the time, a blind pool, in every sense of the term. Nothing like it could occur under the present listing requirements. I do not believe that anything of the kind would be possible in the Curb Market's new Exchange. Modern methods of publicity are so much better than those of twenty years ago that a movement of such a nature would not last for a week before it met the active and effective opposition of the banks. No financial clique, like that which constituted the Standard Oil group, is likely to acquire in the future the unwholesome power which was exercised at the time we have had under review. But the best of all protections is the greatly enlightened public opinion. Information on financial matters is now incalculably better than it ever was before. The cure for corruption is publicity. There is no such sanitary agent as full daylight. People are no longer deceived by the mystery talk which was peddled as news two decades ago. The infallibility of the "insider" has been utterly exploded. The stock market barometer, based upon Dow's theory of the triple simultaneous movement of the market, has increased in dependability as the years have gone by. Certainly it is in no real danger from manipulation, and on that topic I have something further to add.

A Shift of Bad Reporting

Manipulation in the stock market is reported twenty times for once it occurs. It is the inefficient reporter's method of accounting for a stock market movement which he has not taken the trouble to understand. Collection of news in Wall Street is difficult, but not impossible. It requires a higher average of intelligence than news collection anywhere else, and, if it is done properly, entails unremitting hard work. Unremitting hard workers are not much commoner in the newspaper business than elsewhere. The financial reporter is tempted by the fact that he can take refuge in technical terms not understood or correctly appreciated by his employers. Except in such a responsible news agency as the Dow-Jones service, whose very existence depends upon the integrity of what it gathers and sells, financial reporting is apt to become perfunctory, although it is improving.

Always a Reason, and Always News

This is a matter which particularly interests me because some of my earliest work in Wall Street was writing the stock market paragraphs for the Dow-Jones news service. The aim was to get, as far as possible, a reason, if only a tentative reason, for all individual and general fluctuations in the market. Mere generalities were not accepted, and I could tell many stories, ranging from pathos to wild absurdity, of the gathering of news which might be stale in half an hour's time. Such news was, of course, of the highest value to the active brokerage and banking houses, serving as it did to sustain interest in the market. They all had customers whose appetite for such news was insatiable. Even at an interval of twenty years I am humbled by the crudity of some of the reasons I had to give, especially as I was evolving a method out of nothing. But at least it was genuine news collecting, and not guessing. I look back on nothing in my life with greater pleasure than the friendly expressions of regret I received from the active houses in Wall Street when I relinquished that nerve-racking task to take up the editorship of *The Wall Street Journal*. Almost necessarily, a reporter's rewards are those of the tinker's donkey—"more kicks than ha' pence." He has, for compensation, the most interesting work in the world—if he likes to make it so.

Here is a chief reason why the part of the manipulation has been so absurdly exaggerated in the public mind. Every movement in the stock market has a valid explanation. To get at that explanation involves much intelligent research, with a comparison of the carefully sifted expressions of the people concerned in the actual market movement—those who executed the orders on the floor, and, preferably, those who gave them. The research can be carried back to the original source of the orders and the news can be traced further, to the reasons for buying or selling stocks, and the particular stocks involved.

Honest News Protects the Public

Wall Street has a number of maxims more or less of the nature of what is called "dope." One of these is, "There is no news in a bull market." It is not true, except with too many qualifications to justify a general rule. There is news, and plenty of it, in any market if the reporter will only get out and get it. If he is content to turn out perfunctory paragraphic comments on the market for the evening newspapers, or even for the morning press; content to warm over items which he finds in the financial news "slips," he will take refuge in such expressions as "manipulation," "traders selling," "Standard Oil buying," and all the other fudge which some newspaper proprietors still accept as news. Wall Street is the financial news center of the world. News collection there has steadily and greatly improved in my time, but the field is simply inexhaustible.

Chapter XX

WE are nearing the end of our discussions of *The Stock Market Barometer*. From readers of *Barron's* during their serial publication I gathered that this series of papers had been illuminating and widely interesting. It certainly instructed the writer of them, for he did not realize, when the series began, how much could be profitably said upon the subject of Dow's theory of the price movement. It has led us to an analysis of some pretentious theories of what are called "cycles"; to an examination of historical authorities which has shown us how much history could tell us if the records were intelligently compiled, and how little we know of the past, when the importance of commerce in national and world development was so little understood or appreciated. We have reached also a fair and dependable estimate, not only of what the stock market barometer does, but of its limitations. We know, now at least, that it is not a method of beating the speculative market— not an advertised system of stock trading, guaranteed against loss.

Speculation's Prediction Value

So far from limiting the usefulness of the barometer, this really expands that usefulness further than could have been expected when we started to analyze the triple movement of the market—its major swing upward or downward; its secondary reaction or rally; and the never-ceasing ebb and flow of the daily fluctuation. At least we have evolved something of real value to the man whose business is sufficiently extended to make it necessary to foresee the general current of trade. In the chart of the Harvard Committee on Economic Research, for the years from 1903 to 1914 inclusive, the line of speculation is shown as preceding the lines of banking and business. This is a calculation correctly extracted after the event, and such a chart, because of its extreme conservatism and the numerous adjustments made in its construction, will never reach the barometrical value of the stock market averages as recorded from day to day, when considered in the light of Dow's theory of the triple market movement.

A Prophet Who Knows When to Stop

Those who make a living by giving tips on the stock market are active and conspicuous when the market itself shows similar activity. In dull times they are depressing folk to listen to unless you have a patient sense of humor. In those quiet years between the culmination of the bear market of 1910 and the outbreak of the Great War one of them often deplored to me his inability to predict market movements in a market which has ceased to show profitable fluctuations. But our barometer has nothing to take back or regret.   It is almost the only prophet of to-day who stops talking when he has nothing to say.   From the studies in the price movement published from time to time in *The Wall Street Journal* I have offered evidence that the bear market in stocks of 1910 was clearly foreseen in the latter part of 1909.   The market took a turn for the better after June, 1910.

Although the recovery was slow and hesitating the general trend was upward.   There was a secondary reaction of recognizable dimensions about midsummer, 1911.   The top of the main movement, however, was in the latter part of 1912, and what is most interesting about the four years before the war is the relatively small extent of any of the fluctuations.   The bear market from the latter part of 1909 until the middle of 1910 was well defined, but in both averages was of barely half the extent of the preceding bear market in the panic year of 1907.   The following bull market, if it attains quite that dignity, for it was anything but a boom, showed scarcely a third of the range of the preceding bull market which held from the autumn of 1907 to near the end of 1909.   Altogether, in these instructive years, we can see a general dwindling movement.   Examination of business records for those years will show that there was a corresponding slowing up of activity in trade, not amounting to depression but rather to a dull level of business; not without the improvement to be expected from the country's natural growth; but in no way conspicuous, or strong enough to stimulate any large volume of speculation.

Predicting Small as well as Large Movements

Here again we see another valuable function of our barometer. The major movements do, in this sense, forecast the extent and almost the duration of the coming improvement, or the depth, and even the severity, of the impending business depression. Our discussions of selected periods covered in our twenty-five-year chart have made this sufficiently clear, as anyone can see for himself by comparing the price-movement analyses in previous articles with the subsequent developments in trade. It may be broadly said that business became dull in 1910 and that it did not recover its activity, in any sense greatly worth anticipating in the speculative market, until the boom created by the war.

Here is a period, then, which seems to raise a difficulty for the compilers of business charts, where a certain rhythm is postulated as a normal condition of business. Action and reaction can hardly be called equal in these instructive years, unless it may be the action and reaction of the pendulum of a clock which is running down. Perhaps that is not a bad simile of what took place before the war. It may be said that the demand for war material of all kinds wound up our business clock when it seemed to be slowing down. This is anything but accurate; but it gives a pictorial idea which is useful if not too rigidly applied.

But from the top of the stock market in 1909 we could plot what might be termed, with some show of justice, a bear market lasting nearly five years. It could be called, with a little latitude, a plausible instance of that five-year major swing which Charles H. Dow so hastily assumed when he first formulated his theory. There had unquestionably been over-rapid development of the country's resources, and possibly of its railroad resources, which had culminated in the panic of 1907. We may, I think, cautiously infer that the effects of such major panics as that are not all dissipated by the subsequent and logical stock market rally; as, for instance, that recovery which culminated in 1909. We see that the business of readjustment took much longer.

Where the Cycle Becomes Useful

Here is a case where the "panic-cycle" theory becomes useful (and it has its proper place), even if it is altogether too vague for helpful application to daily affairs. It is immensely interesting historically, and teaches real lessons when seen in its true perspective. After the panic of 1873 there was some stock market rally, but a subsequent general dwindling of business, under entirely different conditions to those existing to-day but sufficiently like the period we are now discussing to afford a useful parallel. It might almost be said that it was not until the resumption of specie payments (1879) was well in sight that the business of the country picked up, going on to that broader development which was checked by the less severe panic of 1884.

In the same way, the panic of 1893 was followed

by a period of depression much longer than that occupied in the break in stocks, although there were narrowing fluctuations up and down which, if charted, would look strikingly like those of the years following the strong stock market rally culminating in 1909. Here we have a uniformity which suggests at least similar laws, governing a movement broader than that of even the major swing which we have been able to deduce by the application of Dow's theory of the stock market movement. We can at least see that it is not a task of months but of years to restore confidence where it has once been successfully assailed.

Contracting Volume and Its Bearing

It has been pointed out already that business in stocks is always far lighter in a bear market than in a bull market. Our twenty-five-year chart, recording as it does the monthly average of daily stock trading, tells us that speculative business, in the years 1911 to 1914 inclusive, was very little if any better in volume than in the four years preceding the re-election of McKinley. The later period, here under our consideration, was followed by the war boom, an event which upset all calculations. The Harvard Committee on Economic Research does not even chart that period, representing as it does a set of world conditions as abnormal as an earthquake or some such natural phenomenon.

And since the war, and the culmination of what may be called the deflation bear market in June–Au gust, 1921, the volume of business has shown a marked contraction. We are experiencing one of the slowest and least spectacular bull movements of which we have any authentic record. Of the fact of the bull market, anticipated in more than one of these articles when published serially, there can be no manner of doubt. The recovery had extended in April, 1922, to twenty-nine points in the industrials and rather more than two-thirds as much in the railroads, with typical secondary movements. In a strong primary swing the secondary movement is correspondingly vigorous. It is noteworthy that neither the upward major swing nor the secondary movement of 1922 has shown a virility which is, as yet, prophetic of a boom in business, as distinguished from a conservative recovery. The barometer is saying that some recovery is due, but that it will come slowly and will take more than the usual time to establish itself. The prediction is rather of a bull market which will not carry prices to new high records, to put it mildly, than a spectacular movement which foreshadows a large and adventurous development of our industrial resources.

Throttling the Railroads

Readers of Chapter XVIII, in which the the broad downward movement of railroad stocks over a period of sixteen years was considered, will easily recognize why the extreme conservatism of the stock market at present, even on its recovery, is justified. In our barometer at least, the twenty active railroad stocks represent one-half of our speculative material and record. Our railroads represent the largest single investment of capital in this country, exclusive of farming. The status of these railroads is anything but reassurring. There is nothing to show that more vexatious regulation may not still further restrict their wealth-creating capacity.

We have falsely and foolishly assumed, through our legislators, that 6 per cent is the very maximum of earnings which should be permitted to a railroad stockholder; while he is to take the risk of anything less, down to a receivership. Obviously capital will never go into the development of transportation on any such terms as this. But we cannot establish such utterly discouraging conditions for one-half of the speculative field without injuriously affecting the other half. Who can foresee what politics may not bring forth if we are running into that populistic condition which marked the middle nineties? We are regulating capital out of public utilities of all kinds. Who is to say that this interference with the earning power of capital will not be extended to the great industrial corporations?

Politics in Industry

This is no idle surmise. It has been so extended. It certainly has not been so exercised with any gain to the public. But the action of the Department of Justice against the United States Steel Corporation (now abandoned) shows what can be done if the dangerous theories of the demagogue are to be forced upon business. It is all very well to say that the tendency of modern production is toward concentration, and that commodities will ultimately be cheaper under one management, like that of the Steel Corporation, than under the score or more separate enterprises comprised in that great and beneficent organization. But if the politician's assumption that mere size is in itself an offense is accepted, as it has undoubtedly been accepted in responsible quarters in the past, we may well look upon the course of business in the next half-decade with serious misgiving.

Mr. Taft's Inherited Policies

It must have been in 1909 or early in 1910 that I saw President Taft at the White House. I pointed out to him how the unrelenting hostility toward the railroads, backed up as it had been by the Administration itself, was paralyzing railroad development, and how our regulatory bodies were adding to the business handicap. Mr. Taft was sympathetic, but cautious. He contended that we could no longer expect the rapid growth of the past, based though it had been upon speculative hope made true by great endeavor. But he said that he was inclined to believe that this was necessarily the price which must be paid for the security of the public through the regulation of these great corporations. This was the "policy" he inherited from Roosevelt, and yet it did not satisfy the Progressives in 1912! It was not a long interview, and that was the end of it. When Mr. Taft, with his unimpeachable honesty, could take that view, what was to be expected of all the little politicians, in the state legislatures and the state regulatory bodies, who were paying off old grudges against the railroads, regardless of the cost to the public?

Our Voluntary Fetters

What is the worth of these voluntary fetters we have assumed? Is it contended that railroad service has been improved by all this meddling? There is not a dining car to-day which gives meals as good as those provided by Harvey for the Atchison twenty years ago. The "standard railroad meal," established by Mr. McAdoo, is recalled like a nightmare by its victims. The railroads have not recovered the old level of service. Both the Pennsylvania and the New York Central once were able to cut the time between New York and Chicago to sixteen hours. But that time has now lengthened to twenty and twenty-two hours. Are the cars any more comfortable than they were? Are the railroad servants any more civil and obliging? When the railroads could discharge an employee for not keeping a car clean without risking an interminable inquiry before the Labor Board, the cars were kept clean. But we have legislated and regulated the spirit of service out of the railroads. Only in a half-hearted way are they competing in making their own route more attractive than that of their neighbors. What inducement is there for the railroads to spend capital in developing such attractions?

Congress has said that they will be robbed of any return from so wise an investment if it exceeds a purely arbitrary figure of 6 per cent—one which makes no real provision for growth out of the earnings.

A True Psychological Condition

We are not wandering from the point. We are tracing one of the causes of the most significant movement shown in our averages. You cannot hit the railroads without hitting everything else, because the manufacturers of railroad supplies, as represented in the imposing list of the Railway Business Association, constitute a part of our national manufacturing industry so large that it swings all industry with it. If there is one word which has grown wearisome, from constant use and misuse in the era of quackery from which we are only slowly emerging, that word is "psychology." But here is a true psychological condition. We have lost trust in ourselves. We have meddled so disastrously with the law of supply and demand that we cannot bring ourselves to the radical step of letting it alone.

You cannot have real freedom in a country where you have no freedom in business. There is no tyranny so hard, because none so stupid, as that of bureaucracy. Take a single illustration: President Rea of the Pennsylvania, not so long ago, asked me how many reports I supposed his railroad made to departments in Washington, principally the Interstate Commerce Commission, in a single year? Knowing how ample that railroad's reports are, I said that it might be safe to take five hundred a year, as all that were really needed, and multiply that figure by twenty; and ventured, on that basis, an estimate of ten thousand reports for a single year. Mr. Rea laughed ruefully. He said, "Last year we made one hundred and fourteen thousand reports for our lines east of Pittsburgh alone!"

A Reform or a Revolution?

And that was for part of one railroad! Multiply that by all the railroads in the country and see what bureaucratic red tape can do in tying up a great utility's service and impairing its efficiency. We have just begun, thanks to General Dawes, to import a little common sense into Washington business methods. But manifestly he has only scratched the surface. The reform which is needed almost amounts to a revolution, for we are to remember that the Department of Commerce and the Department of Labor, to name only two, are making their demands for more light and more figures, more stationery and more wasted time, upon the general business of the country.

One Handicap and Its Consequences

It is a self-imposed handicap. We have only ourselves to thank. Look at what I have recorded of President Taft's acceptance of the position twelve years ago. Who is to take the Old Man of the Sea off Sinbad's shoulders? How can we expect a general boom in business, or a restoration of the railroads to their old conditions of vigor and growth, so long as the politician can inflict such handicaps as these? We are all hit by it. It hits the farmer in Nebraska, who is burning corn because it works out cheaper per ton than coal. It is hitting our foreign trade. Ours are the largest coal resources in the world, but Great Britain is actually landing coal in this country. She has already supplanted us where we were able, through the war, to build up foreign trade. The attitude of Congress toward business is not merely a development of the insane prejudice against the railroads. It amounts, when analyzed, to the bolshevist idea of fettering success—of making large individual wealth impossible. Enterprise will be attacked in the legislatures, not because there is a speculative danger but because, in the development of the country, some individuals may grow rich. You cannot keep those individuals poor without keeping the country poor. Are we to try again the experiment which was made during the second Cleveland administration? Is that era of Populism and depression, of entire lack of confidence or trust in ourselves, what we shall run into when the present bull market culminates and begins to give signals on the bear side?

Chapter XXI

WHEN *The Stock Market Barometer* first appeared serially in the columns of *Barron's*, mostly in the latter part of 1921, the order of the chapters adopted in the subsequent publication of the book was not used. Indeed, this study of Dow's theory of the price movement did not start out with the intention of making a book of itself. It was what an incurable newspaper man like myself would call a newspaper assignment. It partook, to some extent, of the character of contemporary criticism. This is curiously true of one of the most important chapters, the fifteenth, "A Line and an Example—1914." That article was submitted to the editor of *Barron's* with an entirely different line for illustration.

A "Line" in Illustration

All students of the averages will remember the broad rule that a "line" in the daily average indicates distribution or accumulation; and that after either saturation or scarcity has come about the movement of the averages above or below the line gives an important indication of the future movement of the market. Obviously, their advance above a "line" representing many days' trading and all within a range of three points or so indicates that the floating supply of stocks has been exhausted and that it is necessary to bid up in order to tempt a new volume of selling. Conversely, a movement below that line indicates the familiar saturation point, where the clouds resolve themselves into rain. There follows a marked recession in the market, to a point where stocks once more become attractive to buyers.

That fifteenth chapter was submitted to the editor of *Barron's* at the bottom of a major bear movement. The line first chosen for illustration was that which was then in the making. He considered such prediction altogether too daring, although I was willing enough to put Dow's theory and my conception of it to the hazard of such a test. The result would have been a remarkable vindication of the theory. But counsels of prudence prevailed and the illustrative line taken shows the action, or rather the inaction, of stocks during May, June and July of 1914, before the outbreak of the World War. There can be no question that the illustration chosen was the right one, both for historical purposes and for the subsequent authority of the book, which has, to my gratification, assumed a position of its own, with several times the circulation which the cautious publishers anticipated.

What is true enough to have become familiar and, therefore unimpressive, is that the book itself applied Dow's theory to an actual market and predicted, in the most positive way, the major bull movement which set in during the time of publication, serially, in the columns of *Barron's*. I have been asked to bring the topic down to date for this new edition, pointing out how the theory has been verified, or modified, in the three years which have elapsed since The Stock Market Barometer was first published. The topic should be interesting and useful, and I hope that a lifelong sense of humor will keep me from indulging in boasts about my inspiration as a prophet, even if it is necessary to furnish a few illustrations, from these columns and those of *The Wall Street Journal*, of the way in which the application of Dow's theory has been successsfully made since 1922.

Some Successful Forecast

Since the publication of The Stock Market Barometer the market has experienced a major upward (bull) movement in which the industrials, between Aug. 24, 1921, and March 20, 1923, advanced over 61 points, while the railroads between June 20, 1921, advanced from 65.52 to 93.99 on Sept. 11, 1922, or 28.47 points, and had only lost about three points of this when the high point of the industrials was recorded in the following March. *The Wall Street Journal* and *Barron's* were both entirely clear on this bull movement, the former saying, on Feb. 11, 1922: "At present the major swing of the market is upwards." The final paragraph of that study is significant:

"The answer to inquirers, therefore, is that we are still in a bull market and that it should run much further, possibly well into 1923, and certainly for a time well beyond the improvement in general business which it forecasts."

That was sufficiently explicit, not merely as regards the movement of the stock market interpreted by the Dow theory but upon the improvement in general business which, in due course, followed the rise in the barometer. When the twenty industrials had advanced 26 points, or in the following June, it was said: "There is no reason to suppose that the present bull market is within months of its culmination." Remember that the bull movement really ran into March, 1923. The presence of a line was noted May 8, 1922, although no bearish inference was drawn. On the 22nd of May the resumption of the bull movement was noted, while its continuance "well into 1923" was again inferred. I note that in an interview given in Boston on June 16 I repeated the conviction that the stock market was likely to run further in the upward direction and that it would be all the better for the secondary reaction which had occurred about that time. A tendency to check in the railroad averages was noted in the "Study in the Price Movement" published July 8, but it was then said: "With this proviso it may be said that the indication in the averages is distinctly bullish."

A Secondary Reaction

It has been said elsewhere in these pages that the prediction of secondary reactions is a chancy sort of business and is not here encouraged although in September *The Wall Street Journal* and *Barron's* rather looked for a reaction, recognizing it on September 19. This may be called merely a good guess, by the scoffer, especially if he was wrong on the market, but at any rate on September 30 the industrials had reacted nearly six points from the high of the bull movement and the railroads more than four points. On October 18 the "Study in the Price Movement" said:

"The stock market today, after a typical secondary reaction, is pointing clearly to the resumption of the major upward movement which developed in August, 1921."

It would be wearisome to recall all such predictions. I prefer to call them inferences. The bullish inference was again drawn on November 3. As late as Jan. 16, 1923, the "extended but by no means unprecedented secondary reaction" was discussed, but the primary upward movement was shown still to dominate.

A Short Bear Movement

For purposes of convenience the short major bear swing may be said to have set in after the top of the industrials was reached in March, 1923. On April 4 the "Study in the Price Movement" called attention to a bearish indication from the line of distribution. Taken all through, the bear market did not last long, and it is noteworthy that while the studies in "the Price Movement" were bearish they were slow to concede the primary reaction, evidently influenced by the fact that the previous bull movement had been decidedly slow. The decline continued to look rather like a secondary reaction in a bull market. The total recession worked out to 20 points in the industrials, culminating Oct. 27, 1923, as far as the industrials were concerned, while at that date the railroads were down rather more than 17 points, although the actual low had been early in the previous August. Rather for convenience of record this conspicuously short bear movement has been taken as primary, but a plausible case might be put up for dating the present bull market from the turn in 1921, when *The Stock Market Barometer* was appearing serially and was even charged with being indelicately bullish.

Influence of Taxes

What was unquestionably a new influence in the stock market had made itself felt in the averages. Congress had been in session all summer and on Aug. 29, 1923, *The Wall Street Journal* had a careful study of the way politics, by dangerous interference with business, had falsified, or to a large extent neutralized, the very barometers of business itself. Income tax and surtax were then at their highest points and *The Wall Street Journal* said:

"There is a reason why the barometer in the past few months has been deflected by an influence not felt before in a major bull market. This influence undoubtedly is the cumulative effect of the income surtax.

"Brokers can tell how steadily the dividend-paying common stocks, representing thirty out of the forty taken in the two averages, have been sold by large holders on any development of comparative strength. It is correct to call this a new factor, although it has been germinating since the bull market started in the autumn of 1921. The whole theory of the stock market barometer is based upon the assumption that pressure on stocks can only forecast coming liquidation of general business. But here, for the first time in the history of the averages, is a pressure of stock for sale which bears no reference to coming events.

"It is as though a hot coal or a lump of ice had been applied to the bulb of a thermometer. If it is too much to hope that Congress may see a return to sanity in taxation, this is a condition which will nevertheless cure itself, but only over a period of time beyond present calculation. That stage will be reached when every one of the twenty active railroad common stocks and the twenty industrials is as widely held as the stock of the Pennsylvania Railroad, where the average holding is round about fifty shares per stockholder.

"A rich man cannot afford to hold a common stock returning him six per cent. on its cost. Not only is he liable to see more than half of the return deducted by the taxgatherer; such a holding pulls up the tax he must pay on all his other income. He, therefore, has been a steady seller for many months past, and this is 'inside' selling with a vengeance. It is well informed selling, in a way, but obviousy it need not predict the general course of business. Congress, in imposing impossible taxes, has not merely laid a handicap on the country's business. It has falsified the very barometer of business."

That temporary influence is now in course of removal so far as Congress is concerned but the State taxes must have some not entirely negligible effect.

A New Bull Market

It would be hypocritical to say that I have really wished I had never written The Stock Market Barometer. It is true to say that I have witnessed with regret the way in which crude adaptations of Dow's complete theory have been taken by tipsters and market quacks to bolster up their unsound conclusions, drawn from an incomplete understanding of the principles involved in reading the averages. On Feb. 4, 1924, after refraining, in disgust at the clamor of tipsters, from discussing the price movement editorially, *The Wall Street Journal* said:

"On the method of reading the averages which is known as Dow's theory, the stock market is in a major bull movement, after the shortest major bear movement of record, one lasting barely eight months. So far as the low of the present movement is concerned, it would presumably date from November 1; but the bull point was given after both the industrial and railroad averages had made one of the most consistent lines of accumulation on record, emerging on the bull side last December (1923)."

It was noted there, as an eminently satisfactory reason for a bull market, that stocks were selling well below the line of values and had not discounted the possibilities of legitimate business expansion. Here again the barometer was right. The business expansion came in due course, slackening in the latter part of the year. This was curiously matched by a substantial secondary reaction in both averages from the high in the industrials of 105.57 on August 20 to the low of 99.18 recorded October 14, paralleled by a reaction of more than six points in the railroads, the averages having seen the low of that movement on October 14.

Since that time the bull movement has been in full swing, developing great activity immediately after the election, when a number of stock tipsters advised taking profits, and selling the market short, on the theory that "the good news was out." As the real odds were something like forty to one that Coolidge would beat

Davis,—they were openly twelve to one before the election—the "good news" was really the resumed expansion of general business which the market barometer had been predicting.

A Changed Technical Condition

There is a technical condition which has developed in the present bull market and one which did not exist before. Here is substantially what I have had to say about it in another place:

Studies of the stock market, based upon Dow's well known theory of the triple market movement as disclosed by the average prices of the industrials and the railroads taken separately for comparison, have been astonishingly right in forecasting the broad upward movement of the stock market and indicating its continuance. The present major bull market, however, is subject to a condition which did not exist before, and it is important to consider the bearing of that limitation.

While the Stock Exchange Governing Committee has been strengthening its control over the conduct of business for a good many years past and certainly since the time when the unlisted department was abolished, the more stringent regulation has been of entirely recent development. It has only been in the past year or two that the governors have assumed to tell the strongest brokerage houses how much of an account they may carry on their capital. In the not very old days a Stock Exchange house took all the sound business it could get, trusting to its own ingenuity to find a means of carrying an expanded account in a big bull market.

This has been drastically changed, and it is now an open secret that a considerable number of brokerage houses are carrying for customers all the stock the Exchange's law allows. Their position is eminently safe, but their policy is obviously changed. The way to make money in a bull market is to buy what you can afford when the upward movement is fairly assured, expand your bull account on the profits, hold on to the larger part of your interest, selling in periods of marked strength, and making up to the proportion you can afford in the inevitable secondary reactions.

But this is not the kind of customer a Stock Exchange house wants. It means the tying up of a substantial amount of capital, with commissions for purchases or sales only earned once in a few weeks. The broker likes the customer to pay commissions every day, although it is anything but profitable to the latter, because the attempt to guess the daily fluctuation is far more like gambling than speculation.

One result of the broker's new limitations is that stock in small quantities has been widely bought for cash and that wealthy customers are financing their own bull account through their own bankers in many parts of the country outside New York. This leaves some uncertainty as to the real extent of the bull account, but also a hitherto unknown degree of stability, because there is less likelihood of a flood of selling orders all at one time.

In the natural way of evolution the result will probably be to concentrate business among fewer houses, each with a much larger working capital than has hitherto been considered necessary. What is at least certain is that there is nothing in the new condition to change the rules for reading the stock market barometer.

Barometrical Indications

It would be timid to conclude this discussion without saying what I think of the barometrical indications writing in August, 1925. There is obviously a strong and well distributed bull account, and there is absolutely no indication in the averages that the bull market has culminated. Counting from the end of the short bear market in the latter part of 1923, the duration of the major swing has not been long and there are still many stocks which are demonstrably selling below the line of values. I think this assumption, if we could calculate an average line of values, would be true of the railroad and partly true of the industrial groups, in spite of their considerable advance.

All indications point to a further upward movement carrying into next year, although secondary reactions of substantial proportions would be very much in order.

Nothing has developed since the first publication of The Stock Market Barometer to shake my faith in the great utility of a common-sense interpretation of the price movement. It may be valueless for individual stocks, except that these do not commonly make serious advances except when the general trend of the market is upwards. The one chosen by the speculator may lag behind and never catch up. I am not greatly interested in encouraging people to speculate in Wall Street, but I am humbly gratified that the business of the country has had its attention drawn to such a barometrical guide. It has been freely criticised by authorities of some weight, but has continued its useful service to the general business of the country.

Chapter XXII

SOME THOUGHTS FOR SPECULATORS

MANY years ago one of the Southern states, which need not be otherwise identified, had a law which prohibited the playing of games of chance where any stake was involved. It need hardly be said that a law so foolish was "more honored in the breach than the observance." The sheriff of one of the smaller towns, however, determined to enforce the law and captured a party of young men playing euchre in a barn. Courts were not overburdened with formalities in those days. It was not considered out of the way, or a departure from dignity, when counsel for the prisoners, while admitting that his "unfortunate clients" had been playing euchre, submitted that it was not a game of chance. As the court and the gentlemen of the jury habitually played the game themselves, the contention was received with incredulity. Nothing daunted, however, the counsel for the defense said: "If your honor will allow me to demonstrate the game to the jury for a short time I am sure I can convince them that euchre is not a game of chance."

Not a Game of Chance

This seemed eminently fair, and the jury and the lawyer were accordingly locked up together. In a

short time various members of the jury sent out to
borrow a little change from their friends. After an
hour or so of "demonstration," the jury returned to
court with the unanimous verdict that euchre was not
a game of chance.

These articles would not be complete if I did not
say something about speculation and, incidentally, give
some practical counsel to the speculator. Speculation
necessarily involves a large element of chance. It is
the speculator himself who too often makes it a sheer
gamble. I do not know what the Southern lawyer in
the story did to convince the jury of the certainties
underlying the game of euchre. But certainly, if the
amateur is to come into Wall Street and "speculate"
with the stupidity he so frequently exhibits, the professionals there can show him that his kind of speculation is not a game of chance, and they will not have
to cheat to do so.

Real Protection in the Barometer

It cannot too often be said that Dow's theory of
the stock market movement is not a "system" for
beating the market—a get-rich-quick scheme which
converts the Wall Street district into a sort of Tom
Tiddler's ground, where any man with a few dollars
for margin can pick up gold and silver. But if the
intelligent speculator of to-day (who in many cases is
the intelligent investor of to-morrow) cannot find
means of protecting himself in the stock market by an
earnest study of the stock market barometer, then

these chapters have, in that respect, failed. He has already gained something tangible if he has correctly understood the major movement. If he comes into Wall Street on a mere tip from somebody he trusts about a stock of which he never heard before, without ascertaining whether the general market is in an upward or a downward major swing, he stands an excellent chance of losing all he brings in the way of margin, without a fair "run for his money." But if he has learned what the market movement means and appreciates the opportunity given to him in the dulness after a typical reaction in a bull market, he stands more than an even chance of making a profit. That profit will depend on a number of considerations which, apparently, do not enter into the minds of many people who come to Wall Street only to lose money, spending the rest of their lives denouncing the Stock Exchange as a gambling hell.

Speculation and Gambling

To these people all stocks look alike. But they are not alike. So far as well-protected speculation is concerned, there is all the difference in the world between such a stock as United States Steel common, with a well-established market—a stock well distributed and widely held—and the latest motor or oil proposition floated on the Curb for the purpose of distribution. The latter may be good, but it is at least untested, not only as regards the business the new company purposes doing, but in the market aspect of its stock.

It is a sound general rule that the outsider, when he buys a Curb stock, should do so outright. His purchase on margin is largely in the nature of a gamble. I am not laying down any law about the morality of gambling. Unless it comes under the head of covetousness, I do not know of any commandment against it; and, like an Episcopalian bishop of my acquaintance, with whom I have played auction bridge for small cash points, I am not in the business of inventing new sins. But margin trading in a security of which the amateur trader knows nothing that he has not had at second hand, in a market which only exists artificially by the manipulation of people who want to sell the stock, is the merest gambling. The man who chooses to speculate in it should regard his venture as on the same level with a bet on a horse race. He should see that his loss is limited to such amount as he could afford to lose on a bet.

Speculation is a different matter, and I hope the day will never come when the speculative instinct is not at least latent in an American's mind. If ever that day does come, if ever prohibition extends to the taking of a chance involving the risk of whole or partial loss, the result may be "good" Americans, but of a merely negative type of goodness. If as you enter Wall Street you will pause a moment in Broadway, to look through the railings of Trinity churchyard, you will see a place full of good Americans. When speculation is dead this country will be dead also.

Selecting a Stock

Let us suppose, then, that the outsider has considered the character of the major movement and tendency of the stock market. His next business is to select his stock. Here again the amateur, who wants quick action for his money, will not take the trouble to inform himself properly upon the stock in which he purposes to risk his small capital.

It is a good standing rule that in a stock for which no permanent market has been created—a new flotation or one which is still notoriously, by majority holdings, in control of the people who dictate the policies of the corporation—the small speculator should not trade on margin at all. This is, of course, a counsel of perfection, but at least he should make it a rule to take only a small risk in such a venture and to buy only what he can in some way finance himself if necessary.

By the time a stock is listed in the Stock Exchange there is generally a dependable market for it at most times although here the danger of too much ownership in few hands, as in the case of Stutz Motor, still exists. Such stocks are good to let alone; and only where the nature of the speculator's own business gives him access to special information should he embark his money in stocks of such a character, and even then his margin should be of the most ample kind.

On the Matter of Margin

This brings us to the question of margins. A complete misunderstanding of what constitutes a sufficient margin is responsible for many needless losses in Wall Street. Brokers are looking for business, and they tell the tyro that ten points margin is good enough if he can guarantee the firm that amount against fluctuations. This would mean $1000 on one hundred shares of stock at par. That margin is not enough, or nearly enough. Writing twenty-one years ago, Charles H. Dow pointed out that "the man who buys a hundred shares on a 10 per cent margin, and stops his loss at 2 per cent, has lost (with commissions) nearly one-quarter of his capital." Obviously it does not take long to wipe him out. Dow was ultra-cautious, but he was not wide of the mark when he said that if such a man had begun with ten-share lots he would have been able to see a substantial loss and yet have averaged his purchases to yield him an ultimate profit, granting he was correct in his first surmise that the stock was selling much below its value. Certainly a trader with $1000, and no more, has no business to start with a hundred shares of stock unless it be something at a very low price. There was a time when Steel common could have been bought below $10 a share.

Little Traders and Large

Another delusion of the small trader is that he should buy part of the quantity he contemplates, adding to his holdings on each point of decline until he completes the amount he thinks he can carry. But why not buy it all at the last price? If he proposes to buy one hundred shares in twenty-share lots, and expects that there will be a decline of five points in the market, he is really contradicting the assumption upon which he originally decided to trade. He has not considered all the facts of the case. If the stock can go down five points the purchase is not so good a one as he supposed. It is quite true that great operators, like Jay Gould, did buy stock in that way. But they were not trading on margin, except in the respect that they financed their stocks mostly through their own banks. And they were buying upon considerations which would seem hopelessly remote to the small speculator who wishes to test his judgment in Wall Street. Such a man as Jay Gould, moreover, could himself give value to the things he purchased. He might well start to buy into a company during the course of a major bear swing, knowing that he could not get all the stock he wanted in a bull market.

The small speculator cannot afford to take any such view, unless he purposes to devote such exclusive attention to stock trading as he would give to any other business. There are plenty of people who do that, and I have in previous discussions given instances of their success. But we are talking now of the man who speculates on his judgment while interested in some other business. There is no reason why a speculator of this class should not have more than an even-money chance in the market if he would only bring a little common sense to bear. But if he will listen to the first casual friend who tells him to "buy a hundred shares of A. O. T., and ask no questions," and risks his only thousand dollars in doing so, he cannot complain if he loses. He is a gambler and not a speculator. He would have much more fun if he took his dollars to the races. He would have a healthy day in the open air and find the racehorse a much more amusing spectacle than the ticker.

A Quotation from Dow

In an editorial published in *The Wall Street Journal* on July 11, 1901, Charles H. Dow said:

"If people with either large or small capital would look upon trading in stocks as an attempt to get 12 per cent per annum on their money instead of 50 per cent weekly, they would come out a good deal better in the long run. Everybody knows this in its application to his private business, but the man who is prudent and careful in carrying on a store, a factory or a real estate business, seems to think that totally different methods should be employed in dealing in stocks. Nothing is further from the truth."

In the same article Dow went on to say that the speculator can avoid tying himself up in a financial knot at the outset by keeping his transactions down to a limit which, compared with his capital, leaves his judgment clear and affords ample ability to cut loss after loss short; to double up; to switch to some other stock, and generally to act easily and fearlessly instead of under the constraint which comes from a knowledge that his margin of safety is so small as to leave no room for anything except a few anxious gasps before the account is closed.

This is as good sense now as on the day it was written. The speculator who comes into Wall Street must learn to take losses, and take them quickly. I have said before that more money has been lost in Wall Street from sheer pride of opinion than from any other single cause. If you buy a stock and find that it is falling rapidly, you have not considered all the facts of the case. You cannot consider them impartially so long as you are under the terror of losing all your capital. You cannot take a clear, unbiased view unless you get out and look at the thing objectively. When you are tied up in a losing speculation you are in the position of the man lost in the forest who cannot see the wood for the trees.

Avoiding Inactive Stocks

Readers will remember the story I told of the young man who refused a partnership offered to him by Jay Gould because, in executing Gould's orders on the floor of the Stock Exchange, Gould seemed to him to make nothing but losses. He was not broad enough to see that these unsuccessful attempts were merely testing purchases, and that Gould probably employed some other broker when he was quite sure that he had caught the turn of the market. Here is where the purchase of a stock only occasionally active becomes so dangerous. The broker may be able to carry it very well to-day, although inactive stocks are not looked upon with favor in bank loans.

But the broker himself does not know whether he

can carry the stock so conveniently to-morrow. The peculiar circumstances which started the movement in that stock may be fully discounted in a few days' active trading, and the event will be a market without a single transaction for days together, where the seller is obliged to make concessions to find a buyer—generally a professional, who charges all the traffic will bear for such a service. Such a stock should not be carried on margin at all. But the man whose business is in some intimate connection with the steel trade or the textile industry may well take hold of Steel common or Bethlehem Steel or American Woolen, feeling that there is a permanent market if not always an active one.

A Word for the Consolidated Exchange

I have many friends in the New York Stock Exchange, but I have also friends elsewhere in Wall Street. The odd-lot brokers, of whom there are fewer than ten firms specializing in that way, make the market in lots of less than a hundred shares. But the Consolidated Stock Exchange makes a regular market for those small quantities all the time. It is in every way a reputable institution, whose members are open to the same scrutiny the speculator ought to apply to any broker he employs. Our small amateur trader can do his business just as well on the Consolidated Exchange, provided he chooses really active stocks. Such stocks are "seasoned" and thoroughly well distributed, and this is not true of those which make up the list of the Curb Association. I am not saying one word against the latter, but the securities in which it deals are seldom popular in bank loans, and I should have the strongest suspicions of a Curb house which professed to trade for its customers indiscriminately on a 10 per cent margin.

By all means get the idea of such a margin out of your head. The margin should be as good as you can make it. If you are engaged in business or living upon an income from investments with people dependent upon you, your losses in speculation should be limited to an amount which will not cause you serious compunction. It is probably heterodox to say so, but there is common sense in the proposition that gambling begins where we risk what we cannot really afford to gain something we have not earned.

A Glance at Short Selling

How can the stock market barometer help the speculator? In many ways. He cannot expect any stock, except under most unusual circumstances, to advance profitably against the general current of the market. He must be most unusually well informed, an almost instinctive reader of the market, if he can speculate successfully on the occasional rallies which take place in a major downward swing. I am saying little about short selling. The man who tries short selling in a bull market is merely guessing at the secondary reactions, and unless he is a trader on the floor or devoting all his attention to the business of speculation, he is certain to lose his money. I am not discussing the morality of short selling, because I do not believe the moral question enters into speculation at all, provided it does not degenerate into gambling with what is, in effect, other people's money. In every market in the world there is necessarily a great deal of short selling. The tourist in San Francisco whose stocks are locked up in his safe deposit box in New York cannot afford to miss his market by waiting until he returns across the continent. If he sells he is short of the market, and a borrower of stocks until he can make his delivery good. But on the law of averages, far more money has been made on the bull side than has ever been made on the bear side, if only for the reason that bull markets are generally much longer in their duration than bear markets. Short selling is an operation which may well be left to the professional, especially by the man who is only a student of the market learning the rules of the game.

Buying on Reactions

No knowledge of the stock market barometer will enable any of us to call the absolute turn from a bear market to a bull market. There may be weeks of narrow fluctuations before a definite trend is established, as we have seen in our previous studies of the market movement. All of these indecisive fluctuations eat up the speculator's capital, in broker's commissions and interest, to say nothing of the market turn. But when once the major bull swing is estab-

lished the successful purchase of stocks for a rise becomes a feasible proposition. If on the completion
of his purchase a stock reacts, carried down by a
similar reversal of movement in the general market,
the speculator should take his loss without hesitation
and wait for that inevitable period of dulness which develops after a secondary reaction in a major bull swing.

Here again he may buy his stock, and instead of
purchasing on the way down, on the fallacious assumption I exposed earlier in this article, he may well add
to his holdings as the market rises. Each advance
adds to his margin of safety, and, provided he does not
"pyramid" too much, and conceding that his holdings
are not overextended so that his own account would
be a tempting object of attack, the speculator may
well, if he protects himself with "stop-loss" orders,
make profits much more substantial than he at first
expected. We hear a great deal about people who
lost money in Wall Street but very little about those
who made substantial profits there. The latter, as a
class, are inarticulate, in my experience; and a man
seldom cares to ascribe his prosperity to successful
speculation. He prefers to call it judicious investment.
There is little difference between a purchase of a house
on mortgage and a purchase of stocks on margin, provided the purchaser can meet his contracts. In these
great uplifting times, when everybody is minding
everybody else's affairs, I am still disposed to say that
it is nobody's business how our speculator carries his
stocks so long as he does so out of his own resources,
which include his borrowing credit at the bank.

Ways of Losing Money

There is another class of speculator, all too common, who loses money by forgetting why he went into the market in the first place. Knowing me personally, he asks me my opinion of Atchison common. I tell him what the road's prospects are, what the earned margin may be over and above the dividend, and the general railroad outlook in that part of the country. He concludes that Atchison common (here chosen merely for example) is cheap, and buys himself some of it. If he would protect his broker with ample margin, or pay for the stock outright, and ignore fluctuations, he would probably make money.

But he listens to every bit of gossip, particularly stories of "traders selling," "Congressional investigation," "threatened strikes," "crop failures," and all the rest of it. He forgets that the market has made allowance for everything of the kind in the broad estimate of the prospective value of the stock. He becomes nervous on a minor fluctuation, takes a loss and decides never to ask my opinion again. At least I wish he would so decide; but, unfortunately, he does not. He comes to me again to see if I cannot say something to upset what he calls his judgment, based, this time, upon the opinion of somebody else.

Another Way of Losing Money

Take another easy way of losing money in Wall Street. The speculator is informed, correctly, of a coming quick movement, perhaps covering four points

in a particular stock.   He notices that the stock has
been active, without paying much attention to the fact
that a point and a half of the expected four points is
already shown in the advance of the price.   After
some hesitation he buys, when the movement is almost
completed.   He sees a small profit, and then the stock
becomes dull.   The special movement is over.   The
attention of the professionals is turned to some other
security, and his own stock sags with the market or
eats its head off in interest.   But he is still fatuously
holding on instead of realizing that he has missed
his opportunity and has had what, if he would look
at it sensibly, is really a cheap and most instructive
lesson.

Here again he forgets why he originally bought the
stock, just as he did when he purchased on permanent
value.   If the special movement he anticipated fails to
materialize he should take his loss, or his disappoint-
ingly small profit, and wait for another chance.   But
the trouble with most of the speculators of my acquaintance is that they lack not only memory but the
virtue of patience.   They must be dabbling all the
time; and sooner or later they get tied up with an
account, extended to their full resources, which seems
to have run aground, with the general current of the
market swinging past it.

A Final Thought

This brings me to the conclusion of my discussions
of the stock market barometer.   I would not have it

on my conscience that I had encouraged any weakling to gamble, or had expedited, by a day, the inevitable parting of a fool from his money. At least in that respect every man is a free agent. In spite of all sorts of personally regulatory legislation, he has still that much freedom allowed to him. We can imagine laws which would make speculation impossible, even if, as they certainly would, they paralyzed the business of the United States. But we cannot imagine any law which would compel a man to trade in Wall Street if he did not choose to do so. All I have tried to do here is to show him how he can protect himself, and at least feel that not only has he had a fair run for his money but that he has earned the prize at the end of the run.

APPENDIX

APPENDIX

RECORD OF THE DOW-JONES AVERAGES TO
AUGUST 31, 1925

Dow, Jones & Co. began the publication of average closing prices of active representative stocks in 1884. The original list of stocks used was as follows:

Chicago & North Western	Union Pacific
D., L. & W.	Missouri Pacific
Lake Shore	Louisville & Nashville
New York Central	Pacific Mail
St. Paul	Western Union
Northern Pacific pref.	

The first average found in the files, of these eleven stocks, nine of which were rails, was 69.93 as of July 3, 1884.

The following is a complete statement of the record from 1896 to date:

Railroads

The railroad stocks used in January, 1897, were:

Atchison	Mo., Kansas & Texas pref.
Burlington	Missouri Pacific
C., C., C. & St. Louis	New York Central
Chesapeake & Ohio	Northern Pacific pref.
Chicago & North Western	New York, Ontario & Western
Erie	Reading
Jersey Central	Rock Island
Lake Shore	St. Paul
Louisville & Nashville	Southern Railway pref.
Manhattan Elevated	Wabash pref.

281

Changes have been made as follows:

In July, 1898, Metropolitan Street Railway, Union Pacific common and Northern Pacific common were substituted for Lake Shore, New York, Ontario & Western and Northern Pacific preferred.

In July, 1899, Brooklyn Rapid Transit, Denver & Rio Grande preferred and Norfolk & Western preferred were substituted for Metropolitan Street Railway, Reading and Erie.

In July, 1900, Southern Pacific common and Union Pacific preferred were substituted for Wabash preferred and Norfolk & Western preferred.

In June, 1901, Baltimore & Ohio, Illinois Central, Southern Railway common, and Pennsylvania were substituted for Burlington, Southern Pacific common, Southern Railway preferred and Northern Pacific common.

In September, 1902, Reading, Canadian Pacific, Delaware & Hudson and Minneapolis & St. Lous were substituted for Missouri, Kansas & Texas preferred, Rock Island, Chesapeake & Ohio and Jersey Central.

On May 18, 1904, Southern Pacific common was substituted for Minneapolis & St. Louis.

On June 27, 1904, Wabash preferred and Metropolitan Street Railway were substituted for C., C., C. & St. Louis and Denver preferred.

On April 12, 1925, Erie was substituted for Wabash preferred.

In May, 1905, Northern Pacific common and Norfolk & Western were substituted for Manhattan and Union Pacific preferred.

On May 4, 1906, Twin City Rapid Transit was substituted for Metropolitan Street Railway.

On April 25, 1912, Rock Island and Lehigh Valley were substituted for Brooklyn Rapid Transit and Twin City Rapid Transit.

On December 12, 1914, Chesapeake & Ohio, Kansas City Southern and N. Y., N. H. & Hartford were substituted for Chicago & North Western, Missouri Pacific and Rock Island.

On April 10, 1924, D., L. & W. and St. Louis Southwestern were substituted for Kansas City Southern and Lehigh Valley.

The railroad list now (August 31, 1925) is as follows:

Atchison	Illinois Central	Reading
Balt. & Ohio	Louisville & Nash.	St. L. Southwestern
Canadian Pacific	New York Central	St. Paul
Chesapeake & Ohio	New Haven	Southern Pacific
Del. & Hudson	Norfolk & Western	Southern Railway
Del., Lack. & W.	Northern Pacific	Union Pacific
Erie	Pennsylvania	

Basis of Calculation

Originally quotations were all in percentages. On October 13, 1915, the Stock Exchange ruled that all stocks should sell on a dollar-share basis. For the sake of continuity the averages of Pennsylvania, Reading and Lehigh Valley, all having $50 par values, have ever since been computed on a percentage basis, which was obtained by doubling their market quotation. Lehigh having been dropped, it is now necessary to double the quotation only in the cases of Pennsylvania and of Reading, all the railroad stocks being adjusted by this arrangement to both the dollar and the percentage basis.

Industrial Stocks

The twelve industrial stocks used in January, 1897, were:

American Cotton Oil
American Spirits Mfg.
American Sugar
American Tobacco
Chicago Gas
General Electric

Laclede Gas
National Lead
Pacific Mail
Standard Rope & Twine
Tennessee Coal & Iron
U. S. Leather pref.

Changes have been made as follows:

In November, 1897, Peoples Gas was substituted for Chicago Gas.

In September, 1898, U. S. Rubber common was substituted for General Electric.

In April, 1899, Continental Tobacco, Federal Steel, General Electric, American Steel & Wire were substituted for American Spirits Mfg., American Tobacco, Laclede Gas and Standard Rope & Twine.

In June, 1901, Amalgamated Copper, American Smelting & Refining, International Paper preferred, U. S. Steel common and U. S. Steel preferred were substituted for American Cotton Oil, Federal Steel, General Electric, Pacific Mail and American Steel & Wire.

In January, 1902, American Car & Foundry and Colorado Fuel & Iron were substituted for Continental Tobacco and International Paper preferred.

In April, 1905, U. S. Rubber 1st preferred was substituted for U. S. Leather preferred.

In November, 1907, General Electric was substituted for Tennessee Coal & Iron.

In May, 1912, Central Leather common was substituted for Colorado Fuel & Iron.

The list, therefore, when the Stock Exchange closed on July 31, 1914, because of the war, was:

Amalgamated Copper	National Lead
American Car & Foundry	Peoples Gas
American Smelting	U. S. Rubber com.
American Sugar	U. S. Rubber 1st pref.
Central Leather	U. S. Steel com.
General Electric	U. S. Steel pref.

In March, 1915, General Motors was substituted for U. S. Rubber 1st preferred.

In July, 1915, Anaconda was substituted for Amalgamated Copper.

In September, 1916, a list of twenty industrials, all common, was substituted for the old list of twelve. National Lead, Peoples Gas, General Motors and U. S. Steel preferred were dropped and twelve new companies were added. The list became:

American Beet Sugar	General Electric
American Can	Goodrich
American Car & Foundry	Republic Iron & Steel
American Locomotive	Studebaker
American Smelting	Texas Co.
American Sugar	U. S. Rubber
American Tel. & Tel.	U. S. Steel
Anaconda Copper	Utah Copper
Baldwin Locomotive	Westinghouse
Central Leather	Western Union

All Quotations on Dollar Basis

At this time (1916) Stock Exchange quotations were all in dollars instead of percentages, so the fact that Utah had a par of $10 and Westinghouse a par of $50 caused no immediate confusion in the new averages. However, in order to make continuity for the industrial averages, the records of the twenty new stocks were figured backward to the reopening of the Stock Exchange on December 12, 1914, after the war closing, so that the present published record of averages is as if the twenty stocks mentioned above had been quoted on the dollar basis from that date.

Changes since made are as follows:

On March 1, 1920, Corn products was substituted for American Beet Sugar.

On January 22, 1924, American Tobacco, du Pont, Mack Trucks and Sears-Roebuck were substituted for Corn Products, Central Leather, Goodrich and Texas Co.

On February 6, 1924, Standard Oil of California was substituted for Utah.

On May 12, 1924, Studebaker non-par and Woolworth $25 par were substituted for old Studebaker and Republic Iron & Steel.

After the change from twelve to twenty industrials, in 1916, Texas Co. reduced its par from $100 to $25. Then American Locomotive changed from $100 par to non-par, issuing two new shares for one old share. Studebaker changed from $100 par to non-par, issuing two and a half shares of new for one of old. The complication arising from the Texas, American Locomotive and Studebaker changes brought about new adjustment.

Texas Co. and Corn Products were dropped. American Locomotive was retained at the actual new quotation. These changes, made on January 22, 1924, were so fitted into the scheme of quotations that while the closing prices on a Tuesday averaged 97.41 on the old stocks, the average on the new stocks was 97.23, all being figured on the dollar basis.

This made the industrial list for July, 1924, as follows:

American Can	General Electric
American Car & Foundry	Mack Trucks
American Locomotive	Sears-Roebuck
American Smelting	Standard Oil of California
American Sugar	Studebaker
American Tel. & Tel.	U. S. Rubber
American Tobacco	U. S. Steel
Anaconda	Woolworth
Baldwin	Westinghouse
du Pont	Western Union

On August 31, 1925, General Motors, International Harvester, Kennecott, Texas Co. and U. S. Realty were substituted for Anaconda, Baldwin, du Pont, Standard Oil of California and Studebaker in the industrial list. These changes made no appreciable difference in the averages.

The industrial list now (August 31, 1925) is as follows:

American Can	Kennecott
American Car & Foundry	Mack Trucks
American Locomotive	Sears-Roebuck
American Smelters	Texas Co.
American Sugar	U. S. Realty
American Tel. & Tel.	U. S. Rubber
American Tobacco	U. S. Steel
General Electric	Western Union
General Motors	Westinghouse
International Harvester	Woolworth

All stocks used in both lists are common stocks. Within the last year capital readjustments of American Car & Foundry and American Tobacco resulted in the issue of two new shares for each old share, splitting the quotation. To maintain the consistency of the averages it is necessary to double the price of Car & Foundry and Tobacco, as in the case of Pennsylvania and Reading.

The averages are compiled from closing prices. In case there is no sale of a particular stock, the last previous close is used. The total sum of the closing quotations for the twenty rails, with Pennsylvania and Reading doubled, is then divided by twenty. The total

sum of the closing quotations of the twenty industrials,
with Car & Foundry and Tobacco doubled, is then divided by twenty.

THE FOLLOWING PAGES GIVE
THE AVERAGE CLOSING PRICES
1897-1925

1925—INDUSTRIALS

Date	Jan.	Feb.	Mar.	Apr.	May	June	July	Aug.
1	†	*	*	118.07	121.10	129.69	131.76	134.55
2	121.25	120.46	123.93	117.61	121.96	130.42	131.53	*
3	122.20	120.08	125.25	117.40	*	130.41	131.52	135.81
4	*	120.56	123.26	118.25	122.86	128.89	†	136.38
5	119.46	120.83	124.81	*	123.63	128.98	*	135.73
6	121.13	121.48	125.68	119.43	124.32	128.85	132.31	135.71
7	121.18	121.50	124.98	118.78	125.16	*	132.70	137.40
8	121.61	*	*	118.90	124.74	127.12	133.07	137.98
9	122.32	122.37	124.33	119.06	124.64	127.21	131.83	*
10	122.16	121.73	122.62	†	*	126.75	131.33	137.41
11	*	121.23	123.26	119.33	124.14	127.85	131.43	137.80
12	123.21	†	124.60	*	124.45	128.38	*	137.48
13	123.56	121.73	123.25	120.18	124.21	129.38	131.71	138.60
14	122.97	120.86	124.16	121.54	124.16	*	132.95	139.51
15	121.38	*	*	121.11	126.00	128.43	133.40	140.20
16	121.71	117.96	120.76	120.67	126.50	129.66	133.50	*
17	123.13	118.48	118.53	121.41	*	129.80	134.00	141.56
18	*	120.07	118.25	122.02	127.09	129.88	134.68	142.60
19	122.35	119.71	119.38	*	128.38	129.26	*	141.82
20	121.74	121.64	120.91	121.23	128.68	129.16	135.00	141.66
21	122.11	121.85	119.60	119.53	128.70	*	134.93	142.63
22	123.60	*	*	120.52	128.95	128.25	133.87	142.87
23	123.09	†	116.82	120.82	128.85	127.17	135.33	*
24	122.98	121.48	116.78	119.74	*	127.80	135.58	142.76
25	*	122.15	118.71	119.75	127.78	128.28	135.63	143.18
26	121.90	122.86	116.78	*	128.43	129.17	*	141.88
27	121.53	122.24	117.48	119.46	129.13	129.73	136.50	141.54
28	121.98	122.71	116.30	120.00	129.60	*	135.62	141.13
29	122.44		115.00	120.40	129.95	129.23	134.48	141.26
30	123.49		116.75	120.01	†	131.01	134.16	*
31	123.22		115.00		*		133.81	141.18
High	123.60	122.86	125.68	122.02	129.95	131.01	136.50	143.18
Low	119.46	117.96	115.00	117.40	121.10	126.75	131.33	134.45

*Sunday †Holiday

1925—RAILROADS

Date	Jan.	Feb.	Mar.	Apr.	May	June	July	Aug.
1	†	*	*	94.29	96.56	99.10	98.85	99.02
2	99.22	99.63	100.76	94.03	97.08	98.81	99.08	*
3	99.33	99.41	100.96	93.84	*	98.80	98.95	99.32
4	*	100.46	100.12	94.71	97.75	98.41	†	99.56
5	99.14	100.49	100.56	*	97.66	98.41	*	100.02
6	100.27	100.46	100.72	95.81	97.65	98.60	99.02	99.78
7	100.35	100.29	100.24	95.67	97.68	*	99.38	100.63
8	100.19	*	*	94.88	97.36	97.22	98.89	100.63
9	100.78	100.10	99.50	94.79	97.09	97.15	98.60	*
10	100.40	100.15	98.58	†	*	96.98	98.48	100.58
11	*	99.69	98.87	94.97	96.43	97.38	98.43	100.58
12	100.47	†	98.65	*	97.11	97.67	*	100.83
13	100.53	99.44	98.96	94.96	97.13	98.26	98.71	101.23
14	99.59	98.88	99.17	95.46	96.85	*	99.15	101.88
15	98.36	*	*	95.91	97.20	97.80	99.16	101.99
16	98.41	97.83	97.63	96.13	97.25	98.09	99.42	*
17	99.30	98.33	96.96	96.59	*	98.14	99.23	103.28
18	*	99.55	96.46	96.64	97.50	97.58	99.19	103.30
19	99.05	99.18	96.68	*	97.93	98.27	*	102.96
20	98.46	99.97	97.81	96.31	98.03	98.33	99.28	102.93
21	98.49	99.89	97.35	95.09	98.27	*	98.91	103.00
22	98.77	*	*	95.61	99.05	97.77	98.61	103.28
23	98.93	100.15	95.66	95.52	99.01	97.50	99.19	*
24	98.86	100.30	94.32	95.26	*	98.06	98.90	103.53
25	*	100.86	95.31	95.75	99.15	98.04	99.03	103.38
26	98.35		94.51	*	98.83	98.41	*	103.08
27	98.45	99.72	94.70	95.68	99.53	98.57	99.22	102.88
28	99.18	99.88	93.73	96.18	99.26	*	99.75	102.80
29	98.58		*	95.98	99.98	97.80	99.31	102.36
30	98.96		92.98	96.15	†	98.41	99.08	*
31	99.26		93.94		*		98.74	101.95
High	100.78	100.86	100.96	96.64	99.98	99.10	99.75	103.53
Low	98.35	97.83	92.98	93.84	96.43	96.98	98.43	99.02

*Sunday †Holiday

1924—INDUSTRIALS

Date	Jan.	Feb.	Mar.	Apr.	May	June	July	Aug.	Sept.	Oct.	Nov.	Dec.
1	†	100.70	97.49	93.50	92.12	*	96.45	102.12	†	104.08	104.17	110.44
2	95.65	100.84	*	94.50	91.68	90.15	96.38	102.89	104.95	103.63	*	110.71
3	94.88	*	97.10	94.33	91.93	91.23	96.48	*	104.02	102.64	103.89	110.83
4	95.40	101.08	97.50	94.69	*	90.72	†	103.28	102.77	102.85	†	111.56
5	95.26	101.08	97.55	94.05	92.23	90.41	96.43	102.52	101.07	*	105.11	111.26
6	*	101.31	98.45	*	92.24	89.18	*	102.57	100.76	102.58	104.06	111.10
7	96.54	100.99	98.61	93.03	92.47	89.52	96.91	102.30	*	102.38	104.86	*
8	96.77	100.20	98.25	92.85	92.04	*	97.56	101.79	101.26	102.60	105.53	111.30
9	97.04	100.88	*	92.24	91.40	90.15	97.40	102.08	101.98	101.38	*	112.11
10	97.23	*	97.21	90.86	90.55	90.53	96.65	*	101.13	101.33	105.91	111.07
11	97.46	100.91	97.81	91.71	*	92.00	97.38	102.20	101.79	99.18	107.58	110.84
12	97.25	†	97.58	90.78	89.48	92.19	97.60	101.51	101.91	*	108.14	111.90
13	*	99.81	98.25	*	89.69	92.68	*	101.60	101.97	†	108.58	112.76
14	95.68	100.05	98.86	89.91	88.77	92.85	97.50	102.86	*	100.11	108.96	*
15	96.09	96.63	98.02	90.52	89.18	*	97.40	104.01	101.38	100.16		113.40
16	96.65	98.06	*	90.78	89.78	93.80	96.85	104.62	101.75	100.86	*	113.73
17	96.42	*	96.60	91.34	89.33	93.57	96.85	*	103.49	101.76	110.73	114.35
18	96.28	96.33	96.69	†	*	93.52	97.40	104.99	103.42		110.24	115.17
19	96.60	96.97	96.89	91.13	89.81	93.79	98.09	105.38	103.63	*	110.50	116.13
20	*	96.58	95.88	*	88.33	93.48	*	105.57	103.85	101.14	109.63	116.41
21	97.28	97.40	95.87	89.18	89.35	93.53	99.02	104.83	*	101.85	109.55	*
22	97.23	†	95.72	89.22	90.10	*	99.36	103.89	103.25	101.96	*	116.84
23	97.73	97.88	*	90.43	90.04	92.65	99.40	103.51	104.16	102.18	109.81	115.78
24	98.59	*	95.58	90.44	90.66	93.13	99.60	*	104.68	102.53	110.08	116.74
25	99.81	97.16	94.12	91.51	*	93.67	100.36	103.53	104.13	102.04	110.15	†
26	100.00	96.45	93.67	92.02	90.60	94.71		103.58	103.98	*	†	118.59
27	*	96.75	92.90	*	90.15	95.33	*	103.23	103.93	101.73	111.10	119.18
28	99.35	97.69	92.54	90.99	89.90	95.55	101.09	102.67	*	102.45	111.38	*
29	99.16	97.22	92.28	90.65	89.90	*	100.87	104.14	102.96	102.41	*	118.63
30	99.40		*	90.63	†	96.37	101.16	105.16	103.16	103.00	*	118.02
31	100.66		93.01		†		102.14	*		104.06		120.51
High	100.66	101.31	98.86	94.69	92.47	96.37	102.14	105.57	104.95	104.08	111.38	120.51
Low	94.88	96.33	92.54	89.18	88.33	89.19	96.38	101.51	100.76	99.18	103.89	110.44

*Sunday †Holiday

1924—RAILROADS

Date	Jan.	Feb.	Mar.	Apr.	May	June	July	Aug.	Sept.	Oct.	Nov.	Dec.
1	†	82.15	81.32	81.48	81.63	*	85.83	89.87	†	90.28	89.36	96.28
2	80.79	82.35	*	82.04	81.48	82.15	85.78	90.02	90.58	90.11	*	96.60
3	80.76	*	80.51	82.83	81.51	82.58	86.00	*	90.13	88.97	89.53	97.21
4	81.01	82.61	80.75	83.43	*	82.78	†	89.79	89.45	88.90	†	98.03
5	81.33	82.50	80.90	83.23	81.58	83.22	86.16	89.78	88.90	*	90.80	97.40
6	*	82.48	81.21	*	81.71	82.58	*	89.73	88.76	88.43	91.23	97.25
7	81.78	81.76	81.10	82.80	81.88	82.76	86.66	90.18	*	88.31	93.40	*
8	81.93	81.40	81.09	82.17	81.94	*	87.27	90.20	89.07	88.26	94.10	96.99
9	83.06	81.74	*	81.76	81.83	83.16	87.32	90.74	89.89	88.48	*	96.75
10	82.80	*	80.61	81.00	81.71	83.44	86.83	*	88.92	87.66	93.55	95.78
11	82.59	82.21	80.93	81.51	*	84.30	87.09	92.20	89.06	87.65	94.32	95.76
12	82.63	†	81.03	81.38	81.58	84.60	87.15	91.50	89.45	*	93.63	96.93
13	*	81.62	81.31	*	81.63	85.13	*	91.23	89.56	86.12	93.04	97.30
14	81.75	81.65	81.47	80.55	81.77	85.21	87.51	91.38	*	86.66	93.93	*
15	79.98	80.39	81.39	80.74	82.07	*	87.68	91.91	89.34	86.40	93.88	97.93
16	80.81	81.00	*	81.10	81.85	85.01	88.08	92.10	89.40	87.20	*	98.06
17	80.76	*	81.05	81.64		84.68	88.00	*	89.97	88.04	94.76	99.31
18	80.80	80.23	81.00	†	*	84.75	88.60	92.65	89.69		95.60	99.50
19	80.79	80.68	81.50	81.55	81.88	85.13	88.69	92.10	89.60	*	95.26	99.30
20	*	80.63	81.45	*	81.37	85.32	*	91.44	89.81	87.70	96.19	99.24
21	80.85	81.08	81.46	81.13	82.38	85.23	89.15	90.93	*	88.12	95.77	*
22	80.76	†	81.99	81.20	82.58	*	89.37	90.10	89.50	88.72	95.96	98.71
23	80.67	81.33	*	81.41	82.88	84.66	89.60	89.82	90.03	88.91	*	97.88
24	80.80	*	82.01	81.13	82.96	84.94	90.10	*	90.71	89.33	95.80	98.25
25	81.56	80.96	81.38	81.30	*	86.05	90.40	89.88	90.51	89.23	96.53	†
26	81.89	80.78	81.40	81.25	83.34	86.41	90.41	89.81	90.35	*	96.48	98.89
27	*	80.68	81.29	*	83.02	86.22	*	89.85	90.55	88.71	†	98.90
28	82.16	80.58	81.05	80.95	82.67	86.11	90.36	89.48	*	89.03	96.25	*
29	81.93	81.58	80.95	80.90	82.29	*	90.04	89.83	89.99	88.86	96.35	98.46
30	81.81		*	81.06	†	85.80	89.80	89.60	90.20	88.90	*	97.67
31	82.09		81.26				90.08	*		89.28		98.33
High	83.06	82.61	82.01	83.43	83.34	86.41	90.41	92.65	90.71	90.28	96.53	99.50
Low	80.67	80.23	80.51	80.55	81.37	82.15	85.78	89.48	88.76	86.12	89.36	95.76

*Sunday †Holiday

1923—INDUSTRIALS

Date:	Jan.	Feb.	Mar.	Apr.	May	June	July	Aug.	Sept.	Oct.	Nov.	Dec.
1	†	97.71	104.23	*	97.40	95.36	*	87.96	93.22	88.06	88.41	93.15
2	98.77	98.70	104.65	101.51	98.05	95.75	88.95	88.20	*	88.09	88.91	*
3	99.42	99.33	104.51	101.60	96.30	*	87.87	†	†	90.45	89.63	92.64
4	98.57	*	*	101.40	96.60	96.14	†	87.20	92.25	89.93	*	92.68
5	98.88	100.03	104.77	102.36	96.73	96.29	87.90	88.51	92.98	89.41	89.36	92.81
6	97.77	101.01	104.79	102.36	*	97.24	88.65	89.55	93.00	89.29	†	92.94
7		101.05	105.23	102.56	95.41	97.17	89.41	88.63	92.84	*	89.48	93.80
8	98.06	101.05	104.70	*	96.54	96.66	*	88.67	92.93	88.56	90.75	93.85
9	97.23	101.05	104.48	102.11	98.19	97.10	89.26	†	*	88.06	91.14	*
10	97.29	100.82	103.82	101.86	97.61	*	88.44	89.11	93.31	87.54	91.39	93.86
11	98.12	101.70		101.08	96.45	97.22	87.80	*	93.61	87.16	*	93.65
12	98.63	†	104.22	101.71	95.40	95.97	87.64	88.95	92.05	†	91.08	94.11
13	99.09	102.16	104.79	101.81	*	95.79	89.07	89.60	89.93	87.13	90.75	94.70
14		101.85	105.28	102.09	96.91	95.44	89.40	90.23	89.63	*	90.44	94.93
15	98.04	102.57	104.74	*	95.95	94.86	*	90.86	89.05	88.06	90.87	95.23
16	96.96	103.23	103.93	101.76	95.53	94.73	89.22	91.64	*	86.91	90.33	*
17	97.05	103.21	104.89	102.14	95.41	*	89.50	92.32	89.41	87.56	89.65	95.26
18	98.09	*	*	102.24	95.07	92.64	90.01	†	88.49	87.46	*	93.66
19	97.85	102.96	105.36	102.58	94.70	92.76	91.35	91.71	89.17	87.51	91.35	93.63
20	97.61	103.56	105.38	101.38	*	90.81	91.72	92.18	88.16	87.83	91.26	94.00
21	*	103.59	105.23	101.10	92.77	92.26	91.39	92.13	88.07	*	92.17	93.51
22	97.25	†	105.09	*	93.58	93.55	*	92.04	88.54	87.48	91.83	93.63
23	97.43	103.27	103.98	100.73	93.90	93.30	91.58	91.92	*	87.37	92.13	*
24	97.16	102.85	103.28	101.08	96.03	*	90.16	91.59	89.21	87.13	92.60	94.42
25	97.79		*	101.36	96.65	91.48	90.87	*	87.94	86.43	*	†
26	98.15	102.40	102.36	101.37	97.48	90.11	91.06	92.48	88.53	86.01	92.88	95.61
27	98.00	102.79	103.03	101.16	*	88.66	88.37	93.20	88.53	85.76	92.61	94.98
28	*	103.90	103.45	100.63	97.25	89.38	87.33	93.70	87.97	*	92.41	95.12
29	98.26		102.77		97.66	88.40	*	93.40	87.89	86.20	†	95.23
30	97.75		†	98.38	†	87.85	88.11	93.46	*	88.53	92.34	*
31	97.43		102.75		97.53		86.91	93.70				95.52
High	99.42	103.90	105.38	102.70	98.19	97.24	91.72	93.70	93.61	90.45	92.88	95.61
Low	96.96	97.71	102.36	98.38	92.77	87.85	86.91	87.20	87.89	85.76	88.41	92.64

* Sunday
† Holiday

1923—RAILROADS

Date:	Jan.	Feb.	Mar.	Apr.	May	June	July	Aug.	Sept.	Oct.	Nov.	Dec.
1	†	86.08	89.37	*	84.91	81.42	*	77.91	79.88	78.83	80.01	81.18
2	86.10	86.63	89.66	85.84	85.29	81.59	78.40	77.28	*	78.96	79.95	*
3	86.07	87.34	90.63	86.17	84.22	*	77.15	†	†	80.13	79.93	80.96
4	85.68	*	*	86.30	83.87	82.15	†	76.78	78.96	80.00	*	81.28
5	85.96	88.08	90.51	86.08	84.01	82.41	77.64	*	79.66	79.96	80.03	81.80
6	85.46	88.93	90.25	86.55	*	82.71	77.99	78.02	79.55	80.81	†	82.40
7	*	88.80	89.75	86.53	80.37	83.01	78.70	78.36	79.93	*	79.73	82.43
8	85.41	88.91	89.36	*	81.55	83.31	*	77.86	80.10	80.72	79.92	82.10
9	84.96	89.17	89.19	86.58	82.31	84.92	78.72	77.90	*	80.33	80.28	*
10	84.85	89.56	88.98	86.48	82.15	*	78.38	†	80.31	79.76	80.58	81.64
11	84.59	*	*	86.28	82.20	84.51	78.11	78.11	80.53	79.23	*	80.81
12	85.09	†	89.06	86.29	81.68	83.71	77.73	*	79.30	†	80.50	81.17
13	85.29	89.49	89.66	86.34	*	83.75	78.11	78.10	78.53	79.19	81.20	81.15
14	*	89.05	89.73	87.23	82.71	83.46	79.08	78.31	78.42	*	81.00	80.40
15	85.35	89.14	89.33	*	81.87	83.65	*	78.74	78.03	79.66	80.70	80.65
16	84.60	89.24	88.67	87.09	81.70	83.48	79.20	78.91	*	79.28	80.28	*
17	84.53	89.29	89.11	87.41	81.58	*	79.16	79.17	78.39	78.41	79.80	80.18
18	84.90	*	*	88.56	81.33	82.14	79.33	79.66	78.07	78.42	*	79.42
19	85.33	89.80	89.36	88.00	81.00	81.74	79.25	*	78.48	78.67	80.56	79.34
20	85.36	90.17	89.60	87.35	*	80.60	80.05	79.53	78.36	78.95	80.77	79.80
21	*	90.43	89.67	86.75	80.13	81.24	80.51	79.31	78.37	*	81.45	79.74
22	85.10	†	89.40	*	80.91	82.40	*	78.76	78.76	78.38	81.59	79.67
23	85.77	90.12	88.80	86.47	82.70	82.43	80.75	78.85	*	78.33	81.25	*
24	86.11	90.20	88.78	86.67	82.35	*	79.98	78.92	78.36	78.41	81.20	79.84
25	86.46	*	*	86.76	82.58	81.46	79.45	78.65	78.86	77.78	*	†
26	86.43	89.76	87.69	86.79	83.16	80.23	79.64	*	78.86	77.65	81.52	80.12
27	86.47	89.53	87.71	86.52	*	78.48	80.00	79.04	79.05	77.65	81.48	79.81
28	*	89.56	87.93	86.60	83.09	78.94	78.12	79.57	78.48	*	81.61	80.10
29	87.20		87.26	*	83.04	77.97	*	79.97	78.33	77.86	†	80.62
30	86.58		†	84.86	†	76.85	77.40	80.01	*	77.67	81.09	*
31	86.26		87.15		85.29		78.13	80.30		77.82		80.86
High	87.20	90.43	90.63	88.56	85.29	84.92	80.75	80.30	80.53	80.81	81.61	82.43
Low	84.53	86.08	87.15	84.86	80.13	76.85	77.14	77.28	78.03	77.65	79.73	79.34

* Sunday † Holiday

1922—RAILROADS

Date:	Jan.	Feb.	Mar.	Apr.	May	June	July	Aug.	Sept.	Oct.	Nov.	Dec.
1	*	74.68	77.99	80.68	84.45	85.23	84.45	88.35	92.41	*	89.28	85.56
2	†	75.19	78.31	*	84.34	85.14	*	88.46	92.10	90.76	90.86	85.86
3	73.48	75.88	78.10	81.26	84.44	85.01	84.52	88.65	*	91.96	91.11	*
4	73.91	76.23	77.79	80.86	84.40	*	†	88.55	†	92.15	90.87	85.16
5	73.56	*	*	81.55	84.68	84.94	84.66	89.18	92.16	92.10	*	84.31
6	73.65	76.70	77.21	82.78	84.65	84.78	87.58	*	91.20	91.93	90.16	84.51
7	73.85	76.38	77.87	83.20	*	84.48	87.16	89.79	92.19	91.90	†	84.39
8	*	76.60	77.99	83.91	84.30	84.43	86.11	89.43	93.51	*	90.48	84.56
9	73.43	76.81	78.53	*	83.98	83.37	*	89.43	93.88	92.05	90.43	84.60
10	73.53	76.77	78.68	84.01	83.13	83.25	86.14	89.60	*	91.81	89.50	*
11	74.01	76.81	78.83	83.61	83.12	*	86.45	89.58	93.99	92.50	88.20	84.35
12	74.65	*	*	83.08	83.44	81.81	86.95	89.32	93.42	†	*	84.54
13	74.98	†	78.71	83.46	83.90	82.76	86.47	*	92.55	92.79	87.53	84.83
14	75.36	77.46	79.56	†	*	83.09	86.24	88.06	93.67	93.26	85.85	84.88
15	*	77.49	79.26	84.32	83.58	82.28	86.56	89.01	93.70	*	86.07	84.58
16	75.76	77.50	79.21	*	83.34	81.91	*	89.84	93.38	93.70	85.59	84.59
17	76.56	77.28	79.28	84.77	84.00	81.95	86.55	90.31	*	93.55	86.15	*
18	76.58	77.33	79.53	83.85	84.41	*	86.50	90.55	91.97	92.85	86.10	83.75
19	76.18	*	*	84.32	85.28	81.88	86.82	91.51	92.70	92.59	*	83.98
20	75.85	77.61	79.92	84.74	86.13	82.85	86.60	*	92.70	93.28	86.11	84.31
21	75.68	78.08	80.07	84.80	*	82.62	86.49	93.05	91.36	93.45	85.83	85.24
22	*	†	79.61	84.84	86.17	83.60	86.41	92.54	91.88	*	84.33	85.87
23	75.50	78.38	79.13	*	86.12	83.73	*	92.03	91.82	92.56	83.70	†
24	75.58	78.73	79.08	84.84	85.94	84.46	85.63	92.32	*	92.72	83.46	*
25	75.30	79.16	79.19	85.09	85.66	*	86.14	91.76	91.41	93.06	82.58	†
26	74.83	*	*	84.36	86.33	84.73	85.59	91.54	89.96	91.43	*	85.98
27	74.84	78.52	78.79	83.60	86.66	83.63	87.63	*	89.93	91.90	82.17	85.55
28	74.94	78.66	79.15	84.20	*	83.49	87.70	90.59	90.08	91.71	83.50	84.86
29	*		80.16	84.43	86.83	83.73	88.21	91.92	89.60	*	84.56	85.79
30	74.98		80.66	*	†	84.45	*	92.68		89.84	†	86.11
31	74.73		80.86		85.53		88.98	92.48		89.25		*
High	76.58	79.16	80.86	85.09	86.83	85.23	88.98	93.05	93.99	93.70	91.11	86.11
Low	73.43	74.68	77.21	80.68	83.12	81.81	84.45	88.06	89.60	89.25	82.17	83.75

* Sunday
† Holiday

1922—INDUSTRIALS

Date:	Jan.	Feb.	Mar.	Apr.	May	June	July	Aug.	Sept.	Oct.	Nov.	Dec.
1	*	81.68	85.33	89.08	93.35	96.03	92.90	96.25	101.28	*	96.23	95.73
2	†	82.86	86.03	*	93.64	96.36	*	96.51	101.29	97.67	98.50	95.91
3	78.91	82.93	86.46	90.05	93.81	96.31	92.92	96.81	*	98.90	99.29	*
4	79.61	83.61	85.91	89.30	93.18	*	†	97.11	†	99.93	99.06	95.10
5	78.68	*	*	90.67	93.18	95.98	92.97	97.03	101.67	100.34	*	95.03
6	78.96	83.70	86.30	90.80	93.59	95.59	93.97	*	100.60	100.81	98.45	96.75
7	79.12	83.38	86.90	90.80	*	95.15	94.63	97.37	101.05	100.50	†	96.91
8	*	82.74	86.73	90.63	92.84	95.11	93.53	97.07	101.22	*	99.53	97.88
9	78.87	83.60	86.95	*	92.57	93.60	*	96.93	101.68	102.26	98.98	97.72
10	78.59	83.05	87.18	91.11	91.58	93.20	93.90	96.51	*	101.55	97.50	97.85
11	80.03	82.96	87.93	91.91	91.50	*	94.17	96.82	102.05	101.72	95.88	97.75
12	79.96	†	*	91.77	92.50	90.73	94.88	97.04	101.88	†	*	98.28
13	80.82	83.81	87.56	92.48	92.93	92.04	94.65	*	101.10	102.60	95.37	98.19
14	81.23	84.09	87.92	†	*	93.08	94.96	96.21	100.79	103.43	93.61	98.03
15	*	83.98	87.30	93.06	92.08	91.25	95.35	96.90	100.99	*	95.11	*
16	81.36	83.88	88.11	*	92.63	91.11	*	97.41	100.43	102.76	94.72	97.64
17	81.90	84.28	88.46	92.75	93.71	91.45	95.26	97.93	*	102.60	95.09	98.23
18	82.33	*	88.47	91.15	93.91	*	96.53	98.60	98.88	102.00	95.36	97.52
19	81.91	*	*	92.52	94.80	91.95	96.69	99.01	99.93	101.21	95.82	97.88
20	82.95	84.85	88.28	92.43	94.65	93.51	96.76	*	100.14	102.01	95.59	98.62
21	82.53	85.81	88.11	93.21	*	93.02	96.13	99.71	98.37	101.95	94.29	†
22	*	†	87.26	93.46	*	93.15	95.78	100.75	98.55	*	94.08	*
23	82.29	85.36	86.90	93.00	94.86	93.07	94.64	100.32	99.10	100.11	94.10	†
24	82.43	85.18	87.40	92.72	94.66	93.16	95.69	99.71	*	100.10	92.78	99.04
25	82.57	83.33	87.08	91.96	94.70	*	94.84	99.82	98.90	99.55	*	99.22
26	81.54	84.58	86.60	91.10	94.36	93.48	96.36	100.05	98.45	98.00	92.03	98.14
27	81.34	85.46	87.20	91.93	95.05	92.47	96.69	99.21	96.81	98.76	93.85	98.17
28	81.75		87.90	92.74	95.47	92.24	96.83	100.70	96.58	98.68	94.65	98.73
29	*		88.87		96.41	92.06	*	100.75	97.12	*	†	
30	81.33		89.05		†	92.93	97.05	100.78	96.30	96.90		
31	81.30		89.05		95.63		97.05	100.78		96.11		
High	82.95	85.81	89.05	93.46	96.41	96.36	97.05	100.78	102.05	103.43	99.53	99.22
Low	78.59	81.68	85.33	89.08	91.50	90.73	92.90	96.21	96.30	96.11	92.03	95.03

* Sunday † Holiday

1921—INDUSTRIALS

Date	Jan.	Feb.	Mar.	Apr.	May	June	July	Aug.	Sept.	Oct.	Nov.	Dec.
1	†	75.48	74.71	75.72	*	73.51	68.35	69.68	66.83	71.68	73.44	78.12
2	*	74.98	75.19	75.27	79.65	73.06	†	69.95	68.00	*	73.52	78.73
3	72.67	74.34	75.23	*	79.23	72.37	*	69.71	†	71.61	73.98	79.00
4	72.76	74.74	75.11	75.16	79.61	72.55	†	69.50	*	70.95	73.94	*
5	73.13	75.05	75.25	76.16	80.03	*	67.71	68.61	†	70.46	73.91	78.93
6	74.31	*	*	76.58	79.68	71.18	69.86	68.56	69.12	70.42	*	79.36
7	75.21	74.80	75.26	75.61	79.48	71.56	69.72	*	69.49	70.66	74.20	79.19
8	74.80	75.54	74.91	75.73	*	71.03	68.35	68.63	69.15	71.17	†	78.80
9	*	75.48	74.60		78.81	69.85	68.54	68.00	70.58	*	75.75	79.60
10	76.00	75.59	73.60	*	78.61	69.92	*	66.71	71.92	70.95	75.61	80.16
11	76.14	75.59	72.25	76.15	77.98	69.70	68.69	66.42	*	71.06	†	*
12	75.88	†	72.76	76.28	77.60	*	68.70	66.88	70.68	†	76.46	80.63
13	74.43	*	*	75.93	77.57	70.03	68.65	66.75	71.72	70.90	*	80.69
14	74.48	76.41	72.99	75.06	77.19	70.05	67.85	*	71.68	70.15	75.50	81.04
15	75.14	76.90	73.87	76.18	*	69.00	67.25	66.02	70.68	70.09	75.80	81.50
16	*	77.14	75.20	76.33	77.23	68.16	67.44	65.27	70.95	*	77.13	80.95
17	75.21	76.40	75.44	*	77.65	67.57	*	66.09	70.83	69.46	77.07	80.57
18	75.40	76.28	76.30	76.15	77.51	67.25	67.87	65.96	*	69.81	76.94	*
19	76.76	75.93	76.56	76.10	76.96	*	68.24	65.34	70.06	70.21	77.06	80.31
20	76.08	*	*	76.08	76.07	64.90	68.21	65.09	69.43	70.77	*	80.30
21	74.65	75.10	76.03	76.54	75.65	66.25	68.11	*	69.45	71.00	76.69	79.02
22	74.91	†	76.60	77.63	*	66.23	68.27	64.50	70.25	71.11	76.21	78.76
23	*	75.66	77.78	78.15	75.86	65.36	69.23	64.38	70.90	*	76.34	79.31
24	74.77	74.66	77.39	*	74.43	66.20	*	63.90	70.81	71.81	†	79.61
25	74.98	75.23	†	78.55	74.26	67.85	69.80	63.91	*	72.22	77.31	†
26	75.19	75.46	77.13	78.86	74.81	*	69.20	65.54	70.65	72.27	77.85	80.69
27	75.71	*	*	78.11	74.31	67.03	69.18	65.56	70.30	72.78	*	80.80
28	76.23	74.98	76.19	78.77		67.63	68.18	*	70.14	73.80	78.01	80.34
29	76.34		77.13	78.57	*	68.73	68.37	66.18	71.19	73.93	77.76	80.80
30	*		76.26	78.84	†	68.45	68.86	67.80	71.08	*	77.30	81.10
31	76.13		75.76		73.44		*	67.11		73.21		81.50
High	76.76	77.14	77.78	78.86	80.03	73.51	69.86	69.95	71.92	73.93	78.01	81.50
Low	72.67	74.34	72.25	75.06	73.44	64.90	67.25	63.90	66.83	69.46	73.44	78.12

*Sunday
†Holiday

1921—RAILROADS

Date:	Jan.	Feb.	Mar.	Apr.	May	June	July	Aug.	Sept.	Oct.	Nov.	Dec.
1	†	75.38	72.41	70.41	*	71.89	70.58	74.03	71.31	74.58	72.53	76.22
2	*	75.21	72.83	70.18	71.63	71.75	†	75.21	71.84	*	72.58	75.50
3	75.98	74.41	72.96	*	71.68	71.87	†	74.42	†	74.38	72.70	75.50
4	76.21	74.56	73.23	70.05	72.51	72.38	†	73.97	*	74.06	72.49	*
5	75.91	74.90	73.42	70.46	73.99	*	70.33	72.85	†	73.76	72.43	75.01
6	76.49	*	*	70.56	74.11	71.31	72.26	72.66	72.19	73.55	*	75.24
7	77.03	74.58	72.87	69.98	74.31	70.13	72.49	*	72.92	73.67	72.70	74.60
8	77.21	74.92	72.54	69.59	*	70.57	71.35	72.64	72.62	73.90	†	74.22
9	*	74.66	71.61	69.53	75.38	69.92	71.90	72.61	73.00	*	73.58	74.35
10	77.33	74.42	70.20	*	74.68	69.20	*	72.02	73.41	73.47	73.51	74.48
11	76.99	73.60	69.10	69.36	73.90	68.99	71.65	71.30	*	73.10	†	*
12	77.30	†	69.56	69.79	72.90	*	71.70	71.93	73.28	†	73.51	74.38
13	76.65	*	*	68.88	73.10	68.91	71.10	71.87	74.30	72.46	*	74.21
14	77.15	74.19	69.18	67.86	72.89	69.69	70.96	*	73.92	71.84	72.92	74.08
15	77.56	73.66	70.16	70.28	*	69.64	70.32	71.97	73.28	71.11	73.25	74.20
16	*	74.08	71.62	70.31	73.36	69.31	70.33	71.61	73.39	*	74.08	74.38
17	76.71	73.95	70.76	*	73.26	68.88	*	71.75	73.26	70.00	74.20	74.83
18	76.40	74.15	70.75	69.88	74.16	67.85	70.70	72.28	*	70.60	74.48	*
19	76.45	74.25	70.99	69.33	73.53	*	71.45	72.30	72.78	71.14	74.58	74.95
20	76.22	*	*	69.27	72.02	65.52	71.59	72.16	72.54	71.73	*	74.57
21	75.47	73.87	70.07	69.54	71.36	66.79	71.90	*	72.67	71.53	74.36	73.95
22	75.45	†	70.31	70.10	*	67.00	72.48	71.17	73.75	71.63	74.20	73.47
23	*	74.11	71.04	71.30	71.83	66.45	73.02	70.73	74.69	*	74.10	73.30
24	75.68	73.75	70.90	*	71.26	67.13	*	69.87	74.66	72.40	†	73.67
25	75.70	74.08	†	71.33	71.45	68.80	73.09	70.21	*	71.88	75.17	†
26	76.00	73.75	71.06	71.45	72.38	*	72.93	70.21	74.30	71.46	75.60	*
27	76.19	*	*	70.54	71.98	68.00	73.08	71.16	73.61	72.20	*	73.71
28	76.67	73.32	70.18	71.26	†	68.70	73.58	*	73.45	72.94	76.06	73.88
29	76.60		71.71	71.27	*	69.27	73.33	71.43	74.10	72.80	76.66	73.71
30	*		71.10	71.25	†	71.04	73.68	72.46	74.17	*	76.33	73.86
31	76.17		70.78		71.83		*	72.15		72.56		74.27
High	77.56	75.38	73.42	71.45	75.38	72.38	73.68	75.21	74.69	74.58	76.66	76.22
Low	75.45	73.32	69.10	67.86	71.26	65.52	70.32	69.87	71.31	70.00	72.43	73.30

*Sunday
†Holiday

1920—INDUSTRIALS

Date:	Jan.	Feb.	Mar.	Apr.	May	June	July	Aug.	Sept.	Oct.	Nov.	Dec.
1	†	*	92.40	102.66	†	90.20	91.26	*	86.34	84.00	85.48	76.50
2	108.76	103.01	91.68	†	*	90.65	92.20	84.95	87.22	84.50	†	77.30
3	109.88	99.96	91.95		94.03	90.90		85.54	88.05	*	84.99	77.08
4	*	97.23	94.22	*	94.27	91.90	*	85.58		85.25	84.45	77.63
5	108.85	95.50	94.58	102.98	94.41	92.25	†	84.06	*	85.56	83.48	*
6	107.36	95.75	94.55	104.32	94.17	*	93.00	84.56	†	85.60	82.86	76.73
7	107.55	96.13	*	105.45	93.45	91.13	94.04	84.10	88.21	85.23	*	76.73
8	107.24	*	97.38	105.65	94.75	91.46	94.51	*	87.13	84.40	81.51	75.49
9	106.59	95.73	97.11	105.38	*	92.20	94.43	83.24	88.33	84.42	79.94	74.22
10	106.33	92.12	99.46	105.23	93.33	91.92	94.20	83.20	87.98	*	80.62	73.29
11	*	90.66	99.80	*	92.52	93.06	*	84.83	86.98	84.00	79.95	72.06
12	104.22	†	98.55	103.94	91.29	93.20	92.08	84.75	*	†	77.56	*
13	104.53	92.66	99.31	104.61	90.80	*	91.58	85.89	86.96	84.39	76.90	70.48
14	102.00	94.21	*	105.18	91.35	91.75	91.20	85.57	87.64	85.22	*	72.29
15	103.62	*	100.55	104.41	91.90	91.68	90.26	*	87.82	85.40	76.63	71.28
16	101.94	92.60	100.39	104.73	*	91.75	89.95	85.07	88.63	84.96	76.65	70.60
17	102.43	93.56	102.11	104.45	91.24	91.37	90.24	83.90	89.95	*	75.21	70.26
18	*	94.44	103.98	*	91.21	92.00	*	84.01	89.81	84.31	74.36	69.55
19	102.72	94.15	103.66	101.87	87.36	91.92	90.21	85.31	*	84.60	73.12	*
20	103.48	95.57	103.56	99.48	88.16	*	90.68	86.22	88.88	85.26	74.03	68.52
21	102.62	95.63	*	95.93	88.20	91.32	90.45	86.86	87.96	84.65	*	66.75
22	102.36	*	104.17	97.15	88.40	90.16	90.74	*	87.45	85.06	77.15	67.02
23	101.90	†	103.55	95.46	*	90.83	89.63	85.78	86.47	85.57	77.20	69.63
24	102.65	92.98	100.33	95.76	87.57	90.88	89.85	87.29	85.90	*	76.65	68.91
25	*	89.98	101.54	*	90.24	90.95	*	86.93	86.35	85.73	†	†
26	103.74	91.37	103.63	97.20	90.01	90.88	87.66	87.22	*	85.61	75.53	*
27	104.15	91.18	103.40	96.41	91.01	*	87.68	86.81	83.82	84.92	75.46	68.01
28	103.96	91.31	*	94.75	91.81	90.45	86.96	86.60	84.53	84.61	*	67.96
29	103.60	*	102.23	93.16	92.06	90.36	87.89	*	83.83	85.08	76.18	69.20
30	104.21		102.45	93.54	*	90.76	86.86	86.43	82.95	84.95	76.04	70.03
31	103.82		102.81		†		86.85	86.16		*		71.95
High	109.88	103.01	104.17	105.65	94.75	93.20	94.51	87.29	89.95	85.73	85.48	77.63
Low	101.90	89.98	91.68	93.16	87.36	90.16	86.85	83.20	82.95	84.00	73.12	66.75

*Sunday
†Holiday

1920—RAILROADS

Date:	Jan.	Feb.	Mar.	Apr.	May	June	July	Aug.	Sept.	Oct.	Nov.	Dec.
1	†	*	75.04	75.98	†	72.28	70.97	*	78.22	82.76	83.31	77.45
2	75.62	74.68	74.83	†	*	72.14	71.33	73.07	78.74	84.28	†	77.47
3	76.48	73.56	74.25	†	71.80	71.98	†	74.36	78.88	*	85.37	77.55
4	*	71.97	74.65	*	72.68	72.01	*	74.91	†	84.30	85.09	77.50
5	76.41	71.51	74.51	75.78	73.33	71.95	71.77	74.03	*	83.81	84.98	*
6	75.89	70.83	74.42	76.28	73.54	*	72.42	73.90	†	84.26	84.08	76.28
7	75.90	71.40	*	76.53	73.11	71.68	73.06	73.90	78.79	84.61	*	76.68
8	75.59	*	76.20	76.35	73.76	71.70	74.06	*	78.05	83.84	83.21	76.75
9	75.56	71.09	76.88	75.90	*	71.14	74.43	72.95	78.07	83.50	81.42	75.78
10	75.62	69.00	78.55	75.64	73.53	70.88	*	73.10	77.90	*	82.10	74.73
11	*	67.83	78.46	*	72.80	71.15	74.30	73.70	77.28	83.31	81.99	73.32
12	74.91	†	77.46	74.76	72.36	70.71	73.81	73.40	*	†	78.75	*
13	75.06	69.38	78.73	74.86	71.73	*	73.84	74.05	77.40	84.11	78.10	71.70
14	74.46	70.14	*	75.40	72.29	70.19	73.20	73.93	77.35	84.18	*	73.63
15	74.68	*	78.33	74.86	72.25	70.17	72.65	*	78.31	84.65	78.95	73.10
16	74.61	69.53	77.82	75.16	*	70.78	72.84	73.89	79.01	84.05	79.64	72.89
17	74.96	72.68	77.57	75.30	72.31	70.56	*	73.55	79.61	*	77.72	72.53
18	*	73.02	78.51	*	71.70	71.03	72.84	73.53	80.25	83.44	77.20	71.73
19	74.71	75.46	78.40	74.56	69.99	70.99	72.61	73.90	*	83.85	75.97	*
20	74.68	74.98	78.13	73.26	70.23	*	72.88	74.66	80.19	83.90	77.46	71.36
21	74.46	75.55	*	71.64	70.69	70.87	73.08	74.94	80.11	83.27	*	69.80
22	74.28	*	77.75	72.39	70.62	70.31	73.45	*	80.15	83.43	79.73	70.74
23	74.22	†	77.39	71.65	*	70.36	73.03	75.63	80.14	83.64	78.58	72.63
24	74.29	75.25	76.75	72.01	69.95	70.49	73.00	75.81	79.97	*	78.43	72.33
25	*	73.14	76.36	*	71.28	70.86	*	75.66	80.30	83.22	†	†
26	74.29	74.34	77.30	74.98	71.37	71.08	72.10	76.55	*	83.36	78.83	*
27	74.35	74.67	77.11	73.71	71.72	*	71.98	76.45	79.70	82.83	78.53	72.66
28	74.25	74.77	*	73.38	72.89	70.72	71.80	76.59	80.23	82.10	*	73.05
29	73.90	*	76.61	72.71	73.24	70.85	72.88	*	80.62	82.57	78.52	75.50
30	74.18		76.46	72.21	*	70.91	72.56	77.12	81.33	82.62	77.55	75.56
31	74.68		76.11		†		73.03	77.50		*		75.96
High	76.48	75.55	78.73	76.53	73.76	72.28	74.43	77.50	81.33	84.65	85.37	77.55
Low	73.90	67.83	74.25	71.64	69.95	70.17	70.97	72.95	77.28	82.10	75.97	69.80

*Sunday †Holiday

1919—INDUSTRIALS

Date:	Jan.	Feb.	Mar.	Apr.	May	June	July	Aug.	Sept.	Oct.	Nov.	Dec.
1	†	80.55	84.04	88.84	93.26	*	108.13	107.99	†	111.12	118.63	104.03
2	82.60	*	*	89.30	94.30	106.92	108.56	†	106.26	111.19	*	104.41
3	83.35	80.91	85.58	88.91	94.78	103.83	109.90	*	108.55	108.90	119.62	105.75
4	83.05	81.08	85.10	89.59	*	105.66	†	102.82	108.27	110.26	†	107.97
5	*	80.70	84.24	89.65	94.92	107.55	109.41	102.40	106.96	*	118.48	107.42
6	82.45	79.68	85.64	*	96.16	107.46	*	105.78	106.33	112.04	117.78	107.39
7	82.44	79.35	86.23	90.18	97.65	107.55	109.97	100.80	*	112.55	117.18	*
8	82.60	79.15	87.27	90.59	98.61	*	110.46	101.88	106.51	113.55	115.54	107.88
9	82.76	*	*	91.01	98.19	107.35	110.00	104.33	108.30	113.40	*	106.85
10	82.30	79.65	87.43	90.11	98.53	105.43	109.92	*	107.68	114.42	112.93	107.01
11	81.66	80.25	88.10	89.61	*	105.16	110.71	103.94	107.10	114.39	110.75	105.01
12	*	†	88.30	90.48	99.23	105.05	112.23	105.10	108.30	*	107.15	103.73
13	81.79	81.07	88.18	*	100.37	102.85	*	104.28	108.39	†	110.69	105.61
14	82.00	81.20	87.87	91.47	99.45	105.05	111.66	102.86	*	112.41	110.49	*
15	82.40	81.96	87.68	91.07	99.92	*	111.47	102.25	108.81	112.88	109.81	105.06
16	82.20	*	*	90.88	100.10	102.78	110.65	†	107.55	112.51	*	106.61
17	81.35	82.55	88.41	91.67	99.16	99.56	110.69	*	106.78	112.98	109.09	107.26
18	80.93	81.92	87.87	†	*	103.28	107.24	99.70	105.84	113.20	107.45	103.78
19	*	82.58	88.26	92.21	99.88	105.08	109.34	100.58	104.99	*	106.15	104.63
20	80.14	82.93	87.81	*	99.65	104.49	110.73	98.46	106.30	115.43	108.19	104.55
21	79.88	84.21	89.05	92.24	99.88	106.13	*	99.47	*	115.62	107.73	*
22	80.00	†	88.66	92.36	100.47	*	109.98	100.84	106.89	117.62	108.42	103.55
23	80.20	*	*	91.65	101.60	106.45	110.03	101.44	106.83	114.88	*	103.79
24	81.75	84.62	87.97	92.09	103.80	106.09	111.10	*	107.30	115.57	108.86	103.95
25	81.33	84.61	†	92.48	*	104.58	110.94	101.63	108.66	112.73	109.02	†
26	*	85.60	86.83	93.17	103.58	104.91	109.72	103.29	110.06	*	107.50	105.63
27	81.47	85.68	87.65	*	104.00	105.63	*	101.91		114.88	†	106.08
28	81.60	84.81	88.86	93.51	105.50	106.66	108.91	103.01	*	116.30	103.72	*
29	80.56		88.88	92.88		*	107.16	104.75	110.32	117.43	103.60	105.18
30	80.94		*		†	106.98	107.16		111.42	117.33	*	105.46
31	80.61		88.85					*		118.92		107.23
High	83.35	85.68	89.05	93.51	105.50	107.55	112.23	107.99	111.42	118.92	119.62	107.97
Low	79.88	79.15	84.04	88.84	93.26	99.56	107.16	98.46	104.99	108.90	103.60	103.55

*Sunday   †Holiday

1919—RAILROADS

Date:	Jan.	Feb.	Mar.	Apr.	May	June	July	Aug.	Sept.	Oct.	Nov.	Dec.
1	†	81.76	84.71	83.73	85.63	*	86.28	86.63	†	81.97	80.01	74.93
2	84.31	*	*	83.80	85.98	90.78	86.56	†	81.30	81.51	*	75.27
3	84.84	81.68	84.88	83.71	86.15	89.41	86.89	*	81.48	80.95	79.90	75.65
4	84.48	82.54	83.65	84.79	*	89.63	†	83.22	81.35	82.06	†	75.97
5	*	82.70	82.78	84.62	87.28	90.53	*	83.93	80.60	*	80.23	76.61
6	83.93	82.18	83.33	*	†	90.05	87.66	82.41	80.36	82.48	80.66	76.99
7	84.08	81.85	84.13	84.78	87.48	90.19	87.76	80.66	*	82.23	81.18	*
8	84.43	81.61	84.66	84.50	87.48	*	88.59	79.96	80.27	82.04	80.90	76.85
9	84.33	*	*	84.55	87.01	89.91	87.87	81.31	80.43	81.70	*	76.44
10	84.01	81.65	84.96	84.25	86.78	88.68	88.10	*	†	82.31	79.98	76.02
11	84.06	81.89	85.81	83.76	*	88.35	88.22	81.28	80.15	82.38	79.80	74.29
12	*	†	85.47	83.16	86.75	88.23	*	81.46	79.89	*	78.57	73.63
13	83.90	81.80	85.26	*	87.27	86.92	88.13	81.01	80.63	†	79.32	74.21
14	83.97	82.08	85.00	83.38	88.53	86.76	88.71	81.01	*	81.61	81.65	*
15	83.85	82.31	85.00	83.79	88.43	*	90.24	80.16	81.08	81.50	81.58	73.96
16	83.31	*	*	83.62	89.72	85.85	89.48	80.33	80.63	81.28	*	74.75
17	82.99	82.80	84.73	83.36	90.50	87.08	89.40	*	80.32	81.36	81.86	74.88
18	82.62	83.00	84.73	†	*	87.33	*	†	79.53	81.15	80.34	74.53
19	*	83.16	84.61	83.50	90.10	87.08	88.33	78.89	79.43	*	79.36	75.56
20	81.69	83.19	84.61	*	90.35	87.79	88.73	79.11	78.98	81.14	79.65	75.86
21	80.86	83.64	84.03	83.53	89.53	87.90	88.58	78.60	*	80.85	79.40	*
22	81.40	†	84.26	84.51	89.41	*	88.12	78.60	79.40	80.88	79.39	75.35
23	82.08	*	84.21	84.46	89.87	87.65	88.25	79.63	79.53	81.09	*	74.86
24	82.68	84.18	*	84.24	90.33	87.95	88.40	*	79.60	82.15	79.40	74.93
25	82.70	83.69	83.93	84.58	*	87.29	*	80.05	79.25	80.99	78.87	†
26	*	84.36	83.00	85.81	91.13	86.83	88.20	81.29	79.69	*	77.97	75.48
27	82.51	84.60	83.10	*	91.13	86.78	87.85	81.16	80.11	81.07	†	74.98
28	82.66	84.22	83.53	85.57	90.82	86.76	87.26	79.78	*	80.60	75.33	*
29	82.11		83.41	85.38	91.08	*	86.50	80.33	80.22	80.63	75.86	74.23
30	82.13		*	85.03	†	86.56		81.21	80.62	80.25	*	73.85
31	81.97		†		91.13			*		80.28		75.30
High	84.84	84.60	85.81	85.81	91.13	90.78	90.24	86.63	81.48	82.48	81.86	76.99
Low	80.86	81.61	82.78	83.36	85.63	85.85	86.28	78.60	78.98	80.25	75.33	73.63

*Sunday
†Holiday

1918—INDUSTRIALS

Date:	Jan.	Feb.	Mar.	Apr.	May	June	July	Aug.	Sept.	Oct.	Nov.	Dec.
1	†	79.28	79.93	77.16	78.16	77.93	81.81	80.71	*	83.95	85.53	*
2	76.68	79.77	78.98	76.69	78.90	*	81.98	80.76	†	84.45	85.23	81.13
3	76.18	*	79.01	77.01	78.64	78.55	82.49	80.90	83.84	84.95	*	82.46
4	75.56	†	79.50	77.42	78.59	79.60	†	*	83.61	85.31	85.74	82.45
5	73.75	79.28	79.20	77.03	*	79.54	82.96	81.57	83.63	84.87	†	82.89
6	*	78.93	79.53	77.95	79.36	78.95	83.20	81.13	82.56	*	86.62	82.45
7	74.86	77.78	79.50	*	80.51	78.53	*	80.97	82.91	84.35	87.61	82.71
8	74.63	78.44	79.50	77.69	80.32	79.16	82.60	81.13	*	84.30	87.66	*
9	75.61	78.98	79.71	77.40	81.30	*	82.76	81.65	81.80	83.36	88.06	83.41
10	76.33	*	*	76.85	81.29	78.93	82.09	82.04	81.33	84.15	*	84.50
11	75.00	†	79.78	75.58	81.82	79.10	81.09	*	80.46	84.83	*	84.27
12	74.48	†	78.67	76.25	*	79.76	81.23	81.58	†	†	86.56	83.53
13	*	78.73	78.68	76.01	82.16	80.53	81.15	81.68	80.29	*	86.12	82.65
14	73.48	78.71	79.13	*	82.21	80.61	*	81.70	81.49	86.35	85.53	82.96
15	73.38	79.96	79.06	77.51	84.04	81.21	80.58	81.58	*	86.21	86.15	*
16	74.60	80.08	78.98	77.21	84.03	*	81.71	81.77	81.48	86.63	85.35	83.23
17	74.48	*	*	76.89	83.50	80.61	81.45	81.51	81.80	88.27	*	83.41
18	74.55	81.53	77.93	78.11	83.35	80.98	82.92	*	81.92	89.07	85.01	83.01
19	74.89	82.08	78.13	78.60	*	80.93	82.31	81.63	81.64	88.88	84.68	82.40
20	*	81.28	78.14	79.73	82.47	81.83	82.29	81.92	81.96	*	84.33	81.72
21	76.11	80.53	78.71	*	82.87	81.65	*	81.61	82.33	88.15	83.84	81.89
22	75.75	†	77.71	79.42	82.22	81.95	81.22	81.61	*	87.79	82.60	*
23	75.43	79.88	76.24	78.30	82.21	*	80.51	82.15	82.44	87.10	81.83	81.51
24	75.92	*	*	78.01	81.58	82.50	80.93	82.83	82.80	87.10	*	80.59
25	76.50	79.17	76.45	77.88	81.16	82.40	81.28	*	82.64	86.52	79.87	†
26	76.44	80.65	76.49	78.23	*	83.02	81.51	82.93	82.84	87.70	81.43	80.44
27	†	80.50	76.72	77.86	78.65	82.78	81.49	83.01	84.03	*	80.16	81.17
28	*	80.39	76.41	*	78.42	82.58	*	83.18	83.85	87.28	†	81.55
29	77.13		†	77.79	78.44	82.68	81.10	82.73	*	86.39	80.93	*
30	76.98		76.72	77.51	†	*	80.79	82.46	84.68	84.08	81.13	80.78
31	79.80		*		78.08		81.23	82.84		85.51		82.20
High	79.80	82.08	79.93	79.73	84.04	83.02	83.20	83.18	84.68	89.07	88.06	84.50
Low	73.38	77.78	76.24	75.58	78.08	77.93	80.51	80.71	80.29	83.36	79.87	80.44

*Sunday †Holiday

1918—RAILROADS

Date:	Jan.	Feb.	Mar.	Apr.	May	June	July	Aug.	Sept.	Oct.	Nov.	Dec.
1	†	80.92	81.00	80.20	79.24	82.65	82.67	82.46	*	85.17	88.63	*
2	79.46	81.03	80.40	79.53	79.75	*	82.57	82.51	†	85.25	88.53	87.75
3	80.02	*		79.67	79.48	82.26	82.75	82.56	83.48	85.11	*	87.86
4	80.28	†	80.13	79.81	79.30	83.43	†	*	83.61	84.87	89.71	87.63
5	79.19	80.59	80.20	79.51	*	83.08	83.16	82.69	83.63	84.95	†	87.77
6	*	79.98	80.60	80.08	80.11	82.93	83.10	82.56	85.55		90.57	87.60
7	79.12	79.33	80.61	*	80.63	82.46	*	82.76	85.67	85.39	92.73	87.66
8	79.33	79.34	82.40	79.53	81.81	82.68	82.83	82.84	*	85.04	92.45	*
9	79.76	79.38	81.71	79.21	82.45	*	83.31	83.08	85.11	85.16	92.91	87.72
10	79.53			78.90	82.36	82.53	83.31	83.33	84.50	85.33	*	88.25
11	78.96	*	82.56	78.00	82.31	82.48	82.76	*	83.68	86.17	92.14	87.90
12	78.53	†	81.91	78.45	*	82.95	82.75	84.12	†	†	91.25	87.07
13		79.06	81.76	78.26	82.75	83.23	82.81	85.00	83.32		90.77	86.50
14	77.50	79.87	82.70		84.08	83.27	*	84.57	83.70	87.87	90.88	86.45
15	77.21	80.86	82.06	79.15	84.39	83.38	82.19	84.43	83.59	87.20	90.39	*
16	77.70	80.70	82.23	78.98	84.32	*	82.46	84.65	83.81	87.28		86.54
17	77.90			78.60	84.20	83.25	82.30	84.32	*	88.18		86.58
18	77.91	81.41	81.24	79.28	83.81	83.31	82.99	*	84.13	89.45	89.91	85.88
19	78.14	81.31	81.21	79.38	*	83.26	82.81	84.48	83.76	89.68	89.56	84.79
20		80.98	81.25	79.52	83.59	83.50	82.97	84.83	84.20		89.45	84.25
21	78.14	80.50	81.55	79.55	84.00	83.24	82.80	84.81	84.21	90.34	89.28	84.30
22	77.90	*	80.70	79.45	83.09	83.31	82.36	84.55	*	91.80	88.45	*
23	77.63	80.90	78.73	79.26	82.51	*	82.58	85.45	84.36	90.26	87.51	83.75
24	77.71	†		78.99	82.40	83.42	82.80	86.38	84.42	89.58	*	83.63
25	78.68	80.23	79.16	78.95	83.20	83.36	82.82	*	84.21	88.78	85.10	†
26	79.11	80.95	79.42	78.84	*	83.69	82.86	86.05	84.13	89.55	86.06	83.05
27	*	81.13	79.82	*	82.27	83.37	*	86.09	84.55	*	85.56	83.10
28	†	81.13	79.72	78.84	82.97	83.20	83.13	85.93	84.43	89.21	†	83.76
29	79.63		†		83.50	83.11	82.90	85.90	*	88.85	87.16	*
30	79.36		79.98		†	*	82.86	85.88	85.50	87.46	87.08	83.10
31	81.03		*		82.88		83.31	86.36		88.11		84.32
High	81.03	81.41	82.70	80.20	84.39	83.69	83.31	86.38	85.67	91.80	92.91	88.25
Low	77.21	79.06	78.73	78.00	79.24	82.26	82.19	82.46	83.32	84.87	85.10	83.05

*Sunday †Holiday

1917—INDUSTRIALS

Date	Jan.	Feb.	Mar.	Apr.	May	June	July	Aug.	Sept.	Oct.	Nov.	Dec.
1	†	88.52	91.10	*	93.42	97.89	*	92.26	†	83.58	71.41	72.86
2	96.15	87.01	92.82	97.06	92.48	97.59	95.23	92.87	*	83.49	72.52	*
3	99.18	89.97	93.63	96.34	90.98	*	95.31	92.96	†	82.45	72.32	72.55
4	97.15	*	95.04	95.83	90.45	97.00	†	†	81.20	80.62	*	70.72
5	96.16	92.03	95.30	94.61	90.20	†	93.57	*	83.66	81.75	69.93	71.68
6	96.75	92.81	95.30	†	*	98.43	93.90	93.85	83.42	81.35	†	71.01
7	*	92.19	95.30	93.10	91.20	98.16	94.28	93.30	83.49	*	71.54	70.29
8	96.40	90.94	95.28	*	90.22	98.58	*	91.47	83.18	80.48	68.58	70.31
9	97.64	90.20	96.46	92.41	89.08	99.08	93.64	92.23	*	79.26	69.36	*
10	95.70	91.56	96.78	91.20	90.41	*	93.10	91.90	83.88	77.32	70.30	70.49
11	96.02	*	*	92.82	89.77	97.86	94.14	91.81	83.51	77.83	*	68.78
12	95.75	†	95.03	93.10	89.62	97.52	93.64	*	82.19	†	70.65	67.30
13	95.13	92.37	95.05	93.18	*	98.31	92.33	92.65	83.14		70.35	66.96
14	*	91.86	95.16	93.76	90.78	97.95	92.57	91.69	83.44	*	69.15	68.65
15	95.59	91.65	95.63	*	90.19	97.22	*	92.10	83.04	75.13	69.10	67.53
16	97.55	91.81	95.65	92.21	92.26	96.95	91.38	91.44	*	77.08	69.75	*
17	96.60	92.70	96.22	91.87	92.75	*	91.95	91.61	81.55	76.11	70.41	67.08
18	97.50	*	*	91.63	91.96	94.89	91.05	91.42	81.63	78.21	*	67.31
19	97.35	93.66	96.97	91.83	92.37	95.36	90.48	*	84.01	79.80	71.51	65.95
20	97.97	94.91	98.20	90.84	*	94.78	91.59	91.27	84.82		72.80	67.13
21	*	93.97	97.61	90.98	93.47	95.77	92.61	90.75	85.23	*	73.57	68.25
22	96.60	†	96.78	*	94.09	96.63	*	89.16	84.53	79.06	72.95	68.23
23	96.26	92.56	97.27	90.96	94.26	97.60	91.61	88.15	*	78.50	74.23	*
24	96.66	92.22	97.73	90.66	95.20	*	91.26	88.91	85.70	78.30	73.51	69.29
25	97.41	*	*	92.98	96.76	97.57	91.24	89.06	86.02	77.68	*	†
26	97.36	93.35	96.32	93.06	97.58	96.81	91.42	*	84.61	77.35	74.03	68.33
27	96.71	92.68	96.46	93.10	*	95.98	91.75	88.40	84.60	78.91	73.80	70.49
28	*	91.56	97.01	92.65	97.20	95.41	92.11	86.12	83.46	*	73.25	72.13
29	95.78		96.75	*	97.41	95.38	*	85.95	83.81	76.28	†	72.45
30	95.83		96.72	93.23	†	95.87	92.13	84.51	*	75.53	72.65	*
31	95.43		95.41		97.38		91.75	83.40		74.50		74.38
High	99.18	94.91	98.20	97.06	97.58	99.08	95.31	93.85	86.02	83.58	74.23	74.38
Low	95.13	87.01	91.10	90.66	89.08	94.78	90.48	83.40	81.20	74.50	68.58	65.95

*Sunday
†Holiday

1917—RAILROADS

Date:	Jan.	Feb.	Mar.	Apr.	May	June	July	Aug.	Sept.	Oct.	Nov.	Dec.
1	†	99.31	96.53	*	96.17	94.84	*	93.63	†	85.66	77.21	76.21
2	105.41	97.50	97.00	100.72	95.35	93.78	92.45	93.84	*	85.20	78.00	*
3	105.76	98.16	97.63	99.25	93.39	*	92.93	93.95	†	85.03	77.37	75.55
4	105.02	*	*	99.25	92.13	93.56	†	†	87.06	84.46	*	74.90
5	104.75	98.59	97.76	98.16	91.74	†	92.16	*	87.93	85.81	75.35	77.21
6	104.74	97.93	97.36	†	*	94.20	92.46	93.91	87.88	85.88	†	76.40
7	*	96.97	97.06	97.11	92.41	94.57	93.08	94.16	87.91	*	76.69	75.86
8	104.88	96.75	96.83	*	91.79	95.06	*	93.28	87.84	85.07	74.54	75.74
9	104.56	96.81	97.40	96.15	90.63	95.27	92.80	93.90	*	84.70	75.88	*
10	103.33	96.11	97.30	96.05	91.88	*	93.55	93.20	87.88	83.51	76.58	75.91
11	103.11	*	*	96.88	91.02	94.79	93.94	93.26	87.60	83.38	*	73.43
12	103.41	†	97.75	96.96	91.04	95.27	94.12	*	86.05	†	76.72	72.17
13	103.47	98.08	97.28	97.83	*	95.72	94.02	93.49	86.17	81.50	76.48	72.43
14	*	97.15	96.95	97.81	91.35	95.51	95.09	93.46	86.88	*	75.60	73.98
15	103.65	96.90	97.27	*	90.73	95.27	*	93.45	87.10	83.07	75.70	73.18
16	105.01	97.13	97.67	96.71	92.06	95.32	94.96	92.96	*	82.51	75.01	*
17	104.36	97.61	97.85	96.97	92.89	*	95.05	92.06	85.95	83.66	75.34	72.93
18	105.10	*	*	97.03	92.76	94.66	94.05	92.08	85.58	83.82	*	72.96
19	104.84	98.03	99.55	96.91	92.95	94.68	93.72	*	87.01	84.34	77.05	70.75
20	104.76	98.68	100.18	97.10	*	94.49	93.75	91.41	86.71	83.57	77.58	71.50
21	*	99.05	99.48	96.88	93.21	94.90	94.08	90.96	87.04	*	78.32	72.03
22	104.55	†	99.48	96.58	94.18	95.26	93.66	90.20	87.41	83.17	78.26	71.84
23	104.02	98.60	101.98	96.58	94.11	95.46	93.40	90.31	*	82.65	78.46	*
24	104.87	98.52	102.30	96.27	94.30	*	93.43	91.35	88.03	81.73	78.16	72.80
25	104.47	*	*	97.40	93.88	96.28	93.36	91.38	89.08	81.96	*	†
26	104.40	98.70	100.54	97.90	94.01	96.53	93.36	*	88.23	82.61	78.13	71.61
27	104.16	98.08	100.36	97.61	*	96.01	93.65	91.13	88.12	81.08	77.13	78.02
28	*	97.37	101.27	96.75	95.15	95.60		90.26	86.30	*	76.42	79.86
29	103.68		100.73	*	95.20	95.09	*	90.53	86.55	80.50	†	79.63
30	103.66		100.96	96.80	†	94.20	93.48	89.87	*	79.61	75.80	*
31	102.71		100.33		95.20		93.57	89.45				79.73
High	105.76	99.31	102.30	100.72	96.17	96.53	95.09	94.16	89.08	85.88	78.46	79.86
Low	102.71	96.11	96.53	96.05	90.63	93.56	92.16	89.45	85.58	79.61	74.54	70.75

*Sunday †Holiday

1916—INDUSTRIALS

Date:	Jan.	Feb.	Mar.	Apr.	May	June	July	Aug.	Sept.	Oct.	Nov.	Dec.
1	†	91.93	90.69	93.69	90.30	91.87	88.93	89.05	91.19	*	105.90	106.17
2	*	93.69	90.52	*	89.02	91.22	*	88.34	92.29	103.01	105.70	106.81
3	98.81	94.40	91.71	94.13	88.61	91.53	89.37	88.83	*	103.45	106.28	*
4	97.72	93.19	91.48	93.97	87.71	*	†	88.41	†	103.41	105.93	106.20
5	97.41	93.39	*	94.12	88.51	92.19	90.53	88.55	93.36	104.15	*	106.43
6	96.44	*	92.93	94.46	90.51	91.73	90.40	*	94.51	102.85	107.21	106.76
7	97.34	94.96	92.58	93.38	*	91.84	89.71	88.88	94.59	103.40	†	106.43
8	97.52	94.91	92.58	93.31	90.36	92.01	89.51	88.15	94.63	*	106.83	106.51
9	*	95.86	93.50	*	89.71	92.78	*	90.26	95.53	100.23	107.68	105.68
10	95.69	96.10	93.11	94.22	89.78	92.70	88.60	90.05	*	101.35	107.65	*
11	94.07	96.15	92.90	93.77	90.08	*	87.63	90.32	95.74	99.98	106.72	104.67
12	95.31	†	*	93.28	90.94	93.61	87.63	90.50	96.65	†	*	100.35
13	94.71	*	94.75	91.28	91.71	93.19	86.42	*	97.71	98.94	105.63	102.61
14	96.47	95.28	95.40	91.63	*	93.33	86.95	90.75	97.85	98.98	107.04	98.23
15	96.55	95.26	95.76	91.48	92.43	93.33	87.36	91.48	98.39	*	107.72	97.93
16	*	94.50	96.08	*	92.01	92.49	*	91.91	98.00	101.42	108.48	99.11
17	96.63	94.11	96.00	91.08	91.51	91.90	87.15	92.08	*	102.42	109.62	*
18	96.16	94.35	95.76	90.65	92.05	*	87.25	92.08	98.51	102.35	110.13	98.07
19	95.25	94.77	*	88.46	91.76	90.00	88.10	91.93	98.57	102.55	*	97.76
20	93.60	*	93.60	88.11	91.81	90.57	89.00	*	98.47	103.68	110.10	95.26
21	94.78	94.36	93.58	†	*	90.03	89.03	93.25	99.55	103.88	110.15	90.16
22	94.65	†	93.97	84.96	92.06	89.54	89.75	93.83	100.77	*	108.65	95.09
23	*	94.35	93.76	*	92.10	88.88	*	93.61	101.30	105.17	107.48	94.60
24	93.87	93.37	93.65	87.00	92.37	89.26	89.10	93.66	*	105.15	109.07	*
25	94.24	93.85	93.23	88.12	92.62	*	88.83	92.90	100.89	104.57	109.95	†
26	93.49	92.78	*	87.23	92.29	87.68	88.13	92.91	101.39	104.56	*	96.10
27	92.99	*	93.57	88.78	91.62	88.43	88.00	*	101.85	105.28	108.23	95.63
28	93.25	90.89	93.81	89.65	*	88.29	88.35	92.49	103.11	104.83	107.01	94.01
29	91.93	91.03	93.36	89.78	91.95	89.51	88.79	91.63	103.73	*	105.97	95.00
30	*		92.73	*	†	89.58	*	91.32	102.90	104.30	†	†
31	90.58		93.25		91.80		89.25	92.25		104.61		*
High	98.81	96.15	96.08	94.46	92.62	93.61	90.53	93.83	103.73	105.28	110.15	106.81
Low	90.58	90.89	90.52	84.96	87.71	87.68	86.42	88.15	91.19	98.94	105.63	90.16

*Sunday †Holiday

1916—RAILROADS

Date:	Jan.	Feb.	Mar.	Apr.	May	June	July	Aug.	Sept.	Oct.	Nov.	Dec.
1	†	102.05	100.65	101.61	102.46	107.06	105.78	103.89	104.01	*	110.07	108.69
2	*	102.56	100.69	*	101.66	106.63	*	103.43	104.62	109.96	110.42	109.10
3	107.76	102.88	101.14	101.96	101.24	106.87	106.62	103.28	*	110.83	110.23	*
4	107.50	101.68	100.86	102.10	100.68	*	†	103.34	†	112.28	110.28	108.65
5	107.32	101.84	*	102.73	101.40	106.91	106.91	103.31	104.75	108.88	*	108.92
6	106.75	*	101.35	102.88	102.03	107.29	107.11	*	104.83	111.00	110.96	108.77
7	107.13	102.26	101.31	102.21	*	108.23	106.60	103.21	105.41	111.30	†	108.56
8	107.36	102.16	101.41	102.10	102.69	108.43	106.62	103.59	105.70	*	110.34	108.33
9	*	102.62	101.74	*	103.08	108.80	*	105.51	105.86	109.40	110.00	107.79
10	106.54	103.00	101.72	102.13	102.58	108.53	106.08	104.75	*	110.47	109.61	106.91
11	106.18	103.32	101.66	101.85	102.75	*	105.41	105.16	105.69	109.26	109.11	105.09
12	106.69	†	*	101.79	103.70	109.08	105.45	104.93	105.61	108.89	*	106.73
13	106.48	*	102.20	100.96	103.97	108.63	104.99	*	106.21	109.14	108.17	105.70
14	106.79	102.41	103.37	101.00	*	108.51	105.10	105.28	106.68	110.24	107.76	106.22
15	106.73	102.34	103.73	101.12	104.68	108.26	105.17	105.76	106.68	*	107.23	107.53
16	*	101.45	103.44	*	104.43	107.47	*	106.25	107.59	110.03	108.15	107.53
17	106.56	101.46	103.63	101.08	104.28	107.15	105.21	105.80	*	110.38	108.25	107.41
18	106.22	101.50	103.70	101.28	106.15	*	105.11	105.44	109.16	110.23	108.26	107.31
19	105.90	101.86	*	100.06	106.97	105.60	105.38	105.27	108.76	110.52	*	106.53
20	105.02	*	102.94	100.17	107.35	106.31	104.96	*	108.39	110.34	109.21	103.53
21	105.55	101.73	102.98	†	108.76	105.85	104.73	105.63	107.59	111.03	108.42	105.91
22	105.41	†	103.03	99.11	108.38	105.71	104.89	107.14	108.13	110.40	108.03	106.08
23	*	101.59	103.20	*	107.18	105.30	*	106.99	108.43	110.02	107.59	106.17
24	104.07	101.03	103.08	99.78	106.76	105.45	104.43	106.68	*	109.89	108.02	*
25	103.98	101.69	102.96	100.02	106.58	*	104.15	106.00	108.43	110.18	108.02	†
26	102.74	101.36	*	99.98	106.26	104.04	103.81	106.03	108.53	109.96	*	106.27
27	102.42	*	102.81	101.95	*	104.53	103.40	*	109.33	109.95	107.81	105.42
28	102.37	101.00	102.71	101.78	106.89	104.55	103.54	105.89	110.26	109.95	107.71	105.15
29	101.83	101.13	102.20	101.73	†	105.52	103.73	105.13	109.76	*	107.85	103.53
30	*		101.72	*	†	105.95	*	104.44	110.03	112.28	†	103.53
31	100.75		101.63		106.68		103.65	105.05		108.88		*
High	107.76	103.32	103.73	102.88	108.76	109.08	107.11	107.14	110.26	112.28	110.96	109.10
Low	100.75	101.00	100.65	99.11	100.68	104.04	103.40	103.21	104.01	108.88	107.23	103.53

*Sunday †Holiday

1915—INDUSTRIALS

Date:	Jan.	Feb.	Mar.	Apr.	May	June	July	Aug.	Sept.	Oct.	Nov.	Dec.
1	†	55.59	55.29	61.05	71.51	64.86	69.85	*	81.79	90.88	95.16	95.90
2	54.63	57.26	55.66	†	*	65.72	69.98	76.46	81.03	91.98	†	94.78
3	*	56.90	55.88	61.49	69.54	67.75	69.56	76.71	80.70	*	94.76	95.91
4	55.44	56.83	56.00	*	69.58	67.71	*	77.33	80.90	90.98	96.06	96.78
5	55.50	56.16	56.51	62.29	67.53	68.56	†	77.21	*	89.16	94.81	*
6	55.40	56.33	56.41	62.78	68.23	*	69.87	77.21	†	88.23	94.18	97.86
7	56.08	*	*	62.55	65.13	69.21	68.85	76.71	81.02	90.20	*	97.71
8	56.55	56.31	56.98	63.15	62.77	68.92	68.65	*	81.16	90.50	92.80	98.45
9	56.54	56.85	56.88	65.02	*	67.27	67.88	77.70	81.88	90.63	91.08	97.18
10	*	57.05	56.66	65.15	62.06	69.02	68.38	77.86	80.96	*	92.18	96.13
11	57.37	57.83	56.86	*	64.64	70.55	*	77.45	80.40	92.37	93.64	96.51
12	57.44	†	56.66	64.66	64.46	71.12	70.05	78.14	*	†	94.71	*
13	57.35	57.20	56.35	65.54	63.01	*	70.26	78.38	81.40	93.63	95.33	95.96
14	57.51	*	*	66.14	60.38	70.93	70.80	78.82	81.51	92.76	*	98.30
15	57.90	57.02	56.70	67.42	61.93	71.05	71.50	*	81.91	92.56	95.05	98.18
16	57.19	56.64	56.59	69.36	*	71.30	71.78	81.28	81.71	93.34	96.33	96.57
17	*	55.70	56.67	69.60	63.41	71.16	71.85	81.78	82.54	*	96.18	97.40
18	58.12	55.53	56.57	*	62.70	70.98	*	81.86	83.27	94.61	95.48	97.57
19	58.11	55.38	56.98	67.86	63.08	71.16	70.84	80.31	*	93.38	95.27	*
20	58.42	55.20	57.40	68.64	63.68	*	71.00	79.31	84.26	94.61	95.02	97.70
21	58.51	*	*	68.43	64.88	71.83	72.05	76.76	84.83	95.35	*	97.66
22	58.21	†	58.10	68.20	65.50	71.90	73.82	*	85.88	96.46	95.45	97.98
23	58.52	54.40	59.10	68.65	65.46	71.28	74.10	76.88	85.55	96.11	95.87	98.25
24	*	54.22	59.26	69.64	64.79	69.78	74.18	79.07	86.48	*	97.18	98.36
25	58.06	54.61	59.25	*	64.42	70.23	*	80.65	86.81	95.88	*	†
26	58.24	55.02	59.51	68.97	64.95	70.71	74.60	81.12	*	95.81	97.28	*
27	57.07	55.18	59.60	68.90	65.01	*	74.83	81.88	89.20	94.72	97.07	99.21
28	57.25	*	*	70.22	64.67	70.74	75.53	81.95	89.73	93.34	*	99.16
29	56.54		60.13	70.95	*	70.08	75.79	*	89.90	95.34	97.56	97.96
30	57.16		61.30	71.78	†	70.06	75.53	81.70	90.58	96.02	96.71	98.20
31	*		60.83		†		75.34	81.20	*	*		99.15
High	58.52	57.83	61.30	71.78	71.51	71.90	75.79	81.95	90.58	96.46	97.56	99.21
Low	54.63	54.22	55.29	61.05	60.38	64.86	67.88	76.46	80.40	88.23	91.08	94.78

*Sunday
†Holiday

1915—RAILROADS

Date	Jan.	Feb.	Mar.	Apr.	May	June	July	Aug.	Sept.	Oct.	Nov.	Dec.
1	†	91.91	87.94	92.84	96.94	91.68	92.55	*	93.91	97.68	107.89	105.87
2	88.46	91.52	88.18	†	*	92.46	92.03	92.61	93.49	97.55	†	105.22
3	*	91.21	88.98	93.39	95.97	93.85	91.88	92.88	94.10	*	107.90	105.79
4	89.63	90.89	88.80	*	96.16	93.87	*	92.91	94.95	97.85	108.28	106.09
5	89.95	90.09	89.98	93.91	94.80	93.49	†	93.13	*	97.70	107.05	*
6	89.43	90.11	89.71	94.05	95.33	*	91.81	93.66	†	98.87	106.56	107.20
7	89.94	*	*	93.93	93.53	93.06	90.51	93.42	95.01	99.54	*	106.56
8	89.85	90.38	90.47	93.64	93.09	92.87	89.48	*	94.89	101.80	105.91	106.40
9	89.95	89.81	90.02	95.78	*	92.54	88.66	93.53	95.33	103.20	105.26	105.91
10	*	90.22	89.97	96.44	91.75	93.38	89.51	95.70	95.00	*	106.79	105.21
11	90.83	90.92	90.18	*	93.60	94.10	*	95.69	94.61	103.53	106.53	105.58
12	90.78	†	89.61	95.67	93.26	94.17	90.64	94.93	*	†	106.82	*
13	90.58	90.28	89.71	95.89	92.55	*	90.50	94.00	95.01	102.55	106.80	104.97
14	90.91	*	*	96.16	90.75	93.95	90.43	94.07	94.87	101.40	*	105.90
15	91.22	89.91	89.95	96.26	92.06	93.26	90.86	*	94.82	101.06	106.55	105.71
16	91.28	89.65	89.59	96.47	*	93.69	90.48	94.20	94.60	101.33	107.20	104.88
17	*	89.14	89.56	97.10	92.79	93.36	90.26	94.24	94.82	*	106.91	105.13
18	92.00	89.26	89.45	*	92.16	93.07	*	94.10	95.73	102.48	107.57	105.30
19	92.91	88.96	89.83	97.72	92.16	93.11	90.68	93.48	*	102.15	107.06	*
20	93.18	88.88	89.90	98.75	92.47	*	90.93	93.00	95.95	101.79	106.81	105.50
21	94.05	*	*	98.45	92.75	93.40	90.87	91.95	95.68	101.54	*	105.45
22	93.51	†	90.09	97.91	93.13	94.01	90.29	*	95.94	102.29	106.55	105.38
23	93.46	87.90	91.30	97.58	*	93.80	90.16	92.28	96.27	102.51	106.76	106.54
24	*	87.85	92.01	98.09	92.98	93.08	90.16	92.76	97.91	*	107.15	106.43
25	93.23	87.91	92.56	*	92.56	93.26	*	93.62	98.94	103.06	†	†
26	93.70	88.08	92.88	97.69	92.31	93.77	90.00	93.63	*	103.45	106.80	*
27	92.21	88.21	92.95	97.33	92.50	*	92.50	93.78	98.96	103.35	106.75	107.35
28	92.52	*	*	97.73	92.14	93.47	92.25	93.93	98.31	105.00	*	106.63
29	90.80		93.37	97.96	92.06	92.55	92.17	*	98.15	106.26	106.40	106.53
30	91.60		92.98	97.35	*	92.96	92.05	94.03	97.93	107.04	106.36	106.88
31	*		92.82		†		92.02	94.08		*		108.05
High	94.05	91.91	93.37	98.75	96.94	94.17	92.55	95.70	98.96	107.04	108.28	108.05
Low	88.46	87.85	87.94	92.84	90.75	91.68	88.66	91.95	93.49	97.55	105.26	104.88

*Sunday †Holiday

APPENDIX

1914—INDUSTRIALS

Date:	Jan.	Feb.	Mar.	Apr.	May	June	July	Aug.	Sept.	Oct.	Nov.	Dec.
1	†		*	82.46	80.11	80.98	80.33					54.72*
2	78.59	82.55	81.66	82.47	79.83	80.50	80.64					56.76
3	78.43	83.19	81.72	82.11	*	80.82	81.27					55.60
4		82.90	82.19	82.07	79.89	81.17	†					55.35
5	79.00	82.85	81.75		79.89	81.19	†					55.36
6	79.26	82.34	81.12	82.18	79.78	81.48	81.40					55.09
7	79.17	82.51	81.28	82.18	79.85	*	81.60					55.20
8	78.81		*	81.92	79.16	81.64	81.79					55.20*
9	79.06	82.44	81.36	81.56	79.56	81.81	81.61					
10	79.15	82.36	81.94	†	*	81.84	81.30					
11	*	82.50	81.57	81.30	80.03	81.61	81.25					
12	79.29	†	81.20	81.05	80.10	81.76	80.86					54.46
13	79.62	82.84	81.64	80.55	80.05	81.57	81.11					54.42
14	80.64	83.09	81.94	80.00	81.05		80.34					53.46
15	80.95	*	*	79.90	81.11	81.46	80.43					53.17
16	80.81	82.60	81.68	79.72	80.82	81.28	80.41					†
17	80.77	82.48	82.32	79.86	*	81.03	80.57					
18	*	82.69	82.32	*	81.36	81.25						53.34
19	81.21	82.65	82.54	78.88	81.66	81.33	80.41					*
20	81.01	82.78	83.43	79.35	81.46	81.52	80.76					
21	81.92	82.52	83.02	79.52	80.89	*	80.83					54.55
22	82.66	*	*	78.73	80.85	81.58	80.52					54.58
23	82.70	†	83.19	77.52	81.40	81.19	79.71					54.55
24	82.18	82.34	83.10	76.97	*	80.23	79.67					54.58
25	*	81.31	82.57	*	81.23	79.30	79.07					56.76
26	82.88	81.47	82.31	77.82	81.25	80.06	76.28					53.17
27	82.68	82.00	81.83	78.79	81.56	80.11	76.72					
28	82.12	82.26	81.65	78.61	81.55	*	71.42					
29	81.72			79.12	81.57	80.00	†					
30	82.80		81.64		†	80.66						
31	82.85		82.39		*							
High	82.88	83.19	83.43	82.47	81.66	81.84	81.79					
Low	78.43	81.31	81.12	76.97	79.16	79.30	71.42					

Exchange closed on account of War

†Holiday
*Sunday

1914—RAILROADS

Exchange closed on account of War

Date:	Jan.	Feb.	Mar.	Apr.	May	June	July	Aug.	Sept.	Oct.	Nov.	Dec.
1	†	*	*	104.97	102.45	102.53	102.05					90.21
2	103.72	108.59	104.73	104.98	102.08	101.80	102.24					*
3	103.51	109.07	104.80	104.43	*	102.12	102.68					92.29
4	*	108.70	105.51	104.39	102.66	102.37	†					90.95
5	104.08	108.39	105.13	*	102.43	102.35	*					90.89
6	104.23	107.70	103.70	104.51	102.31	102.91	102.70					90.88
7	104.25	107.48	103.26	104.65	102.03	*	103.05					90.78
8	104.15	*	*	104.16	101.36	103.01	102.76					91.01
9	104.11	106.84	103.40	103.78	101.50	103.38	102.75					*
10	104.35	106.88	103.95	†	*	103.30	101.85					90.13
11	*	106.93	103.58	103.40	102.01	103.02	101.80					89.73
12	104.48	†	103.17	*	102.18	103.28	*					87.91
13	104.60	107.26	103.65	103.13	101.96	103.20	101.06					87.40
14	105.92	107.18	103.79	102.82	102.90	*	101.34					†
15	106.65	*	*	102.48	103.06	103.14	100.70					*
16	106.52	106.36	103.82	102.41	102.91	102.86	100.63					87.75
17	106.55	106.03	104.25	101.69	*	102.60	100.01					88.80
18	*	106.65	103.94	101.73	103.41	102.78	100.49					88.50
19	107.25	106.69	104.13	*	103.49	102.94	*					88.19
20	107.25	106.76	104.96	100.63	103.37	103.06	98.30					88.53
21	108.13	106.38	104.87	101.45	102.68	*	98.77					92.29
22	108.75	*	*	101.26	102.68	103.54	98.49					87.40
23	109.31	†	105.76	100.53	103.24	102.91	97.95					
24	108.77	106.10	105.60	99.48	*	101.73	97.05					
25	*	105.04	104.91	99.24	103.08	101.63	97.16					
26	108.87	105.17	104.75	*	103.01	100.63	*					
27	108.80	105.67	104.00	99.65	103.64	101.39	96.58					
28	108.33	105.48	103.85	100.96	103.48	*	93.14					
29	107.75		*	100.38	103.11	101.28	94.12					
30	109.29		104.02	101.23	†	102.41	89.41					
31	109.43		104.75				†					
High	109.43	109.07	105.76	104.98	103.64	103.54	103.05					92.29
Low	103.51	105.04	103.17	99.24	101.36	100.63	89.41					87.40

*Sunday †Holiday

1913—INDUSTRIALS

Date:	Jan.	Feb.	Mar.	Apr.	May	June	July	Aug.	Sept.	Oct.	Nov.	Dec.
1	†	83.64	80.62	81.92	79.62	*	75.43	78.21	†	80.79	78.42	75.77
2	88.42	*	*	81.76	79.34	77.27	75.84	78.26	80.94	81.43	*	76.23
3	87.45	83.26	81.33	82.16	79.31	76.68	75.83	*	80.30	80.79	77.76	76.83
4	87.76	83.38	80.71	83.19	*	75.67	†	78.75	80.27	80.59	†	77.01
5	*	83.05	81.69	82.68	79.95	75.07		79.52	81.13	*	78.11	76.89
6	87.20	82.94	81.33	*	79.21	75.21	*	79.16	81.40	79.82	77.33	76.37
7	88.02	83.46	80.60	82.35	79.52	74.98	75.67	79.51	*	79.89	77.04	*
8	88.01	83.54	79.68	82.92	79.40	*	75.52	79.32	81.39	79.17	76.71	76.87
9	88.57	*	*	82.59	79.23	73.90	75.23	79.16	81.50	79.27	*	75.97
10	88.25	82.93	79.27	82.64	78.97	72.34	75.51	*	82.12	79.07	75.94	76.17
11	87.68	82.17	79.95	82.14	*	72.11	75.40	79.73	82.17	78.29	76.36	76.26
12	*	†	79.46	82.16	78.58	74.28	75.62	80.68	82.95	*	76.96	75.59
13	85.96	81.34	79.93	*	79.04	74.58	*	80.93	83.43	†	76.86	75.89
14	84.96	81.79	79.81	82.11	78.72	75.52	75.23	80.46	*	77.64	77.25	*
15	85.47	81.42	79.73	81.09	78.51	*	75.41	79.50	82.81	77.85	77.21	75.27
16	85.75	*	*	81.08	78.83	74.58	76.51	79.85	83.04	77.09	*	75.69
17	85.61	80.57	79.26	81.28	78.71	74.91	76.18	*	82.38	77.37	77.07	75.78
18	85.75	79.82	78.68	81.05	*	75.85	77.10	79.85	82.53	78.00	77.25	75.78
19	*	80.44	78.27	81.00	78.73	75.41	76.94	79.96	82.58	*	76.94	76.71
20	81.55	80.20	78.25	*	79.06	74.91	*	80.37	82.57	78.06	76.48	77.61
21	82.57	79.93	†	81.73	79.01	74.03	78.16	80.14	*	79.60	76.18	*
22	83.34	†	†	81.46	79.50	*	78.09	80.07	83.01	79.02	76.14	78.06
23	82.94	*	*	81.25	79.50	74.33	77.84	80.09	82.72	78.40	*	78.11
24	82.22	79.26	78.91	80.76	79.88	75.28	78.65	*	82.13	78.61	76.11	78.34
25	82.37	78.72	80.20	79.72	*	75.38	78.36	80.30	82.19	78.58	76.86	†
26	*	80.05	80.31	79.41	79.72	74.93	78.47	80.29	81.96	*	76.68	78.85
27	82.53	80.56	79.78	*	79.22	74.70	*	80.15	81.95	79.38	†	78.70
28	83.13	80.32	80.51	79.32	78.48	74.89	79.06	81.33	*	78.94	76.21	*
29	82.92		81.11	78.39	78.38	*	78.93	81.81	81.23	79.13	75.94	78.48
30	83.80		*	78.54	†		78.59	†	80.37	78.60	*	78.26
31	83.72		80.92		†		78.48	*		78.30		78.78
High	88.57	83.64	81.69	83.19	79.95	77.27	79.06	81.81	83.43	81.43	78.42	78.85
Low	81.55	78.72	78.25	78.39	78.38	72.11	75.23	78.21	80.27	77.09	75.94	75.27

*Sunday   †Holiday

1913—RAILROADS

Date:	Jan.	Feb.	Mar.	Apr.	May	June	July	Aug.	Sept.	Oct.	Nov.	Dec.
1	†	115.36	110.95	112.85	108.83	*	104.40	105.29	†	107.42	104.11	102.84
2	117.61	*	*	112.57	108.52	105.55	104.09	105.29	106.43	107.83	*	103.05
3	117.08	115.13	111.83	113.16	108.37	104.96	104.10	*	105.73	107.33	103.59	104.10
4	117.54	114.93	111.18	113.65	*	103.96	†	106.02	105.60	107.23	†	104.19
5	*	114.51	111.59	113.22	109.40	103.56	103.58	106.51	106.15	*	103.83	104.11
6	116.76	114.46	111.21	*	108.42	104.43	*	106.19	106.25	106.66	103.12	104.15
7	117.40	114.63	110.59	112.43	108.78	103.97	103.42	106.72	*	106.78	103.35	*
8	117.66	114.75	109.83	113.08	108.65	102.98	103.11	106.70	105.87	105.96	102.78	104.56
9	118.10	*	*	112.58	108.58	101.18	103.31	106.30	106.13	106.01	*	103.63
10	117.90	113.75	109.04	112.23	108.26	100.50	103.16	*	107.16	105.50	101.87	103.70
11	117.66	113.08	109.70	111.53	*	103.18	103.52	107.10	107.01	104.80	102.29	103.59
12	*	†	109.80	111.87	108.01	103.30	103.41	107.71	108.27	*	103.11	102.71
13	116.25	112.08	110.25	*	108.43	104.75	103.96	107.76	109.17	†	103.38	102.90
14	115.01	112.30	110.03	111.63	107.93	*	104.86	107.28	*	104.19	103.26	*
15	114.57	111.98	109.88	111.29	107.70	103.85	104.61	106.28	108.57	103.99	103.10	102.11
16	114.89	*	*	111.58	108.13	104.25	104.61	106.60	109.00	102.90	*	102.20
17	114.60	110.95	109.35	111.78	107.90	105.05	105.25	*	108.34	102.95	103.27	102.25
18	114.77	110.30	108.94	111.36	*	104.65	104.98	107.03	108.93	103.62	103.08	102.15
19	*	111.15	109.13	111.26	108.04	104.15	105.83	107.73	108.62	*	102.80	103.56
20	114.20	110.92	109.01	*	108.41	102.84	*	107.03	108.65	103.46	102.87	104.21
21	115.21	110.56	†	111.91	108.36	*	105.98	106.59	*	105.42	102.84	*
22	115.93	†	†	111.66	108.90	103.40	105.66	106.74	108.78	104.58	102.93	104.45
23	115.43	*	109.65	111.46	108.88	104.48	106.21	106.91	108.63	104.08	*	103.80
24	114.61	110.11	110.65	110.41	109.51	104.35	106.45	*	108.10	104.71	103.77	104.41
25	114.90	109.45	110.79	109.81	*	104.13	106.61	106.90	107.72	104.62	103.32	†
26	*	110.65	110.26	109.40	109.03	103.65	106.99	106.85	108.05	*	103.18	104.23
27	114.71	111.35	111.09	*	108.71	104.38	*	106.50	108.02	105.26	†	103.94
28	115.27	110.94	111.81	109.14	107.83	*	106.86	107.40	*	104.63	103.03	*
29	115.34			108.14	107.41	103.61	106.11	107.14	107.46	104.90		103.48
30	115.56		*	107.75	†		105.77	107.76	107.01	104.43	*	103.41
31	115.49		111.69		109.51		106.99	*		104.05		103.72
High	118.10	115.36	111.83	113.65	109.51	105.55	106.99	107.76	109.17	107.83	104.11	104.56
Low	114.20	109.45	108.94	107.75	107.41	100.50	103.11	105.29	105.60	102.90	101.87	102.11

*Sunday
†Holiday

1912—INDUSTRIALS

Date:	Jan.	Feb.	Mar.	Apr.	May	June	July	Aug.	Sept.	Oct.	Nov.	Dec.
1	†	80.50	82.07	89.05	90.33	88.32	91.35	90.47	*	93.90	90.51	*
2	82.36	80.51	81.96	88.82	90.40	*	91.69	90.16	†	93.50	†	90.85
3	82.02	80.40	*	88.78	88.96	88.59	91.61	89.93	90.62	94.12	*	90.36
4	82.04	*	82.60	89.52	88.77	89.29	†	*	90.76	93.70	90.29	89.00
5	81.95	80.33	82.83	†	*	90.42	89.60	90.03	91.33	93.94	†	87.88
6	82.14	80.46	82.65	*	87.59	90.67	90.33	89.84	91.18	*	91.94	87.80
7	*	80.62	83.38	90.01	87.68	90.37	*	90.12	91.45	93.93	91.67	87.84
8	82.12	80.80	83.50	90.21	87.86	90.45	89.14	90.00	*	94.12	91.31	86.03
9	81.28	80.67	83.44	90.70	88.41	90.55	89.07	90.19	91.21	93.68	90.37	86.02
10	81.88	80.15	*	90.27	88.97	89.85	88.18	90.53	91.13	93.94	*	85.25
11	81.64	†	83.13	89.90	89.58	89.94	88.06	*	90.38	93.94	89.58	86.05
12	82.00	80.64	83.47	89.18	*	89.95	87.97	90.72	90.53	92.62	90.10	86.18
13	81.76	80.83	83.96	89.12	89.53	89.40	88.06	91.33	90.52	†	89.96	85.78
14	*	81.06	85.12	*	89.83	89.53	*	91.78	90.62	92.40	90.40	*
15	81.48	81.05	85.15	89.71	89.58	*	88.29	91.30	90.67	92.73	90.09	86.22
16	81.63	80.75	84.51	89.22	89.23	89.79	88.71	91.40	91.55	93.70	90.16	86.21
17	81.68	80.85	*	89.31	89.35	89.70	89.18	91.19	91.66	93.52	*	85.66
18	81.59	*	85.12	89.22	90.32	89.53	89.45	*	92.27	93.61	89.97	86.78
19	81.96	81.05	85.35	89.16	*	90.07	89.77	91.23	92.79	93.46	90.05	87.85
20	82.32	81.15	85.52	89.19	90.34	90.87	89.70	91.70	*	92.31	90.30	87.72
21		80.78	86.57	*	90.48	90.65	*	91.62	93.08	92.41	91.43	87.22
22	81.98	†	86.92	88.72	89.97	*	89.75	91.11	93.43	91.60	91.01	87.36
23	81.88	81.27	87.60	89.58	89.77	90.06	89.38	91.34	93.38	91.58	90.52	†
24	81.73	81.17	88.39	89.37	90.25	89.86	89.45	91.40	93.42	90.91	*	87.33
25	81.84	*	88.54	90.43	90.37	91.00	90.00	*	93.61	91.14	89.87	87.25
26	81.80	80.98	88.62	90.93	*	90.67	89.50	91.54	94.00	*	90.34	87.14
27	81.27	81.04	88.48	90.81	90.01	91.09	89.45	92.06	*	91.44	90.62	*
28	*	81.57	88.09	*	90.15	90.92	*	91.66	94.15	90.35	†	87.26
29	81.27	81.40	88.23	90.46	89.53	*	88.97	91.63		90.41	91.26	87.87
30	81.27		88.27	90.30	†	91.09	89.18	91.57		90.71	91.40	
31	80.19		*		88.01		89.71	†				
High	82.36	81.57	88.62	90.93	90.48	91.09	91.69	92.06	94.15	94.12	91.94	90.85
Low	80.19	80.15	81.96	88.72	87.59	88.32	87.97	89.84	90.38	90.35	89.58	85.25

*Sunday   †Holiday

1912—RAILROADS

Date:	Jan.	Feb.	Mar.	Apr.	May	June	July	Aug.	Sept.	Oct.	Nov.	Dec.
1	†	115.07	115.98	119.43	121.40	118.71	119.93	121.71	*	124.03	120.45	*
2	117.05	115.06	115.90	119.26	121.74	*	120.14	121.57	†	123.53	†	120.09
3	116.80	115.07	*	119.42	119.92	118.75	120.24	121.63	121.03	124.10	*	119.75
4	116.71	*	116.25	120.11	120.04	119.40	†	*	121.02	123.87	120.76	119.21
5	116.53	114.92	116.32	†	*	120.48	119.75	121.90	121.86	124.35	†	118.65
6	116.74	115.21	116.13	120.66	119.34	120.66	119.90	121.65	121.37	*	122.79	118.55
7	*	115.53	116.80	*	119.93	120.19	119.18	122.26	121.47	123.98	122.28	118.36
8	116.51	115.61	116.86	120.51	119.80	119.81	118.85	122.06	*	123.95	121.68	*
9	115.22	115.69	116.76	121.21	119.78	*	119.18	122.61	121.08	123.47	120.50	116.65
10	115.85	115.22	*	120.58	120.41	120.19	118.18	123.42	120.87	123.60	*	116.80
11	115.58	*	116.38	120.76	120.97	119.78	119.20	*	120.44	121.91	119.83	115.63
12	115.81	†	116.49	119.93	*	118.93	117.68	123.57	120.50	†	120.85	116.15
13	115.51	115.61	116.56	119.96	121.06	119.11	117.89	123.65	120.77	*	120.67	116.16
14	*	115.53	117.16	*	121.56	119.30	*	124.16	120.63	121.68	121.11	115.61
15	115.53	115.80	117.28	120.93	121.68	118.65	118.35	123.67	*	122.24	120.77	*
16	116.10	115.41	116.44	120.18	120.87	118.70	118.74	123.68	120.95	122.92	121.01	116.62
17	116.00	115.62	*	120.53	121.15	*	119.51	123.15	122.13	122.56	*	116.15
18	115.72	*	116.96	120.37	121.47	118.94	119.50	*	121.89	122.66	120.79	115.86
19	116.73	115.69	117.13	120.24	*	118.86	119.86	123.23	121.84	122.56	120.43	116.58
20	117.03	115.75	118.19	120.09	121.08	119.05	119.68	123.32	123.09	122.56	120.68	117.55
21	*	115.26	117.91	*	121.03	119.73	*	123.09	123.21	121.36	121.36	117.06
22	116.83	†	118.02	119.87	120.43	119.58	119.75	122.14	*	121.43	121.03	*
23	116.72	115.62	118.41	121.00	120.43	*	119.27	122.11	123.33	120.54	120.70	116.69
24	116.39	115.52	*	120.70	120.61	119.24	119.12	122.16	123.70	120.51	*	116.83
25	116.60	*	118.56	121.80	120.80	119.32	119.79	*	123.56	120.28	119.91	†
26	116.54	115.16	118.76	121.80	*	120.33	120.02	121.98	123.37	120.68	120.36	116.85
27	115.56	115.16	118.49	122.12	120.48	120.15	119.88	122.88	124.13	*	120.10	116.48
28	*	115.83	118.74	*	120.31	119.91	*	122.53	124.16	120.96	†	116.25
29	115.50	115.73	119.15	122.09	120.10	119.77	119.56	122.46	*	119.57	120.44	*
30	116.07		119.26	121.58	†	*	119.74	122.24	123.95	120.01	120.75	116.07
31	115.06		*		118.37		120.67	†		120.38		116.84
High	117.05	115.83	119.26	122.12	121.74	120.66	120.67	124.16	124.16	124.35	122.79	120.09
Low	115.06	114.92	115.90	119.26	118.37	118.65	117.68	121.57	120.44	119.57	119.83	115.61

*Sunday †Holiday

1911—INDUSTRIALS

Date:	Jan.	Feb.	Mar.	Apr.	May	June	July	Aug.	Sept.	Oct.	Nov.	Dec.
1	*	85.33	84.53	83.40	84.14	85.79	85.93	85.47	79.17	*	77.69	80.31
2	†	85.97	82.66	*	83.69	86.17	*	84.80	†	76.75	78.07	80.68
3	82.11	85.60	82.32	83.33	83.87	86.18	85.64	84.40	*	76.52	78.19	*
4	82.26	86.02	81.80	83.32	83.16	*	†	82.95	†	76.15	78.38	80.54
5	82.09	*	*	83.02	83.15	86.35	85.28	82.65	79.77	76.70	*	80.31
6	82.44	85.84	82.47	82.93	83.04	86.25	85.80	*	80.28	76.50	79.00	80.31
7	82.75	85.87	82.81	82.89	*	86.50	86.22	83.15	79.63	76.53	†	79.82
8	*	85.48	82.46	83.06	82.88	86.31	86.26	82.53	79.09	*	78.14	79.34
9	82.51	85.67	82.37	*	82.85	86.02	*	81.85	78.67	76.52	80.42	79.19
10	81.88	85.42	82.54	83.08	82.60	86.35	86.28	81.43	*	76.85	81.01	*
11	81.70	85.57	82.39	82.82	83.04	*	86.38	80.71	78.79	77.15	80.55	79.41
12	82.05	*	*	82.89	82.92	86.70	86.17	80.40	79.07	†	*	80.33
13	82.96	†	83.00	82.81	82.68	86.94	86.22	*	78.21	77.94	79.98	80.43
14	83.07	85.47	83.98	†	*	87.02	85.98	81.31	78.13	78.66	79.92	81.51
15	*	85.41	84.09	†	82.71	86.63	86.03	81.28	77.88	*	79.71	81.61
16	82.46	84.51	83.73	*	84.63	86.61	*	80.18	78.87	78.34	79.91	81.97
17	83.38	85.09	83.15	82.56	85.41	86.68	85.72	80.05	*	78.11	81.08	*
18	83.32	85.30	83.35	81.56	86.17	*	86.37	80.86	78.66	77.77	81.12	82.48
19	83.52	*	*	81.91	85.78	87.06	86.44	81.38	77.75	77.64	*	81.89
20	83.80	85.59	84.13	81.86	86.08	86.62	86.33	*	77.01	78.11	80.59	82.27
21	83.53	85.58	84.03	81.84	*	86.61	86.47	80.51	75.53	77.75	81.56	82.30
22	*	†	83.72	81.32	86.32	86.14	86.45	80.64	74.15	*	81.47	82.22
23	83.37	85.70	83.71	*	86.25	86.33	*	80.55	73.62	77.77	81.86	82.11
24	83.78	84.33	83.40	82.12	85.78	86.76	86.22	79.73	*	77.68	81.47	*
25	83.44	84.33	83.43	82.20	85.62	*	86.19	79.13	72.94	77.72	81.53	†
26	83.67	*	*	82.32	85.94	86.38	86.26	78.93	73.33	77.14	*	82.08
27	84.02	84.51	83.69	82.45	86.01	86.36	85.92	*	73.51	74.82	81.35	81.84
28	83.89	85.02	84.00	83.31	*	86.06	85.73	79.31	73.05	75.36	81.50	81.30
29	*		83.58	83.65	86.40	86.32	85.90	79.13	75.15	*	80.97	81.58
30	84.93		83.86	*	†	85.98	*	79.00	76.31	75.06	†	81.68
31	84.93		83.27		85.55		86.02	79.25		75.79		*
High	84.93	86.02	84.53	83.65	86.40	87.06	86.47	85.47	80.28	78.66	81.86	82.48
Low	81.70	84.33	81.80	81.32	82.60	85.79	85.28	78.93	72.94	74.82	77.69	79.19

*Sunday †Holiday

1911—RAILROADS

Date:	Jan.	Feb.	Mar.	Apr.	May	June	July	Aug.	Sept.	Oct.	Nov.	Dec.
1	*	119.40	117.14	117.80	119.23	121.65	122.76	121.92	113.10	*	115.81	116.54
2	†	119.65	115.75	*	119.00	122.28	122.28	120.71	113.78	111.24	115.72	117.28
3	115.13	119.14	115.78	117.84	119.45	122.36	122.00	120.30	*	111.35	115.96	*
4	114.89	119.76	115.87	118.20	118.30	*	†	118.81	†	111.41	116.60	117.25
5	115.21	*	*	118.13	118.28	122.43	121.09	118.44	114.11	111.75	*	116.79
6	115.38	119.51	116.27	118.11	118.31	122.33	121.98	*	112.83	111.55	117.11	116.12
7	115.93	119.97	116.63	117.72	*	123.01	122.06	119.07	111.89	111.55	†	115.68
8	*	119.66	116.07	117.72	118.24	122.96	122.05	118.43	111.06	*	116.48	115.47
9	115.59	119.70	116.16	*	118.23	123.10	*	116.92	111.18	111.79	117.79	115.74
10	115.45	119.56	116.34	117.57	118.06	123.23	122.24	116.41	*	112.08	118.53	*
11	114.96	119.67	116.25	117.37	118.55	*	122.81	115.19	111.28	112.49	118.15	116.79
12	115.23	*	*	117.51	118.23	123.21	122.70	114.76	110.26	†	*	116.86
13	116.55	†	116.61	117.56	118.15	123.08	122.90	*	110.59	113.23	117.44	117.41
14	116.34	119.62	117.73	†	*	122.59	122.81	116.09	110.64	114.06	117.13	117.24
15	*	119.60	117.77	†	118.23	122.36	122.62	115.74	111.95	*	116.75	117.35
16	116.34	118.15	117.38	*	119.96	122.28	*	114.11	111.77	113.75	117.28	117.62
17	117.80	118.68	116.83	117.28	120.70	122.65	122.29	114.48	*	113.80	117.92	*
18	117.51	119.26	117.25	116.05	120.91	*	123.51	115.44	110.75	113.41	117.61	117.16
19	117.68	*	*	116.63	120.71	122.30	123.75	115.88	110.68	113.79	*	117.51
20	117.43	119.45	117.86	116.58	121.00	122.11	123.31	*	110.46	114.13	117.08	117.18
21	117.23	119.23	117.77	116.38	*	121.61	123.86	114.76	110.91	113.66	117.74	116.98
22	*	†	117.63	116.12	121.09	122.25	123.83	114.70	111.00	*	118.03	117.12
23	116.88	119.36	117.63	*	121.07	123.31	*	114.61	110.32	113.79	119.21	†
24	117.13	117.20	117.50	116.48	120.43	123.09	123.42	113.64	*	113.98	118.43	*
25	116.68	117.07	117.43	116.73	120.20	*	123.15	113.05	110.70	114.03	118.36	†
26	117.10	*	*	117.11	120.25	123.31	123.15	112.92	109.80	113.87	*	117.11
27	117.85	116.90	118.06	117.15	120.43	122.71	122.40	*	110.90	112.97	118.03	116.79
28	117.98	117.34	118.73	117.66	*	123.06	122.29	113.09	110.51	113.56	118.06	116.15
29	*		118.33	118.25	120.71	122.77	122.62	112.66	111.28	*	117.24	116.57
30	118.36		118.53	*	†		*	112.60		113.85	†	116.83
31	118.82		117.71		120.55		123.00	112.91		114.46		*
High	118.82	119.97	118.73	118.25	121.09	123.31	123.86	121.92	114.11	114.46	119.21	117.62
Low	114.89	116.90	115.75	116.05	118.06	121.61	121.09	112.60	109.80	111.24	115.72	115.47

*Sunday
†Holiday

1910—INDUSTRIALS

Date:	Jan.	Feb.	Mar.	Apr.	May	June	July	Aug.	Sept.	Oct.	Nov.	Dec.
1	†	91.33	91.77	89.71	*	85.69	81.64	76.14	78.58	79.95	85.10	81.43
2	*	90.40	92.62	89.71	85.51	85.25	†	77.69	78.68	*	85.45	80.60
3	98.34	87.50	92.61	*	84.72	82.70	*	77.14		80.68	85.85	80.77
4	98.30	87.77	92.83	89.75	86.41	83.06	†	77.04	*	81.34	85.64	*
5	97.06	88.39	92.98	90.96	87.32	*	80.23	77.58	†	80.76	85.82	81.00
6	97.62	*	*	91.16	86.51	82.05	80.27	78.19	78.35	81.46	*	79.68
7	97.67	85.35	94.35	90.89	86.72	84.50	80.66	*	78.43	81.48	85.70	80.46
8	97.87	85.03	94.56	89.53	*	84.55	80.83	78.13	78.39	81.51	†	80.50
9	*	87.32	94.30	89.36	88.03	84.89	81.19	79.30	78.44	*	84.29	81.00
10	97.10	87.85	93.92	*	88.63	83.46	*	79.20	78.57	81.91	83.50	81.54
11	96.64	89.07	92.63	91.10	88.73	83.39	81.07	78.78	*	82.38	83.53	*
12	95.85	†	92.78	90.92	88.52	*	80.14	79.65	79.13	†	83.55	80.96
13	96.16	*	*	92.10	88.72	83.88	80.79	80.05	79.71	84.06	*	80.77
14	93.69	89.65	93.10	92.36	89.13	84.28	81.41	*	79.40	84.63	84.40	81.47
15	94.45	89.23	91.92	92.04	*	83.84	81.29	79.77	78.38	85.27	84.88	81.28
16	*	90.09	91.35	92.62	88.78	84.12	81.08	81.04	78.55	*	85.21	81.20
17	93.75	90.65	92.14	*	88.62	84.26	*	81.41	78.65	85.63	84.57	81.43
18	93.92	90.92	92.71	91.67	88.26	84.43	80.89	80.85	*	86.02	85.12	*
19	92.35	91.14	92.14	91.78	88.71	*	81.22	80.31	78.48	85.11	85.40	82.16
20	93.29	*	*	90.37	89.34	85.08	81.53	80.44	78.37	86.00	*	81.80
21	94.41	90.70	92.33	90.52	89.66	85.29	79.21	*	79.17	85.35	84.90	81.94
22	94.52	†	92.36	89.97	*	86.28	77.78	79.47	79.08	85.94	84.84	81.42
23	*	90.62	91.30	90.09	88.77	86.01	77.16	79.68	78.65	*	85.05	81.33
24	93.08	91.22	91.31	*	89.06	84.93	*	78.96	78.51	85.01	†	†
25	90.66	91.31	†	88.73	88.67	85.25	75.87	78.59	*	84.61	85.32	*
26	92.69	90.64	†	88.83	88.14	*	73.62	79.28	79.19	84.59	85.30	†
27	91.62	*	*	88.18	87.86	83.14	75.81	79.19	79.01	85.51	*	80.45
28	91.91	91.34	89.72	86.29	†	83.14	78.09	*	78.96	85.45	83.28	80.65
29	92.42		90.21	87.17	*	81.60	77.57	79.67	79.07	84.96	83.62	81.76
30	*		89.47	86.20	†	81.18	76.48	79.59	79.72	*	82.52	81.41
31	91.91		89.71		86.32		*	79.68		84.77		81.36
High	98.34	91.34	94.56	92.62	89.66	86.28	81.64	81.41	79.72	86.02	85.85	82.16
Low	90.66	85.03	89.47	86.20	84.72	81.18	73.62	76.14	78.35	79.95	82.52	79.68

*Sunday
†Holiday

1910—RAILROADS

Date:	Jan.	Feb.	Mar.	Apr.	May	June	July	Aug.	Sept.	Oct.	Nov.	Dec.
1	†	122.11	123.62	121.73	*	118.32	112.09	108.38	111.08	114.69	117.06	112.59
2	*	121.36	124.40	121.80	117.47	118.01	†	110.43	111.01	*	117.21	112.01
3	129.48	119.80	124.22	*	117.25	115.64	*	110.04	†	115.21	117.69	112.30
4	129.90	120.33	124.09	121.69	119.18	115.68	†	109.96	*	115.18	117.13	*
5	128.53	121.11	124.22	122.87	120.28	*	110.63	110.33	†	114.33	117.31	112.62
6	128.85	*	*	123.17		114.59	111.22	110.83	110.57	115.01	*	111.33
7	129.05	119.06	125.41	122.71	119.20	117.38	111.75	*	111.11	115.06	117.43	111.95
8	129.19	118.95	125.64	121.43	*	117.10	111.54	110.94	110.92	115.06	†	112.30
9	*	121.10	125.59	121.22	119.66	117.73	112.33	112.50	111.27	*	115.76	112.97
10	127.47	121.11	125.43	*	120.73	116.85	*	112.01	111.29	115.60	115.19	113.20
11	126.85	121.85	124.48	123.23	121.59	116.28	112.66	112.13	*	115.81	115.09	*
12	125.98	†	124.75	122.73	121.55	*	111.69	113.38	111.71	†	115.02	112.65
13	126.57	*	*	124.00	121.51	117.08	112.70	113.75	112.88	116.68	*	112.63
14	123.90	122.56	124.79	124.36	121.73	117.44	113.65	*	112.63	117.36	115.82	113.07
15	124.74	122.06	123.54	124.14	*	117.30	113.02	113.27	111.41	117.66	116.36	113.18
16	*	122.98	122.96	124.35	121.66	117.46	113.66	114.83	111.65	*	116.56	113.36
17	123.53	123.28	123.50	*	121.82	117.67	*	115.47	111.90	118.00	115.73	113.63
18	123.35	124.06	124.16	123.61	121.50	118.15	112.48	113.96	*	118.44	116.45	*
19	122.51	123.43	123.33	123.81	121.33	*	112.64	113.74	111.96	117.67	116.79	114.46
20	123.71	*	*	122.59	122.01	118.78	112.33	113.51	112.08	118.43	*	114.10
21	124.46	123.33	123.66	122.67	123.10	118.38	111.73	*	113.45	117.88	116.11	113.91
22	124.27	†	123.88	122.06	*	119.40	110.51	112.20	112.99	118.11	116.11	113.46
23	*	123.27	123.33	122.06	122.43	118.83	109.57	112.46	112.60	*	116.28	113.34
24	122.78	124.41	123.34	*	122.79	117.73	*	111.49	112.59	117.07	†	†
25	120.91	123.80	†	120.49	121.50	117.73	108.24	110.88	*	116.80	116.48	*
26	122.70	123.10	†	120.58	122.30	*	105.59	111.83	113.59	117.32	116.50	†
27	121.85	*	*	119.66	121.96	115.49	108.02	111.71	113.61	117.13	*	112.98
28	122.38	123.55	121.98	118.16		115.17	110.70	*	113.58	116.70	114.25	113.08
29	122.98		122.45	119.61	*	112.96	110.18	112.28	113.95	116.76	114.68	114.04
30	*		121.63	118.29	†	111.63	109.19	112.26	114.45	*	113.19	114.11
31	122.73		121.83		119.62		*	112.10		118.44		114.06
High	129.90	124.41	125.64	124.36	123.32	119.40	113.65	115.47	114.45	118.44	117.69	114.46
Low	120.91	118.95	121.63	118.16	117.25	111.63	105.59	108.38	110.57	114.33	113.19	111.33

*Sunday
†Holiday

1909—INDUSTRIALS

Date	Jan.	Feb.	Mar.	Apr.	May	June	July	Aug.	Sept.	Oct.	Nov.	Dec.
1	†	84.44	82.72	85.37	88.32	92.38	92.95	*	97.50	100.36	99.44	96.88
2	86.27	85.03	83.28	85.37	*	92.64	93.14	97.52	98.12	100.50	†	96.66
3	*	84.67	82.58	85.94	88.76	94.06		98.14	98.47	*	100.23	97.46
4	85.26	84.69	81.79	*	89.22	94.16	*	98.00		100.19	100.44	98.08
5	84.85	84.86	82.10	86.92	89.32	94.46	†	97.07	*	99.02	99.80	*
6	85.14	84.64	82.21	86.81	90.13	*	93.13	98.30	†	98.73	99.33	97.52
7	86.95	*	*	86.90	91.40	93.97	93.16	98.48	97.41	98.88	*	98.28
8	86.22	85.61	82.20	87.78	91.56	93.98	93.04	*	97.05	98.07	99.41	98.13
9	85.36	85.60	81.64	†	*	93.78	92.90	98.37	95.86	98.00	98.67	98.69
10	*	85.76	81.78	88.11	90.94	93.85	92.98	98.37	97.22	*	98.78	98.41
11	85.28	86.22	81.90	*	91.25	93.98	*	99.02	96.19	96.95	98.77	98.47
12	85.05	†	82.03	87.56	91.08	94.05	93.40	99.11	*		98.77	*
13	84.60	†	82.03	87.43	90.79	*	92.82	98.85	96.17	96.79	99.16	99.00
14	84.77	*	81.88	87.16	90.93	94.19	93.06	99.26	96.93	98.06	*	98.58
15	84.48	86.72	82.65	86.56	90.82	92.62	93.45	*	98.29	98.57	99.31	98.67
16	85.31	86.42	83.06	87.65	*	92.32	94.09	98.35	99.06	98.64	99.21	98.61
17	*	85.93	82.81	87.81	90.84	91.16	94.19	98.91	99.16	*	99.53	98.86
18	84.79	84.76	*	*	91.36	91.34	*	98.14	99.08	98.78	100.34	99.04
19	85.11	84.33	82.40	87.86	91.41	91.18	94.33	97.71	*	98.15	100.53	*
20	84.76	82.82	82.33	87.65	90.88	*	94.68	97.50	99.73	98.02	100.02	98.84
21	85.72	*	*	87.65	91.15	89.66	94.03	98.23	99.92	98.11	*	98.87
22	85.72	†	83.28	88.10	91.51	90.03	94.19	*	99.13	96.82	98.98	98.85
23	85.83	79.91	82.94	87.66	*	91.29	93.39	98.89	99.08	95.70	98.35	98.56
24	*	81.44	83.32	88.12	91.76	91.86	94.32	99.06	99.17	*	98.03	98.61
25	85.86	80.57	83.22	*	91.58	91.51	*	98.51		96.83	†	†
26	85.69	81.34	83.60	87.63	91.18	91.38	94.02	96.30	*	96.21	98.73	*
27	85.77	81.85	84.73	87.44	91.65	*	94.51	97.18	99.32	97.04	97.81	98.28
28	85.10	*	*	88.13	92.18	91.59	94.90	96.78	100.12	98.03	*	98.63
29	84.62		85.31	88.03		92.82	95.31	*	99.94	98.97	95.89	99.28
30	84.09		85.29	88.29	*	92.28	96.17	98.32	99.55	99.07	96.02	99.18
31	*		86.12		†		96.79	97.90		*		99.05
High	86.95	86.72	86.12	88.29	92.18	94.46	96.79	99.26	100.12	100.50	100.53	99.28
Low	84.09	79.91	81.64	85.37	88.32	89.66	92.82	96.30	95.86	95.70	95.89	96.66

*Sunday †Holiday

1909—RAILROADS

Date:	Jan.	Feb.	Mar.	Apr.	May	June	July	Aug.	Sept.	Oct.	Nov.	Dec.
1	†	117.00	116.90	122.22	123.57	126.11	127.56	*	130.16	132.55	129.91	126.51
2	120.93	117.87	117.18	121.11	*	125.96	127.93	131.55	130.94	132.61	†	125.92
3	*	117.91	116.51	121.70	124.18	127.14	†	131.58	131.10	*	129.96	127.05
4	119.76	117.94	115.96	*	124.44	128.23	†	131.54	†	132.64	129.79	127.78
5	118.76	117.94	116.26	122.80	123.90	128.21	*	131.08	*	131.58	129.56	*
6	118.67	117.65	116.06	121.94	123.88	*	128.08	132.35	†	131.45	128.98	127.43
7	119.95	*	*	122.29	124.66	127.79	128.20	132.48	129.35	131.69	*	128.10
8	119.59	118.03	116.44	122.68	124.76	128.21	127.67	*	128.99	130.60	128.69	128.08
9	118.50	117.88	115.99	†	*	127.95	127.53	132.61	127.48	130.48	128.08	128.88
10	*	118.10	116.19	†	124.35	128.15	127.66	132.60	130.30	*	128.08	128.38
11	118.16	118.61	115.86	*	125.40	128.28	*	133.61	129.68	129.20	128.36	128.58
12	117.63	†	116.35	122.96	125.68	128.23	128.15	134.08	*	†	127.86	*
13	117.67	†	116.16	122.17	126.13	*	127.78	133.76	129.10	129.64	128.20	129.13
14	118.26	*	*	122.66	125.78	128.11	128.00	134.46	130.10	130.48	128.44	128.78
15	118.28	119.90	115.95	122.46	125.70	126.97	128.08	*	130.10	130.83	128.03	129.08
16	119.38	119.78	116.68	121.21	*	127.28	128.21	133.87	131.25	130.83	127.76	129.28
17	*	119.33	117.41	122.00	125.18	126.18	128.90	134.31	131.96	*	128.10	129.71
18	119.05	118.08	117.33	*	125.61	126.50	*	133.03	132.73	130.83	128.67	130.03
19	119.72	117.98	116.99	123.00	125.75	126.50	128.93	131.41	132.76	130.40	128.93	*
20	119.35	117.15	116.93	123.25	125.09	*	129.36	131.36	*	129.93	128.08	129.58
21	119.97	*	*	122.75	125.23	124.92	128.59	132.56	132.88	130.20	128.08	129.34
22	119.32	†	118.15	123.48	125.80	125.03	128.65	*	132.58	128.71	*	129.30
23	119.32	113.90	117.66	122.85	*	126.30	128.85	132.72	131.16	127.29	127.61	129.18
24	*	115.56	118.40	123.05	125.79	127.05	128.95	132.70	130.97	*	127.46	129.41
25	119.25	114.92	118.55	*	125.43	126.93	*	131.28	130.77	128.23	127.35	†
26	119.15	116.21	118.56	122.39	124.93	126.75	128.78	128.71	*	127.46	†	*
27	119.30	116.36	119.51	122.33	125.37	*	129.35	129.66	131.09	128.36	128.38	129.06
28	118.33	*	*	123.25	125.51	127.15	129.60	128.85	132.48	128.63	127.73	129.18
29	117.81		120.72	123.13	†	127.60	130.35	*	132.69	129.84	126.30	129.99
30	116.93		120.55	123.45	*	127.15	130.95	130.79	132.31	129.61	126.05	130.04
31	*		121.64		126.13		131.24	130.70		132.64		130.41
High	120.93	119.90	121.64	123.48	126.13	128.28	131.24	134.46	132.88	132.64	129.96	130.41
Low	116.93	113.90	115.86	121.11	123.57	124.92	127.53	128.71	127.48	127.29	126.05	125.92

*Sunday
†Holiday

1908—INDUSTRIALS

Date:	Jan.	Feb.	Mar.	Apr.	May	June	July	Aug.	Sept.	Oct.	Nov.	Dec.
1	†	61.83	*	67.84	69.92	74.38	72.76	80.57	84.55	79.50	*	87.63
2	59.61	*	61.09	67.82	70.05	74.03	72.87	*	83.76	80.53	82.90	87.67
3	60.62	61.82	60.97	67.22	*	73.89	73.12	81.07	82.57	81.20	†	86.58
4	60.87	62.14	61.19	67.15	69.78	72.66	†	82.13	83.55	*	84.87	87.26
5	*	61.02	61.29	*	70.62	73.16	*	82.07	†	80.56	85.81	86.68
6	61.75	61.15	61.68	67.04	71.09	73.67	74.50	83.80	*	80.93	87.28	*
7	61.42	60.77	63.23	67.48	70.91	*	74.84	84.46	†	81.33	87.77	86.38
8	61.75	59.90	*	67.81	71.26	73.38	75.83	84.89	83.67	80.68	*	87.02
9	63.50	*	63.66	68.64	71.78	72.91	76.37	*	83.61	80.64	87.47	87.42
10	63.01	58.80	63.50	68.76	*	73.40	75.63	85.40	82.95	80.75	87.54	87.35
11	64.27	59.11	63.87	68.47	72.47	73.42	75.34	84.43	82.00	*	87.09	86.61
12	*	†	64.13	*	72.30	72.82	*	84.69	82.43	81.49	87.62	86.47
13	64.98	58.62	65.15	68.17	73.09	72.90	76.06	83.71	*	81.21	88.38	*
14	65.84	59.73	66.11	68.52	73.95	*	76.87	82.08	82.48	81.54	88.09	85.31
15	65.44	59.17	*	68.01	74.38	72.93	76.72	81.61	82.42	81.65	*	85.15
16	64.19	*	65.23	68.44	74.56	73.48	76.81	*	80.21	81.81	87.68	85.88
17	64.53	58.88	65.78	†	*	73.12	77.08	82.61	79.00	81.35	87.69	83.99
18	64.45	58.84	65.07	*	75.12	73.55	78.28	83.00	79.85	*	86.87	83.91
19	*	59.08	65.77		73.78	72.65	*	82.51	78.66	81.26	86.70	83.71
20	63.19	59.68	66.41	67.94	73.83	72.71	78.75	82.57	*	82.21	86.69	*
21	63.21	60.20	67.26	68.32	74.21	*	78.62	82.15	77.68	82.82	86.19	83.46
22	62.10	†	*	68.38	73.73	71.71	79.13	82.29	77.07	82.83	*	84.57
23	61.44	*	68.32	69.10	72.43	71.70	79.56	*	78.87	82.44	86.17	85.48
24	61.31	60.00	69.08	70.01	*	71.90	78.55	81.91	79.59	82.48	87.61	85.68
25	61.76	59.92	69.92	69.93	73.04	72.33	79.64	82.03	80.19	*	87.15	†
26	*	59.98	69.43	*	72.40	72.34	*	82.65	79.25	82.22	†	*
27	62.06	60.16	69.78	69.80	72.64	72.22	79.10	83.84	*	83.55	87.61	
28	62.53	61.07	68.69	70.23	72.15	*	79.36	84.10	79.58	82.72	87.63	86.97
29	62.08	60.54	*	70.29	72.76	72.91	79.46	84.56	79.23	83.15	*	86.22
30	62.32		68.64	69.55	†	72.59	79.61	*	79.93	82.92	87.30	85.91
31	62.70		67.51		*		80.34	84.66		82.53		86.15
High	65.84	62.14	69.92	70.29	75.12	74.38	80.34	85.40	84.55	83.55	88.38	87.67
Low	59.61	58.62	60.97	67.04	69.78	71.70	72.76	80.57	77.07	79.50	82.90	83.46

*Sunday
†Holiday

1908—RAILROADS

Date:	Jan.	Feb.	Mar.	Apr.	May	June	July	Aug.	Sept.	Oct.	Nov.	Dec.
1	†	91.26	*	92.38	98.35	102.05	99.92	106.90	109.13	105.91	*	117.13
2	89.81	*	86.87	92.45	98.72	102.35	99.74	*	109.19	107.26	110.46	116.21
3	90.38	90.90	86.80	91.78	*	101.90	99.96	106.41	108.03	108.05	†	116.35
4	90.37	91.49	87.15	92.43	98.11	100.30	†	106.99	109.13	*	112.48	117.20
5	*	90.52	87.26	*	98.65	100.65	*	106.78	†	107.45	111.93	116.70
6	91.12	90.45	87.79	92.23	99.42	101.34	101.24	107.45	*	107.69	113.63	*
7	91.15	89.60	89.45	92.20	99.02	*	101.58	107.58	†	107.90	114.53	116.54
8	90.82	88.34	*	93.51	99.90	101.21	102.73	108.01	109.50	106.52	*	117.39
9	92.86	*	90.71	94.30	100.58	100.70	102.95	*	110.33	106.35	114.45	117.80
10	92.03	86.21	90.03	94.18	*	101.03	101.91	109.12	110.14	106.28	115.47	118.05
11	93.75	86.46	91.10	93.77	101.37	100.95	101.65	107.97	109.14	*	115.08	117.81
12	*	†	91.18	*	100.55	99.65	*	108.71	109.50	107.79	115.46	118.18
13	94.27	86.18	91.88	93.53	101.54	99.85	102.36	107.73	*	108.00	116.73	*
14	95.06	87.53	92.84	93.94	102.24	*	103.15	106.05	110.14	107.96	116.53	118.00
15	95.10	86.55	*	93.69	102.56	99.90	103.23	106.17	108.87	108.46	*	117.36
16	94.68	*	91.93	94.06	103.10	100.76	103.12	*	107.55	108.19	116.94	117.98
17	95.27	86.04	92.60	†	*	100.44	103.13	106.76	106.00	107.54	117.51	116.43
18	95.75	86.60	91.11	†	104.45	100.65	104.17	106.77	107.41	*	116.80	116.58
19	*	86.95	91.50	*	103.16	99.08	*	106.09	105.77	107.92	115.78	116.03
20	94.67	87.43	91.98	93.51	102.71	99.25	105.25	106.41	*	109.03	115.95	*
21	93.09	87.61	92.25	93.93	103.42	*	104.20	106.20	103.78	109.73	114.77	115.20
22	92.76	†	*	93.88	102.50	97.96	105.68	106.22	103.43	109.78	*	117.19
23	92.46	*	93.10	94.96	100.26	97.97	106.76	*	104.18	109.26	114.94	118.14
24	91.66	87.29	93.83	96.41	*	98.19	105.09	106.21	105.97	109.40	116.58	118.15
25	92.22	86.79	94.06	96.22	101.32	98.89	106.15	106.08	106.38	*	116.01	†
26	*	86.66	93.16	*	99.65	98.47	*	107.31	105.68	109.88	†	†
27	92.73	86.77	94.40	96.95	99.15	99.16	105.25	108.83	*	110.15	117.23	*
28	93.40	87.36	93.46	97.68	98.53	*	105.80	108.67	105.45	109.51	117.01	119.80
29	92.40	86.52	*	97.86	99.14	100.06	105.63	109.11	105.43	109.95	*	119.28
30	92.44		93.21	96.95	†	99.88	105.77	*	105.95	110.16	117.10	119.43
31	92.19		92.00		*		106.26	109.10		109.57		120.05
High	95.75	91.49	94.40	97.86	104.45	102.35	106.76	109.12	110.33	110.16	117.51	120.05
Low	89.81	86.04	86.80	91.78	98.11	97.96	99.74	106.05	103.43	105.91	110.46	115.20

*Sunday †Holiday

1907—INDUSTRIALS

Date:	Jan.	Feb.	Mar.	Apr.	May	June	July	Aug.	Sept.	Oct.	Nov.	Dec.
1	†	90.59	90.12	82.30	83.87	77.93	81.27	78.36	*	67.95	57.56	*
2	94.25	90.48	89.62	81.84	84.57	*	80.90	78.87	†	67.62	57.39	60.14
3	94.35	*	*	81.94	85.02	77.40	81.38	78.48	73.51	67.94	*	59.47
4	95.98	90.50	88.00	83.13	84.50	79.11	†	*	72.74	67.76	58.48	60.11
5	96.17	91.60	86.44	83.96	*	78.62	81.85	77.41	73.59	67.31	†	61.16
6	*	91.45	87.28	84.22	84.31	78.83	82.52	76.55	73.89	*	57.75	61.77
7	96.37	92.35	86.52	*	83.54	79.35	*	74.91	73.56	67.56	56.39	61.01
8	95.65	92.46	85.21	84.36	83.48	79.92	82.52	75.29	*	67.05	56.68	*
9	96.07	92.13	84.89	84.70	83.28	*	81.57	74.72	73.44	65.51	56.48	59.72
10	95.89	*	*	84.78	83.06	79.95	80.64	73.31	71.68	65.50	*	58.51
11	95.53	92.94	85.70	84.19	82.85	79.15	80.61	71.18	70.96	63.51	56.88	58.22
12	95.78	†	86.53	83.85	*	79.07	80.71	72.37	69.86	62.34	55.87	58.17
13	*	93.39	83.12	82.23	83.56	78.62	81.46	69.63	69.69	*	55.37	57.29
14	95.58	92.73	76.23	*	83.42	78.01	*	70.32	68.30	62.14	54.36	57.33
15	95.36	93.07	81.33	81.40	83.84	77.66	81.20	69.29	*	62.09	53.00	*
16	94.41	93.19	83.69	82.84	83.42	*	81.51	69.36	68.14	60.46	53.89	57.03
17	94.34	*	*	82.89	83.10	77.90	80.40	*	69.17	60.53	*	56.85
18	92.62	92.81	82.13	83.07	82.71	78.11	80.77	69.50	69.05	59.13	55.05	57.71
19	92.58	92.28	81.55	83.11	*	78.09	81.16	69.80	69.80	58.65	53.45	58.08
20	*	92.11	80.94	83.10	80.79	77.86	81.33	70.01	70.10	*	53.18	58.98
21	93.28	91.87	81.97	*	78.77	77.43	*	69.25	70.45	60.81	53.27	59.46
22	93.66	†	80.40	84.80	79.33	77.44	81.11	70.37	*	59.11	53.08	*
23	93.90	†	78.76	84.63	79.04	*	80.98	69.27	69.53	58.21	55.02	58.21
24	94.03	*	*	83.94	79.45	77.93	81.32	69.25	69.82	58.18	*	58.00
25	93.00	90.33	75.39	83.88	79.00	79.53	81.11	*	69.43	58.30	53.63	†
26	92.72	90.61	77.78	83.51	*	79.44	81.25	70.43	69.01	58.31	55.05	57.60
27	*	89.75	77.38	83.95	77.30	80.22	81.21	70.27	67.72	*	55.55	58.65
28	91.89	90.54	78.21	*	77.32	80.00	*	70.97	67.16	58.13	†	58.83
29	91.76		80.15	84.37	78.27	80.36	80.10	71.18	*	57.23	57.51	*
30	90.77		*	84.30	†	*	79.86	72.28	67.72	58.42	58.41	59.47
31	91.70		†		78.10		78.87	†		57.70		58.75
High	96.37	93.39	90.12	84.80	85.02	80.36	82.52	78.87	73.89	67.95	58.48	61.77
Low	90.77	89.75	75.39	81.40	77.30	77.40	78.87	69.25	67.16	57.23	53.00	56.85

*Sunday
†Holiday

1907—RAILROADS

Date:	Jan.	Feb.	Mar.	Apr.	May	June	July	Aug.	Sept.	Oct.	Nov.	Dec.
1	†	120.28	117.98	107.70	109.28	100.42	105.72	104.96	*	98.73	84.36	*
2	129.90	120.20	116.96	107.16	109.41	*	104.78	105.37	†	98.08	84.14	88.28
3	129.71	*	*	106.88	110.36	99.50	105.70	105.27	99.44	97.81	*	87.32
4	131.60	119.58	114.77	109.05	109.64	100.78	†	*	98.68	97.56	85.05	89.11
5	131.95	120.76	112.56	110.48	*	100.45	106.34	103.71	100.11	98.11	†	90.30
6	*	120.67	114.31	109.83	108.87	101.03	107.23	102.34	100.45	*	85.72	90.56
7	131.63	122.00	112.51	*	108.14	102.06	*	100.90	100.26	97.31	84.27	90.12
8	130.38	121.59	110.86	109.77	108.23	102.96	106.84	101.35	*	95.56	85.09	*
9	129.74	120.82	111.09	109.30	107.58	*	105.48	100.36	100.38	95.77	85.07	89.19
10	129.65	*	*	109.32	106.76	102.81	103.99	98.51	98.91	94.50	*	87.88
11	128.78	121.70	111.83	108.69	107.08	101.76	104.48	*	99.02	93.34	85.91	87.85
12	129.56	†	112.53	108.36	*	101.95	105.66	95.87	98.30	92.83	85.41	87.85
13	*	122.81	107.52	106.72	108.04	101.65	105.68	97.66	99.10	*	84.80	86.94
14	128.53	121.90	99.71	*	107.25	100.73	*	95.25	98.44	93.18	84.15	87.76
15	128.53	122.13	105.95	105.56	106.52	100.36	106.38	96.16	*	92.03	82.50	*
16	127.18	122.94	108.71	107.29	106.06	*	105.60	95.31	98.88	92.48	82.97	86.73
17	126.80	*	*	106.57	105.72	100.90	106.00	95.22	99.91	90.88	*	86.61
18	124.55	122.14	106.71	107.16	105.16	100.75	106.94	*	99.78	90.30	84.60	87.23
19	124.25	121.25	105.51	107.20	*	100.96	107.20	95.52	100.36	92.23	82.93	87.39
20	*	120.78	105.73	107.51	103.57	100.83	106.91	96.49	100.36	*	82.38	88.78
21	125.22	120.30	106.21	*	102.45	100.44	*	95.88	101.03	88.73	81.41	89.35
22	125.25	†	103.15	109.65	103.38	100.42	106.68	96.63	*	86.69	81.49	*
23	125.75	†	100.77	109.70	102.70	*	107.68	95.14	100.19	84.82	83.40	88.11
24	125.68	*	*	108.65	103.40	101.18	107.37	94.93	100.38	85.90	*	87.61
25	124.08	117.71	98.27	108.83	102.50	103.11	107.36	*	100.01	85.88	81.72	†
26	123.68	118.26	101.94	108.45	*	102.86	107.51	96.39	99.28	86.13	83.51	87.01
27	*	117.15	102.56	108.93	99.98	103.75	106.23	96.41	98.27	*	84.09	88.41
28	122.34	118.68	103.23	*	99.95	103.77	*	97.41	97.21	83.49	†	88.35
29	122.18		†	109.73	101.33	105.06	106.41	97.11	*	84.85	85.80	*
30	121.52		105.85	109.97	†	*	105.26	97.83	98.35	84.02	87.13	89.50
31	122.25		*		100.92		107.68	†				88.77
High	131.95	122.94	117.98	110.48	110.41	105.06	107.68	105.37	101.03	98.73	87.13	90.56
Low	121.52	117.15	98.27	105.56	99.95	99.50	103.90	94.93	97.21	83.49	81.41	86.61

*Sunday †Holiday

1906—INDUSTRIALS

Date:	Jan.	Feb.	Mar.	Apr.	May	June	July	Aug.	Sept.	Oct.	Nov.	Dec.
1	†	101.55	93.83	*	88.03	94.01	*	93.72	94.42	95.77	93.80	95.16
2	95.00	101.71	93.86	97.84	87.16	94.38	86.12	93.37	*	95.42	94.28	*
3	95.63	99.77	93.85	98.19	86.45	*	86.64	92.44	†	95.22	94.17	95.35
4	94.44	*	*	97.48	89.08	95.19	†	91.67	93.31	94.66	*	95.23
5	96.09	100.05	92.90	97.00	89.75	95.04	86.58	*	93.77	95.48	94.60	95.27
6	97.09	100.39	94.00	97.09	*	95.21	87.79	92.85	94.63	95.88	†	94.82
7	*	99.60	94.09	96.56	90.78	95.12	87.97	92.97	94.22	*	93.93	95.30
8	98.03	99.50	94.69	*	92.08	94.50	*	92.10	94.50	96.53	93.58	95.19
9	97.85	99.93	96.43	95.93	92.86	93.99	87.87	91.70	*	96.75	93.37	*
10	98.09	99.76	96.33	95.05	93.21	*	87.26	91.92	94.55	96.51	93.32	95.58
11	99.06	*	*	96.44	93.41	94.38	86.37	92.03	94.53	96.65	*	95.89
12	100.25	100.08	96.40	96.02	93.13	94.10	85.70	*	95.38	96.58	92.38	95.36
13	99.79	99.27	96.96	96.51	*	93.63	85.18	92.53	95.27	96.04	93.06	94.10
14	*	97.88	96.44	97.02	92.80	92.91	85.40	92.70	95.89	*	94.01	94.82
15	100.80	97.31	95.79	*	93.06	92.25	*	92.94	95.53	95.78	94.25	95.46
16	100.81	96.51	95.33	97.01	93.77	91.02	86.45	92.59	*	96.14	94.76	*
17	101.67	97.31	95.10	96.84	93.05	*	86.91	93.38	95.63	95.78	95.20	94.50
18	102.26	*	*	95.67	92.75	90.66	86.54	95.34	95.84	95.65	*	93.54
19	103.00	97.07	93.05	94.23	92.68	91.43	87.21	*	95.47	94.77	94.92	93.11
20	102.72	96.25	94.35	95.29	*	92.00	88.12	95.96	96.07	92.76	95.04	93.81
21	*	96.76	94.38	95.25	92.20	90.55	88.51	95.60	96.00	*	95.32	94.59
22	102.37	†	94.96	*	92.15	90.95	*	95.09	95.50	94.58	95.25	93.45
23	102.50	96.87	95.06	93.46	92.16	89.85	88.59	95.36	*	94.47	95.33	*
24	102.53		94.77	93.60	92.76	*	88.12	96.07	95.92	93.85	94.57	92.94
25	102.66	*	*	93.02	93.42	89.02	89.59	96.08	94.68	93.12	*	†
26	102.90	97.38	96.25	92.44	93.15	89.38	90.03	*	94.82	93.16	94.77	93.13
27	101.86	96.44	95.82	89.92	*	87.71	91.41	95.19	94.77	93.47	95.05	94.34
28	*	93.94	96.64	88.70	93.29	88.70	91.80	94.01	94.98	*	95.27	94.28
29	99.32		96.43	*	93.69	87.29	*	94.89	94.84	93.85	†	93.63
30	98.31		96.60	90.53	†	87.01	91.72	94.31	*	93.68	95.12	*
31	100.69		96.95		93.75		92.41	94.01		92.91		94.35
High	103.00	101.71	96.96	98.19	93.77	95.21	92.41	96.08	96.07	96.75	95.33	95.89
Low	94.44	93.94	92.90	88.70	86.45	87.01	85.18	91.67	93.31	92.76	92.38	92.94

*Sunday
†Holiday

1906—RAILROADS

Date:	Jan.	Feb.	Mar.	Apr.	May	June	July	Aug.	Sept.	Oct.	Nov.	Dec.
1	†	135.93	129.98	*	120.70	128.82	*	130.45	136.10	136.86	132.93	136.30
2	133.12	135.70	130.13	133.13	120.61	129.35	121.76	131.11	*	136.57	133.49	*
3	133.23	133.89	130.00	132.60	120.30	*	122.41	130.40	†	136.24	133.70	136.86
4	132.36	*	*	132.68	123.29	129.98	†	129.70	136.09	135.98	*	136.60
5	133.73	133.73	128.54	132.05	124.01	129.44	122.88	*	136.41	136.87	133.91	136.11
6	134.48	134.50	129.48	132.34	*	129.93	124.73	130.99	137.16	136.53	†	135.37
7		133.73	129.22	131.76	124.25	130.55	124.96	131.21	136.62	*	133.55	136.65
8	134.76	133.83	130.46	*	126.10	130.56	*	131.08	137.05	136.68	132.88	136.28
9	134.73	135.34	131.40	130.45	126.14	129.71	124.81	130.18	*	136.78	132.67	*
10	134.65	134.87	130.88	130.07	126.91	*	124.24	130.62	137.09	137.65	132.24	136.61
11	135.58	†	*	131.85	128.16	131.05	123.54	131.07	135.77	137.68	*	137.56
12	136.65	135.23	130.53	131.45	127.60	130.82	122.43	*	137.72	137.60	131.45	136.63
13	136.80	134.66	131.46	132.13	*	129.96	122.45	131.71	136.61	136.78	132.28	134.93
14		133.55	130.85	132.56	127.23	129.25	122.71	131.93	137.68	*	134.08	136.73
15	136.86	132.28	130.40	*	127.05	128.40	*	132.10	137.82	136.84	134.35	136.78
16	137.12	132.06	130.59	132.66	127.83	127.21	124.03	131.39	*	136.76	135.42	*
17	137.06	131.10	130.41	132.66	127.46	*	124.33	133.63	137.84	135.98	136.13	135.36
18	137.07		*	131.14	126.90	126.77	123.55	135.41	137.75	135.86	*	133.14
19	138.29	132.60	128.96	128.36	126.91	128.48	124.47	*	137.03	134.12	136.44	130.84
20	138.25	132.41	130.16	129.01	*	129.53	125.46	136.98	137.83	131.62	136.06	131.23
21	*	131.47	129.63	128.96	126.93	128.23	125.82	135.60	137.70	*	136.83	131.31
22	138.36	†	130.50	*	126.75	128.76	*	134.83	136.92	133.87	136.68	129.65
23	138.11	132.06	130.87	126.56	126.29	127.64	126.01	136.95	*	133.43	136.31	*
24	137.20	131.79	130.75	126.76	127.78	*	125.27	135.15	137.26	133.27	135.01	128.37
25	137.45		*	126.18	128.31	126.72	126.83	137.06	135.71	132.05	*	†
26	137.79	132.58	132.03	125.73	128.03	127.10	127.71	*	135.69	132.17	134.90	128.51
27	136.36	131.24	131.32	122.95	*	124.89	128.08	136.04	135.25	132.34	135.96	130.34
28	*	129.56	132.53	121.89	127.89	125.93	129.02	135.04	135.89	*	135.90	130.02
29	133.98		132.17	*	128.41	123.91	*	135.96	135.92	132.70	†	128.95
30	133.55		132.70	124.06	†	123.31	128.31	135.34	*	132.60	136.01	*
31	135.34		132.73		128.61		129.11	135.20		131.37		129.80
High	138.36	135.93	132.73	133.13	128.61	131.05	129.11	137.06	137.84	137.68	136.83	137.56
Low	132.36	129.56	128.54	121.89	120.30	123.31	121.76	129.70	135.25	131.37	131.45	128.37

*Sunday †Holiday

1905—INDUSTRIALS

Date:	Jan.	Feb.	Mar.	Apr.	May	June	July	Aug.	Sept.	Oct.	Nov.	Dec.
1	70.91	70.91	76.06	80.67	76.90	73.17	77.48	81.35	79.66	*	84.14	89.62
2	†	71.19	76.81		77.77	73.31	*	81.31	79.71	82.17	83.92	89.50
3	70.39	71.47	75.92	81.13	76.51	73.43	78.70	81.63	†	82.62	83.78	*
4	70.22	71.53	76.14	81.31	74.68	*	†	81.90	80.73	82.38	82.93	89.56
5	70.23	*	*	82.17	76.82	73.51	78.65	81.75	78.92	82.78	*	90.82
6	69.46	71.80	76.33	82.76	76.17	72.53	79.33	*	78.60	82.55	83.32	90.91
7	69.23	72.63	76.02	83.12	*	72.94	79.54	82.20	79.78	82.02	†	92.37
8	*	72.54	76.29	82.45	74.52	73.05	79.47	81.90	79.02	*	82.17	93.20
9	69.52	72.26	77.36	*	75.78	73.27	*	81.83	*	81.65	81.56	92.84
10	70.10	73.27	77.88	82.20	76.34	74.68	79.47	82.03	79.06	82.02	82.57	*
11	70.03	73.34	77.72	81.93	77.15	*	78.02	82.20	80.13	80.83	82.25	93.59
12	69.61	*	*	82.64	78.05	74.61	79.09	82.01	79.43	80.96	*	95.13
13	70.31	†	78.22	83.23	77.45	73.95	78.93	*	80.11	81.54	80.83	95.68
14	70.70	73.48	78.17	83.75	*	74.11	78.56	82.12	80.52	81.47	81.67	95.47
15	*	73.57	77.89	83.12	77.46	73.76	78.68	82.35	81.11	*	82.77	96.05
16	70.94	73.63	77.81	*	76.89	73.96	*	82.45	*	81.48	82.47	96.09
17	70.67	73.92	77.18	83.41	76.65	73.36	79.10	82.73	81.38	81.43	84.19	*
18	70.98	74.23	77.27	82.60	74.63	*	79.10	82.03	80.77	80.96	84.53	95.71
19	70.67	*	*	83.44	73.87	73.68	79.26	82.14	81.45	81.41	*	95.64
20	70.63	74.94	78.02	80.95	73.22	74.43	79.60	*	81.77	82.27	85.22	94.61
21	70.14	75.51	77.51	†	*	75.19	79.30	82.26	81.91	82.83	85.84	94.20
22	*	†	76.44	*	71.37	75.70	78.05	82.10	81.78	*	86.11	94.43
23	69.45	75.34	77.42	79.97	71.57	75.78	*	82.82	*	82.86	85.93	95.05
24	69.39	76.11	79.27	80.85	73.75	75.69	78.69	82.61	81.05	82.84	85.81	*
25	68.76	76.16	78.89	81.26	72.91	*	78.36	82.37	81.30	82.66	86.94	†
26	70.07	*	*	78.53	73.01	77.45	78.66	82.61	81.13	82.08	*	95.84
27	70.43	75.75	78.58	77.87	72.91	77.45	79.27	*	80.92	81.97	89.43	94.04
28	70.82	75.15	78.13	76.08	*	77.78	80.46	82.22	81.39	81.51	89.77	95.37
29	*		78.70		74.12	77.19	80.64	82.79	81.90	*	89.89	96.56
30	70.77		79.23		†	76.87	*	82.05	*	82.33	†	96.20
31	71.33		80.02		74.32		81.70	80.63		83.77		*
High	71.33	76.16	80.02	83.75	78.05	77.78	81.70	82.82	81.91	83.77	89.89	96.56
Low	68.76	70.91	75.92	76.08	71.37	72.53	77.48	80.63	78.60	80.83	80.83	89.50

*Sunday †Holiday

1905—RAILROADS

Date:	Jan.	Feb.	Mar.	Apr.	May	June	July	Aug.	Sept.	Oct.	Nov.	Dec.
1	*	120.70	124.95	124.98	119.81	117.00	123.38	125.63	127.91	*	132.37	130.00
2	†	121.30	125.20	*	120.63	117.19	*	125.58	129.08	131.99	132.23	129.93
3	118.50	122.03	124.51	125.43	119.44	117.16	124.65	126.35	*	132.42	132.47	*
4	118.16	121.63	125.05	125.03	117.35	*	†	126.84	†	131.47	131.45	129.65
5	118.12	*	*	125.43	118.96	117.58	124.05	126.80	130.32	131.40	*	130.81
6	117.38	121.30	125.25	126.21	118.35	116.59	124.58	*	128.19	131.53	131.99	130.64
7	117.03	121.95	124.65	125.88	*	117.30	124.93	127.78	127.37	130.92	†	130.98
8	*	122.36	125.19	125.41	117.61	117.42	124.90	127.88	128.92	*	130.51	131.04
9	117.35	122.20	125.90	*	118.47	117.55	*	127.83	128.33	130.35	129.00	131.33
10	117.55	122.40	126.46	125.62	118.23	119.42	124.58	127.47	*	131.26	129.83	*
11	117.74	122.25	126.70	125.41	119.36	*	123.17	130.11	128.76	130.04	128.91	131.95
12	117.21	*	*	125.90	120.02	119.13	125.17	130.07	129.83	130.10	*	132.03
13	117.96	†	127.16	126.24	119.42	118.35	124.82	*	129.45	131.01	127.91	132.81
14	118.49	122.42	126.78	127.01	*	118.93	124.92	130.83	130.50	130.73	129.34	132.08
15	*	122.75	126.75	126.28	119.85	118.56	125.19	130.36	130.00	*	130.08	131.90
16	118.31	122.36	126.45	*	119.33	118.78	*	131.10	130.93	130.80	129.37	
17	118.16	122.23	125.21	126.39	119.24	118.35	125.25	131.28	*	130.49	130.69	*
18	118.63	122.43	124.87	124.70	117.44	*	125.01	130.25	131.43	130.13	130.95	131.28
19	118.60	*	*	125.66	116.91	118.86	125.38	130.53	130.54	130.51	*	131.71
20	119.40	122.86	126.00	123.40	115.88	119.69	125.04	*	131.60	131.82	131.97	131.93
21	119.24	123.50	125.14	†	*	120.67	124.16	131.54	131.91	132.62	132.13	132.26
22	*	†	123.91	†	114.52	121.27	122.95	131.58	132.33	*	131.98	133.05
23	118.18	122.94	124.65	*	114.76	121.50	*	132.17	132.19	132.65	132.00	133.14
24	117.59	124.63	125.26	122.57	117.36	120.91	123.73	132.06	*	132.61	131.26	*
25	117.26	125.48	125.51	123.80	116.47	*	123.79	131.75	130.97	132.49	131.65	†
26	118.97	*	*	124.04	116.70	122.07	123.95	131.83	131.27	131.95	*	133.17
27	119.14	125.08	124.48	120.88	116.90	122.01	124.92	*	131.38	131.36	132.26	131.08
28	120.30	123.78	123.46	120.48	*	123.37	126.03	131.31	130.93	130.70	131.63	132.30
29	*		124.69	117.81	118.57	122.46	126.06	132.19	131.38	*	131.34	133.54
30	120.58		124.45	*	†	122.57	*	131.30	131.86	131.25	†	133.26
31	121.05		124.89		119.30		126.28	129.57		132.33		*
High	121.05	125.48	127.16	127.01	120.63	123.37	126.28	132.19	132.33	132.65	132.47	133.54
Low	117.03	120.70	123.46	117.81	114.52	116.59	122.95	125.58	127.37	130.04	127.91	129.65

*Sunday †Holiday

1904—INDUSTRIALS

Date:	Jan.	Feb.	Mar.	Apr.	May	June	July	Aug.	Sept.	Oct.	Nov.	Dec.
1	†	49.03	47.86	†	*	48.26	49.31	52.73	54.94	58.05	63.72	72.05
2	47.38	48.69	47.87	49.08	48.42	48.10	†	52.68	55.15	*	64.76	72.46
3	*	48.40	48.00	*	48.33	48.17	*	52.75	†	58.65	64.87	72.86
4	47.77	48.35	47.90	48.68	48.60	48.17	†	52.70	*	58.27	65.31	*
5	48.09	47.87	47.28	48.89	48.56	*	49.62	52.85	†	58.18	65.25	73.23
6	47.07	47.65	*	49.30	48.71	48.08	50.09	52.90	55.38	57.59	*	72.57
7	47.16	*	47.18	49.98	48.59	48.27	49.96	*	55.68	57.96	66.21	68.97
8	47.92	48.10	47.72	49.59	*	48.60	50.44	52.73	55.94	58.22	†	68.00
9	48.02	46.98	47.04	49.65	48.71	48.66	50.84	53.03	56.54	*	67.07	69.22
10	*	46.76	46.93	*	48.42	49.06	*	53.13	57.43	58.75	67.58	70.01
11	47.82	47.76	46.46	49.98	48.30	49.12	50.67	53.28	*	59.03	68.03	*
12	47.63	48.16	46.41	49.58	47.93	*	51.37	53.39	56.46	59.23	68.19	65.77
13	47.77	48.11	*	49.73	47.72	48.88	51.73	54.03	56.32	60.16	*	66.42
14	47.85	*	46.50	49.41	47.72	49.05	51.87	*	57.10	61.42	68.78	66.17
15	47.97	48.86	47.73	49.35	*	48.86	52.06	53.98	56.66	62.07	69.17	66.62
16	48.08	48.39	47.77	49.38	47.56	48.83	52.50	53.54	57.19	*	69.11	68.73
17	*	48.16	48.30	*	47.67	48.73	*	54.08	56.58	62.06	70.08	68.47
18	48.82	47.90	47.91	49.33	47.43	48.89	52.50	54.25	*	62.16	69.69	*
19	48.65	47.51	48.76	48.92	47.45	*	52.96	53.76	56.55	61.72	70.01	68.48
20	48.58	47.31	*	48.62	47.53	48.97	52.80	53.35	55.67	62.12	*	69.09
21	49.38	*	48.26	49.10	48.06	49.03	52.47	*	56.00	62.35	70.62	68.38
22	49.94	†	48.50	49.09	*	49.46	52.65	53.13	55.72	62.97	69.80	67.87
23	49.91	46.86	48.62	49.12	48.53	49.47	53.14	53.91	56.31	*	69.89	68.47
24	*	46.71	48.16	*	48.00	49.32	*	54.13	56.50	63.17	†	†
25	49.61	47.47	48.15	48.65	48.14	49.12	52.98	54.41	*	62.68	70.83	*
26	50.18	47.14	48.21	48.81	48.23	*	52.27	54.44	56.91	62.63	71.56	†
27	50.50	47.08	*	48.95	48.26	49.29	52.43	54.47	57.14	61.97	*	69.13
28	49.42	*	48.68	48.86	†	49.12	52.39	*	57.44	63.39	72.36	70.20
29	49.11	47.53	48.60	48.90	*	49.08	52.12	54.61	57.11	64.54	72.35	71.07
30	48.91		48.77	48.80	†	49.25	52.13	54.44	57.59	*	72.02	70.05
31	*		49.12		48.18		*	54.57		63.03		69.61
High	50.50	49.03	49.12	49.98	48.71	49.47	53.14	54.61	57.59	64.54	72.36	73.23
Low	47.07	46.71	46.41	48.62	47.43	48.08	49.31	52.68	54.94	57.59	63.72	65.77

*Sunday
†Holiday

1904—RAILROADS

Date	Jan.	Feb.	Mar.	Apr.	May	June	July	Aug.	Sept.	Oct.	Nov.	Dec.
1	†	97.70	92.61	†	*	94.33	97.53	101.20	105.31	109.11	113.30	118.68
2	96.30	97.55	92.80	95.96	95.22	94.15	†	100.85	106.31	*	114.06	119.33
3	*	96.96	92.90	*	95.37	94.41	*	101.29	†	109.19	113.95	119.46
4	96.55	96.61	93.09	96.04	95.60	94.41	†	101.30	*	109.56	113.78	*
5	97.08	95.50	92.40	96.25	95.17	*	98.63	101.51	†	110.00	113.47	119.36
6	95.61	95.50	*	96.93	95.36	94.54	99.55	101.60	107.12	109.23	*	118.67
7	95.88	*	92.77	97.15	95.23	94.80	98.72	*	106.81	109.68	114.37	116.82
8	96.65	93.90	92.36	96.81	*	95.13	99.47	101.50	107.28	110.31	†	116.26
9	97.23	94.75	92.33	96.98	95.23	95.43	99.63	101.98	107.83	*	115.28	116.94
10	*	94.05	92.31	*	94.87	95.77	*	102.25	108.12	110.32	115.32	117.31
11	97.33	94.06	91.66	97.58	94.93	96.04	99.26	102.99	*	110.85	116.72	*
12	96.39	†	91.53	96.75	94.45	*	100.40	103.13	106.91	110.92	116.92	113.53
13	96.67	94.11	*	97.13	94.10	95.66	100.79	103.56	106.81	110.95	*	114.00
14	96.85	*	91.31	96.57	93.83	96.48	100.50	*	107.86	112.31	116.31	113.78
15	96.81	94.54	93.10	96.57	*	96.04	100.89	104.02	107.67	113.06	117.21	114.60
16	96.80	94.61	93.33	96.35	93.55	96.26	101.11	103.83	107.89	*	116.82	116.07
17	*	94.23	94.35	*	93.90	95.86	*	104.15	107.38	113.22	117.46	116.15
18	97.73	93.76	93.81	96.22	93.88	96.16	101.62	104.48	*	113.58	116.85	*
19	98.21	93.51	95.08	95.96	93.75	*	102.24	103.98	106.90	113.40	117.00	116.16
20	98.45	93.18	*	95.96	94.11	96.45	102.21	103.31	106.30	113.69	*	116.91
21	99.43	*	94.51	96.65	94.74	96.85	101.85	*	107.05	114.60	117.27	115.94
22	99.76	†	95.86	96.85	*	97.17	102.01	104.50	106.43	114.78	116.41	115.30
23	99.78	92.17	95.88	96.90	95.20	97.23	102.06	104.40	106.96	*	116.54	115.92
24	*	91.83	94.90	*	94.90	97.25	*	104.71	107.01	114.72	†	†
25	98.73	92.65	94.65	96.37	94.39	97.17	101.60	105.30	*	114.63	117.01	*
26	99.26	92.18	94.80	96.45	94.43	*	100.80	105.32	107.53	114.04	117.54	†
27	99.50	92.13	*	96.68	94.41	97.05	99.75	105.50	107.97	113.01	*	116.85
28	98.21	*	95.92	96.57	†	97.00	101.21	*	108.32	114.42	118.22	117.68
29	98.06	92.28	96.50	96.14	*	97.30	100.81	106.10	108.00	115.20	118.27	118.55
30	97.90		96.35	96.04	†	97.32	100.52	105.83	108.78	*	118.93	117.90
31	*		96.49		94.36		*	105.22		113.36		117.43
High	99.78	97.70	96.50	97.58	95.60	97.32	102.24	106.10	108.78	115.20	118.93	119.46
Low	95.61	91.83	91.31	95.96	93.55	94.15	97.53	100.85	105.31	109.11	113.30	113.53

*Sunday
†Holiday

1903—INDUSTRIALS

Date:	Jan.	Feb.	Mar.	Apr.	May	June	July	Aug.	Sept.	Oct.	Nov.	Dec.
1	†	*	*	63.47	63.84	59.59	58.81	50.75	52.75	47.06	*	44.35
2	64.60	65.53	66.01	62.63	63.86	59.87	58.08	*	52.60	47.62	45.46	45.50
3	64.65	66.06	65.68	62.55	*	59.90	58.21	50.57	51.85	47.53	†	46.23
4	*	66.40	65.81	62.28	64.06	58.86	†	49.22	51.93	*	44.90	46.50
5	65.38	66.55	64.70	*	64.01	58.53	*	47.98		47.05	43.60	46.06
6	65.88	66.38	64.82	62.40	63.89	58.50	58.08	49.36	*	47.23	43.94	*
7	65.73	66.47	64.13	62.09	63.55	*	57.84	48.64	†	46.96	43.71	47.40
8	66.33	*	*	62.28	63.70	57.97	57.95	47.38	51.53	45.51	*	47.34
9	66.21	67.10	64.42	62.32	63.55	57.37	56.97	*	51.39	45.34	42.15	47.34
10	65.85	67.22	63.90	†	*	56.78	56.61	48.06	51.00	44.71	43.34	46.35
11	*	67.19	64.28	†	63.76	58.28	55.89	48.67	50.93	*	42.83	46.12
12	65.65	†	63.92	*	63.50	59.38	*	50.31	50.80	43.67	42.93	46.03
13	64.98	66.93	64.11	60.79	63.63	58.94	56.12	51.36	*	43.20	43.41	*
14	64.89	67.05	64.31	62.12	63.15	*	54.92	52.80	50.16	43.42	43.13	46.70
15	64.50	*	*	62.14	63.01	57.75	54.37	52.97	50.30	42.25	*	46.83
16	64.80	67.70	64.19	62.87	62.69	57.84	54.10	*	49.82	44.41	43.36	46.86
17	65.07	67.69	64.51	63.84	*	57.55	54.73	53.88	49.44	45.07	43.50	46.70
18	*	67.32	64.86	64.14	62.12	56.89	54.10	53.61	48.73	*	44.20	47.16
19	64.52	66.69	65.40	*	62.28	57.48	*	51.43	48.50	43.19	44.53	47.33
20	64.19	67.26	65.75	64.43	61.25	57.12	52.76	51.76	*	44.75	44.19	*
21	65.00	†	65.69	64.56	61.95	*	51.95	51.45	48.45	45.10	44.15	46.95
22	64.83	†	*	†	62.56	56.65	52.01	51.63	48.43	44.77	*	46.63
23	64.30	67.43	65.39	64.21	61.40	57.61	50.83	*	47.75	44.59	44.55	47.55
24	64.31	67.09	64.43	64.07	*	57.60	49.84	51.36	46.62	44.48	43.64	47.75
25	*	66.52	63.96	63.79	60.67	57.31	49.08	52.27	46.64	*	43.91	†
26	64.90	66.16	64.15	*	61.53	57.27	*	52.32	46.19	45.33	†	48.64
27	65.36	66.19	63.45	63.48	61.16	57.64	50.11	52.38	*	45.41	44.25	*
28	65.37		63.44	63.77	60.52	*	51.52	53.02	45.09	45.46	44.14	49.35
29	65.55		*	64.09	60.27	58.77	51.02	53.17	46.67	45.21	*	49.06
30	64.96		62.86	63.78	†	59.08	50.72	*	45.80	44.82	44.33	49.11
31	65.18		63.64		*		50.76	53.19		45.13		49.35
High	66.33	67.70	66.01	64.56	64.06	59.90	58.81	53.88	52.75	47.62	45.46	49.35
Low	64.19	65.53	62.86	60.79	60.27	56.65	49.08	47.38	45.09	42.25	42.15	44.35

*Sunday †Holiday

1903—RAILROADS

Date:	Jan.	Feb.	Mar.	Apr.	May	June	July	Aug.	Sept.	Oct.	Nov.	Dec.
1	†	*	*	110.01	109.56	103.35	104.01	96.37	97.46	91.45	*	94.41
2	119.17	119.33	114.58	109.15	109.55	104.20	102.91	*	97.67	92.77	93.23	94.36
3	119.05	119.26	113.91	109.60	*	104.23	103.05	95.90	96.99	91.99	†	95.60
4	*	119.86	114.34	109.16	110.82	102.69	†	93.84	97.90	*	92.68	95.79
5	119.56	120.00	112.22	*	110.62	102.45	*	91.93	97.20	91.19	91.41	95.42
6	121.02	119.55	113.20	109.42	110.73	102.44	103.06	93.32	*	91.01	91.75	*
7	120.20	119.58	111.38	109.14	110.03	*	103.07	92.89	†	91.31	92.18	96.28
8	121.00	*	*	109.34	109.93	101.41	103.20	90.70	97.41	90.13	*	96.10
9	121.28	120.19	111.82	108.91	109.23	100.46	101.83	*	97.05	90.21	92.15	96.56
10	121.00	120.00	110.51	*	*	99.40	100.53	91.79	97.37	89.90	91.76	95.60
11	*	119.89	111.82	†	109.61	102.18	99.56	92.54	96.83	*	90.98	95.48
12	120.43	†	111.54	105.75	109.47	103.88	*	94.66	95.20	89.63	90.10	95.20
13	120.44	119.92	111.60	107.36	109.24	103.58	99.58	96.13	*	89.65	91.05	*
14	120.33	119.50	111.77	107.20	108.55	*	97.89	98.26	95.50	89.36	90.71	96.23
15	119.89	*	*	108.36	107.98	101.93	97.10	97.96	95.09	89.76	*	96.41
16	120.30	119.80	110.93	108.86	107.75	102.48	97.77	*	94.81	91.85	91.26	96.40
17	120.45	119.35	111.26	109.11	*	102.26	99.20	98.60	94.33	91.88	91.45	95.90
18	*	117.81	112.06	*	106.68	101.81	98.50	98.84	93.91	*	92.54	96.55
19	119.63	117.04	112.86	109.84	107.05	102.45	*	96.88	94.01	89.81	93.43	96.57
20	119.12	117.80	113.62	110.42	105.68	102.25	97.28	96.86	*	91.45	93.00	*
21	120.10		113.48	*	106.59	*	96.99	96.53	93.80	91.96	92.53	96.58
22	119.77	*	*	109.98	106.93	101.70	97.81	96.52	92.80	92.01	*	96.59
23	118.83	†	112.58	110.06	105.12	102.18	96.92	*	91.26	91.52	93.12	97.58
24	118.81	117.26	111.23	109.68	*	101.83	96.40	97.41	91.95	91.58	92.61	97.78
25	*	116.82	110.48	*	103.77	101.63	95.00	97.28	90.51	*	92.91	†
26	119.78	115.86	110.59	108.77	105.10	101.43	*	96.93	88.80	92.84	†	
27	119.43	115.19	109.11	108.65	104.96	102.03	97.00	97.41	*	93.25	93.07	*
28	119.29	115.19	109.38	109.53	104.20	*	97.08	97.56	88.65	93.10	93.06	98.88
29	119.53		*	108.86	103.78	103.63	97.01	*	91.27	92.63	*	98.94
30	118.86		108.76		†	103.67	96.72	98.05	89.75	92.66	93.80	98.36
31	119.06		109.98		*		96.48	98.84		92.81		98.33
High	121.28	120.19	114.58	110.42	110.82	104.23	104.01	98.84	97.90	93.25	93.80	98.94
Low	118.81	115.19	108.76	105.75	103.77	99.40	95.00	90.70	88.80	89.36	90.10	94.36

*Sunday †Holiday

1902—INDUSTRIALS

Date:	Jan.	Feb.	Mar.	Apr.	May	June	July	Aug.	Sept.	Oct.	Nov.	Dec.
1	†	65.04	65.13 *	67.20	67.11	*	64.25	65.91	†	66.45	65.80	62.53
2	64.32	*		67.17	65.89	66.26	64.76	65.83 *	66.55	66.44	*	62.22
3	64.25	64.77	65.30	67.01	66.25 *	66.17	64.89 †		66.64	66.58	65.55	62.06
4	64.59 *	64.62	64.77	66.82		65.96	†	65.96	66.60	65.71 *	†	61.90
5		64.96	64.97	66.84 *	66.06	65.32	†	66.12	66.80		64.55	61.76
6	64.90	64.92	66.16		67.01	65.46	65.09	66.47	66.56 *	64.21	64.37	61.73 *
7	64.22	65.31	65.56	66.60	66.36	65.49 *	64.51	66.52	67.12	63.84	64.19	
8	64.87	64.94	65.60	66.60	66.66		64.27	66.53 †	67.03	64.28	62.90 *	62.14
9	64.08		*	66.76	66.40	65.68	64.65	*	66.89	65.06	*	62.19
10	63.85	64.82	65.11	65.95	65.95 *	66.11	64.50	66.19	66.67	64.76	62.35	60.71
11	64.02	65.16	65.32	66.18		66.20	64.45	66.07	66.05	63.84 *	60.96	59.97
12	*	†	64.88	66.33	65.51	65.94	*	66.48	66.30		61.61	60.19
13	63.31	64.58	65.26	*	65.90	65.94 *	64.64	66.78	*	64.17	61.81	59.85 *
14	62.57	64.61	65.38	66.03	65.95	66.05	64.79	66.59	66.11	65.02	60.62	
15	63.16	64.6-	65.59	66.46	66.06	*	65.55	66.50 *	66.40	65.37	61.60 *	59.57
16	63.59		*	66.86	65.35	65.90	65.90		66.89	66.10		59.71
17	64.02	65.30	65.59	67.44	64.85 *	65.89	66.03	66.38	67.25	66.57	62.19	60.10
18	63.54	64.81	65.9o	67.75		65.43	66.04	66.46	67.77	66.50 *	61.61	61.18
19		65.53	66.50	67.61	64.73	64.91	*	66.28	67.40 *		61.69	61.36
20	63.45	64.68	67.25	*	65.33	64.76	66.01	65.33		66.58	62.04	61.87 *
21	63.44	64.98	67.52	67.10	65.86	64.78 *	66.44	65.80	66.91	65.81	62.94	
22	63.54	†	67.31	66.20	65.88		66.50	65.80	65.45	65.89	62.87 *	62.67
23	64.01		*	66.84	66.44	64.20	66.37	*	65.42	65.78		62.00
24	64.13	65.30	67.30	68.44	66.82 *	63.67	66.59	65.87	65.81	66.37	62.79	62.61
25	63.90	65.58	67.01	67.62		63.82	66.59	65.79	66.34	66.44 *	62.15	†
26	*	65.20	67.25	67.63	66.46	64.04	*	66.19	66.28		61.41 †	*
27	64.17	65.27	67.21	*	66.25	63.73	67.28	66.28	*	66.06	62.14 *	63.21
28	65.17	64.81	†	67.31	66.21	63.87 *	66.51	66.28 †	64.07	65.92	62.05 *	63.69
29	64.76		† *	67.37	66.42 †		66.56	*	66.15	65.13		
30	64.87		67.19	67.01	† *	64.31	65.82	66.78		65.43	65.80	63.30
31	64.95		67.52		67.11		67.28	65.33	67.77	66.06	60.62	63.96
High	65.17	65.58	67.52	68.44	67.11	66.26	67.28	66.78	67.77	66.58		64.29
Low	62.57	64.58	64.77	65.95	64.73	63.67	64.25	65.33	64.07	63.84		59.57

*Sunday
†Holiday

APPENDIX

1902—RAILROADS

Date:	Jan.	Feb.	Mar.	Apr.	May	June	July	Aug.	Sept.	Oct.	Nov.	Dec.
1	†	114.06	113.65	115.78	121.86	*	120.67	125.78	†	124.61	121.29	118.51
2	115.85	*	*	115.84	119.75	119.19	120.90	125.33	127.96	124.19	*	117.57
3	115.08	113.69	114.25	117.13	120.32	119.00	121.66	*	128.55	123.93	120.75	117.47
4	114.95	114.03	113.69	117.56	*	118.99	†	125.43	127.87	122.51	†	116.76
5	*	114.78	114.23	117.48	119.52	118.35	122.21	125.73	128.28	*	119.13	116.59
6	115.40	115.73	114.98	*	121.28	118.38	*	126.04	127.93	120.99	119.39	116.45
7	114.34	115.72	114.55	116.58	120.66	118.47	122.53	126.60	*	119.98	119.41	*
8	114.58	115.60	114.45	117.18	120.86	*	122.39	126.51	128.68	120.58	117.26	116.94
9	114.06	*	*	117.65	120.36	118.53	122.98	125.38	129.36	121.88	*	116.59
10	113.63	115.88	113.71	116.95	119.51	119.31	123.17	*	129.07	120.98	116.79	114.60
11	113.89	115.80	113.70	117.03	*	119.56	123.98	125.42	128.82	119.33	115.25	113.08
12	*	†	114.07	117.36	118.31	119.46	124.06	125.73	127.50	*	115.86	114.01
13	112.92	115.13	114.19	*	119.23	120.21	*	126.29	127.91	118.97	115.76	113.08
14	111.73	115.35	114.65	118.12	119.53	120.40	124.78	125.75	*	120.56	113.70	*
15	112.41	115.21	115.07	118.80	119.94	*	125.02	125.59	127.49	120.95	115.21	113.21
16	112.40	*	*	118.93	118.28	120.61	125.59	125.31	127.77	122.70	*	113.59
17	113.51	115.55	115.44	119.74	117.76	120.76	125.91	*	128.16	123.93	115.68	114.03
18	113.18	115.27	115.64	120.18	*	121.45	125.06	125.93	128.80	123.43	114.81	116.13
19	*	115.50	115.66	120.38	117.46	120.58	125.52	126.48	128.68	*	116.00	115.91
20	112.68	113.63	115.71	*	118.46	120.71	*	125.53	128.31	123.38	116.66	116.06
21	112.68	113.96	116.41	119.67	119.00	120.60	126.17	126.22	*	122.21	118.39	*
22	112.71	†	116.32	118.96	119.25	*	126.33	126.31	127.68	122.33	118.32	117.33
23	113.18	*	*	118.85	119.57	120.31	127.08	127.10	125.23	121.94	*	116.47
24	112.93	113.99	116.48	119.80	119.58	119.63	127.16	126.98	124.70	122.25	118.50	117.19
25	112.45	114.43	115.98	120.17	*	119.72	126.45	126.91	125.01	122.28	117.30	†
26	*	113.97	115.87	120.24	118.88	120.11	125.56	126.70	125.78	*	116.45	117.92
27	112.60	114.05	115.66	*	118.91	120.22	*	127.23	124.98	121.10	†	118.05
28	113.82	113.65	†	120.80	118.91	120.58	126.03		*	121.13	117.78	*
29	113.38		116.08	121.63	119.32	*	125.85		120.41	120.10	117.48	117.12
30	113.99		*	121.26	†	120.38			124.78	120.68	*	118.42
31	114.19		116.48					*		121.68		118.98
High	115.85	115.88	116.48	121.63	121.86	121.45	127.16	127.23	129.36	124.61	121.29	118.98
Low	111.73	113.63	113.65	115.78	117.46	118.35	120.67	125.31	120.41	118.97	113.70	113.08

*Sunday
†Holiday

1901—INDUSTRIALS

Date:	Jan.	Feb.	Mar.	Apr.	May	June	July	Aug.	Sept.	Oct.	Nov.	Dec.
1	†	67.71	67.76	70.91	75.93	76.59	77.08	71.71	*	66.07	64.67	*
2	70.44	†	67.67	71.02	75.19	*	77.07	71.28	†	65.94	64.83	64.02
3	67.97	*	*	71.35	74.37	77.73	76.60	71.22	72.65	64.48	*	64.44
4	69.33	68.46	67.58	72.01	74.90	77.07	†	*	73.27	64.57	64.48	64.87
5	67.68	69.27	67.35	†	*	76.37	†	69.21	73.06	63.48	†	64.84
6	*	69.89	67.39	†	75.55	76.45	74.04	69.05	72.23	*	64.56	63.82
7	67.12	69.33	67.72	*	75.02	76.31	*	69.53	69.03	63.72	64.78	62.96
8	67.65	69.80	67.55	71.47	71.72	76.07	74.66	70.42	*	63.84	65.10	*
9	67.53	70.16	67.30	72.51	67.38	*	72.78	69.66	70.69	64.13	65.66	63.68
10	67.89	*	*	73.11	71.67	76.27	72.22	69.36	71.45	65.36	*	63.27
11	67.85	70.48	67.48	72.62	71.92	76.11	70.77	*	71.01	65.91	66.52	62.75
12	67.36	†	67.28	72.88	*	76.55	71.05	69.91	70.25	65.52	66.35	61.61
13	*	69.45	67.18	73.65	69.59	77.31	69.46	70.33	67.25	*	66.03	61.84
14	67.26	70.62	67.54	*	70.06	77.07	*	70.71	†	65.79	65.36	62.22
15	66.50	70.78	67.33	75.35	70.84	77.43	69.67	71.71	*	65.30	66.10	*
16	65.71	70.18	67.47	75.42	73.09	*	71.55	71.58	70.01	64.91	66.12	61.95
17	65.30	*	*	74.88	73.86	78.26	71.91	71.01	69.87	65.23	*	62.27
18	65.21	68.92	68.42	75.10	72.76	77.82	71.97	*	70.25	65.48	65.87	62.79
19	64.77	68.37	68.73	75.89	*	77.56	71.32	71.01	†	65.81	65.62	62.86
20	*	67.96	68.82	75.66	73.44	77.22	70.43	71.08	70.47	*	65.15	63.17
21	64.92	68.55	68.93	*	73.51	77.94	*	71.40	69.73	65.42	65.45	63.12
22	65.53	†	68.92	74.56	72.83	77.71	71.39	72.10	*	65.66	65.88	*
23	66.37	†	68.82	73.80	73.73	*	70.91	73.03	67.57	65.66	65.68	62.11
24	65.65	*	*	73.21	73.62	77.71	71.69	73.70	67.43	65.44	*	61.52
25	66.16	68.27	68.59	73.63	73.67	76.93	72.13	*	66.22	65.29	65.15	†
26	66.68	67.36	68.52	74.35	*	76.87	72.70	73.83	66.89	65.09	65.18	62.62
27	*	68.11	69.27	†	74.01	76.82	72.94	72.81	67.69	*	65.78	63.31
28	66.29	67.00	69.39	*	74.51	76.47	*	72.71	67.40	64.01	†	63.76
29	66.56		69.43	75.23	75.77	77.94	72.65	72.82	*	64.46	65.01	*
30	66.72		69.92	75.80	†	*	71.63	73.47	66.66	64.86		63.33
31	66.81		*		75.93			73.83		64.45		64.56
High	70.44	70.78	69.92	75.89	75.93	78.26	77.08	73.83	73.27	66.07	66.52	64.87
Low	64.77	67.00	67.18	70.91	67.38	76.07	69.46	69.05	66.22	63.48	64.48	61.52

*Sunday †Holiday

1901—RAILROADS

Date:	Jan.	Feb.	Mar.	Apr.	May	June	July	Aug.	Sept.	Oct.	Nov.	Dec.
1	†	97.61	97.80	105.48	117.86	114.58	115.35	107.74	*	108.18	111.65	*
2	94.79	†	97.90	106.20	117.73	*	115.16	107.08	†	107.69	111.76	113.08
3	92.66		*	107.69	116.25	115.69	114.76	106.78	110.12	107.19	*	113.53
4	95.70	98.90	98.58	107.75	116.60	115.69	†	*	110.92	107.19	111.38	114.52
5	95.50	99.48	99.01	*	*	115.43	†	104.86	110.56	106.63	†	114.56
6	*	99.77	99.37	†	117.68	115.23	*	105.36	110.56	*	113.05	112.91
7	96.48	99.11	99.30	105.65	117.05	115.24	110.61	105.80	106.17	106.20	113.34	112.00
8	96.45	99.28	99.34	107.13	111.62	114.53	112.16	106.68	108.36	106.77	113.74	*
9	96.84	99.02	99.55	108.39	103.37	*	109.64	106.38	109.58	106.96	114.23	112.23
10	96.24	*	*	107.68	110.06	114.45	108.23	106.05	108.52	108.38	*	111.91
11	97.18	99.06	99.55	108.43	*	114.39	106.43	*	108.60	109.48	114.56	111.00
12	97.85	†	99.78	109.25	†	114.91	106.80	106.42	105.30	108.62	113.90	110.08
13	*	97.98	100.09	*	109.63	116.52	*	107.73	†	*	113.93	110.58
14	96.86	98.29	100.25	109.02	104.54	116.73	106.35	108.13	109.01	108.93	112.35	110.75
15	96.45	99.33	100.61	109.49	106.74	117.55	107.11	109.15	108.92	108.63	113.47	*
16	96.03	98.86	101.50	109.36	107.85	*	110.13	108.61	110.10	108.59	113.55	110.96
17	95.52	*	*	110.35	110.25	117.65	110.13	107.83	†	108.87	*	111.82
18	94.65	97.95	102.53	111.83	110.09	116.73	111.50	*	110.30	109.05	113.01	112.18
19	93.56	97.64	102.88	112.68	*	116.46	109.68	108.40	110.82	109.15	112.86	111.96
20	*	97.11	102.66	*	108.79	116.30	108.08	109.13	*	*	113.00	112.81
21	94.16	97.39	102.95	111.71	109.54	117.18	105.81	109.19	109.90	108.98	114.38	112.93
22	94.90	†	103.00	111.05	109.36	116.83	107.65	109.86	109.86	110.00	115.21	*
23	95.00	†	103.25	111.89	108.65	*	106.68	110.52	107.96	110.83	114.94	112.45
24	93.90	*	*	112.89	108.99	117.08	107.15	111.35	108.48	110.70	*	112.27
25	94.83	97.36	102.58	113.70	108.71	116.20	107.68	*	109.29	110.67	114.70	†
26	95.79	97.71	102.85	*	*	115.46	107.93	111.69	109.22	110.88	114.83	113.28
27	*	97.76	103.45		108.53	115.46	*	110.66	*	*	114.98	113.97
28	95.75	97.34	103.70	115.66	109.31	116.39	108.33	110.68	108.21	109.60	†	114.28
29	95.75		104.54	116.35	110.16	117.21	107.76	111.00		110.61	114.57	*
30	96.08		105.03		†	*	107.39	111.54		111.03	114.20	114.21
31	97.16		*		112.15		*	†		110.79		114.85
High	97.85	99.77	105.03	116.35	117.86	117.65	115.35	111.69	110.92	111.03	115.21	114.85
Low	92.66	97.11	97.80	105.48	103.37	114.39	105.81	104.86	105.30	106.20	111.38	110.08

*Sunday

†Holiday

1900—INDUSTRIALS

Date:	Jan.	Feb.	Mar.	Apr.	May	June	July	Aug.	Sept.	Oct.	Nov.	Dec.
1	*	67.34	63.59	*	61.32	59.38	*	57.06	†	54.96	59.18	66.35
2	68.13	67.86	61.95	65.55	61.05	58.80	55.48	57.21	*	54.52	59.39	*
3	66.61	67.88	62.76	65.17	61.02	*	55.67	57.29	†	54.74	59.80	66.43
4	67.15	*	*	65.11	61.18	57.97	†	57.70	58.55	55.29	*	65.42
5	66.71	68.36	62.12	65.47	61.36	57.48	56.51	*	58.58	55.70	60.87	66.05
6	66.02	68.03	61.87	66.15	*	56.98	56.13	57.57	58.50	55.51	†	65.07
7	*	67.94	61.83	66.15	60.62	57.56	56.03	57.71	58.32	*	62.90	64.17
8	66.41	67.46	61.39	*	59.26	56.62	*	57.88	57.88	55.38	63.76	63.98
9	64.99	66.86	61.11	65.46	59.94	56.41	55.76	57.74	*	55.51	65.15	*
10	64.14	66.66	61.68	64.55	60.10	*	56.91	58.00	58.07	54.90	66.48	64.65
11	63.27	*	*	64.78	58.62	56.03	56.77	58.09	58.10	55.34	*	65.54
12	64.93	†	63.31	64.40	58.12	56.15	56.71	*	58.25	56.09	67.33	65.45
13	64.80	67.39	62.88	†	*	57.12	55.98	58.50	58.20	56.58	65.73	64.89
14	*	66.90	62.03	†	57.55	56.51	55.88	58.77	57.47	*	66.23	65.54
15	64.22	67.08	61.81	*	56.62	56.17	*	58.90	56.56	57.90	66.81	65.94
16	64.29	66.40	61.91	61.55	57.12	55.42	56.22	58.86	*	57.82	68.19	*
17	64.56	65.81	62.50	61.80	56.76	*	56.75	58.84	56.67	57.89	68.70	65.70
18	64.28	*	*	61.82	57.76	54.96	56.61	58.69	55.63	58.46	*	66.52
19	65.29	66.25	62.91	62.38	58.18	55.08	57.27	*	55.63	58.73	68.88	67.19
20	64.83	66.16	63.45	62.20	*	54.39	58.35	58.80	54.37	59.54	69.07	67.38
21	*	65.59	64.08	60.47	57.40	54.65	58.41	58.55	54.37	*	68.97	68.63
22	65.37	†	64.06	*	58.10	54.11	*	58.65	52.96	60.63	68.41	70.03
23	64.38	64.52	63.67	61.19	58.35	53.68	59.02	58.42	*	60.79	66.92	*
24	64.72	64.12	64.26	61.69	57.51	*	58.35	58.30	53.13	60.79	66.75	†
25	65.05	*	*	61.89	57.26	53.68	58.18	58.17	53.25	60.64	*	†
26	64.23	63.56	64.06	63.05	57.55	54.00	57.93	*	54.53	60.50	67.23	70.85
27	64.27	63.35	64.71	62.25	*	54.11	58.03	58.22	54.14	60.08	67.01	71.04
28	*	63.96	65.12	61.79	57.67	54.75	57.70	57.79	54.27	*	66.59	69.79
29	64.45		64.07	*	58.01	54.83	*	58.43		59.31	†	70.20
30	66.06		65.39	61.33	†	54.93	57.13	58.39	*	59.53	66.59	*
31	66.13		66.02		59.10		56.80	57.81		59.04		70.71
High	68.13	68.36	66.02	66.15	61.36	59.38	59.02	58.90	58.58	60.79	69.07	71.04
Low	63.27	63.35	61.11	60.47	56.62	53.68	55.48	57.06	52.96	54.52	59.18	63.98

*Sunday
†Holiday

1900—RAILROADS

Date:	Jan.	Feb.	Mar.	Apr.	May	June	July	Aug.	Sept.	Oct.	Nov.	Dec.
1	†	78.17	78.58	*	79.77	79.98	*	76.33	†	76.00	79.73	88.63
2	78.86	78.84	77.86	82.19	79.17	79.71	75.28	76.45	*	75.85	79.71	*
3	77.43	78.86	78.05	82.35	79.51	*	75.23	76.76	†	76.84	80.01	88.59
4	77.95	*	*	82.65	79.68	78.76	†	76.83	77.03	76.79	*	87.58
5	77.94	79.83	78.11	82.23	79.68	78.65	75.77	*	77.33	77.00	81.16	87.87
6	77.51	80.51	78.02	82.30	*	77.99	75.14	76.66	77.45	76.71	†	87.90
7	*	80.11	77.97	82.91	79.21	78.03	74.93	76.51	77.34	*	82.83	87.26
8	77.06	79.61	77.69	*	77.71	77.34	*	76.41	77.13	76.11	83.64	87.21
9	76.17	79.28	77.70	82.59	77.55	77.12	74.96	76.56	*	76.33	84.27	*
10	76.42	78.84	78.32	81.88	78.09	*	75.91	76.77	77.38	76.16	84.34	87.63
11	75.95	*	*	81.96	76.95	76.85	76.50	76.82	77.38	76.04	*	88.53
12	77.10	†	79.05	82.47	76.56	77.06	76.36	*	77.48	76.68	84.64	88.65
13	77.03	79.60	79.14	†	*	76.98	75.47	77.43	77.08	76.88	84.10	88.31
14	*	79.63	78.69		76.91	76.66	75.45	77.81	76.46	*	84.69	89.40
15	76.50	79.16	78.63	*	77.30	75.36	*	78.06	75.38	78.25	85.53	90.15
16	76.83	78.72	78.48	81.45	78.13		75.60	77.65	*	78.38	86.88	*
17	77.06		78.69	80.99	77.91	*	76.24	77.74	75.65	78.31	87.35	90.78
18	77.08	*	*	80.97	78.63	75.03	75.95	77.51	75.89	78.61	*	90.47
19	77.89	79.28	78.82	80.98	79.12	74.87	76.01	*	75.00	79.32	86.76	91.10
20	77.79	79.22	79.58	81.58	*	74.36	76.51	77.31	74.23	79.96	87.80	91.51
21	*	79.10	80.03	80.40	78.15	74.61	76.63	77.35	74.45	*	88.23	92.38
22	78.00	†	80.71	*	78.18	73.90	*	77.48	73.91	80.21	88.42	93.01
23	77.03	78.60	80.17	80.08	78.30	72.99	77.55	77.38	*	80.10	86.84	*
24	77.41	78.13	81.00	79.89	77.90	*	76.75	77.21	73.77	80.40	87.39	
25	77.85	*	*	80.02	77.77	73.28	76.61	76.94	74.35	80.22	*	†
26	76.95	78.23	81.50	80.88	77.80	73.89	76.25	*	74.42	80.50	88.26	93.72
27	*	78.08	81.65	80.11	*	73.55	76.65	76.80	75.70	80.08	88.28	93.88
28	76.96	78.78	82.20		77.70	74.60	76.49	76.60	74.83	*	88.18	94.02
29	77.86		81.99	*	78.30	74.36	*	77.18	75.35	79.46	†	94.55
30	78.08		82.08	79.51	†	74.49	75.75	77.18	*	79.85	88.88	*
31	78.86		82.40		79.15		75.95	77.13		79.55		94.99
High	78.86	80.51	82.40	82.91	79.77	79.98	77.55	78.06	77.48	80.50	88.88	94.99
Low	75.95	78.08	77.69	79.51	76.56	72.99	74.93	76.33	73.77	75.85	79.71	87.21

*Sunday †Holiday

1899—INDUSTRIALS

Date:	Jan.	Feb.	Mar.	Apr.	May	June	July	Aug.	Sept.	Oct.	Nov.	Dec.
1	*	64.44	66.64	75.15	74.59	68.40	70.67	73.89	75.57	*	75.17	75.47
2	†	63.93	65.90	*	76.04	70.11	*	74.29	75.76	70.95	75.72	75.68
3	60.41	63.61	67.02	76.02	76.00	70.13	†	74.61	*	70.97	75.34	*
4	60.69	63.39	66.73	76.04	75.39	*	†	74.68	†	71.73	74.93	74.26
5	60.91			75.87	74.48	69.73	71.48	74.08	77.61	72.03	*	73.57
6	60.86	63.05	65.95	74.17	73.83	70.09	71.92	*	76.97	72.30	75.13	73.53
7	61.35	61.95	66.40	73.08	*	70.71	72.15	73.68	76.61	72.68	†	73.03
8	*	62.23	67.29	73.14	72.18	71.03	71.69	74.23	76.56	*	75.13	70.27
9	61.98	62.10	67.66	*	69.98	72.29	*	74.59	77.01	72.67	74.38	69.26
10	61.45	62.11	68.14	72.60	72.47	72.42	70.55	75.37	*	73.47	73.67	*
11	61.31	†	68.16	74.49	71.88	*	71.35	75.19	75.59	73.00	73.06	67.43
12	61.23		*	75.10	72.18	73.08	71.55	75.79	74.68	72.45	*	67.54
13	61.71	†	68.89	75.33	69.36	71.88	71.67	*	76.11	71.81	74.08	64.03
14	61.43	62.55	68.98	76.04	*	71.92	71.02	76.23	75.65	71.85	74.16	65.26
15	*	62.50	68.90	76.30	69.77	71.71	71.14	75.63	74.55	*	74.67	66.21
16	61.28	62.70	70.71	*	70.96	71.62	*	75.15	73.54	72.47	75.48	63.84
17	61.41	63.13	71.26	75.96	72.75	71.30	70.90	75.62	*	72.22	75.80	*
18	61.93	64.76	72.02	76.36	71.84	*	71.37	75.64	72.39	72.93	75.93	58.27
19	62.30		71.19	76.29	71.81	70.43	71.07	76.06	73.10	72.86	*	61.02
20	62.40	66.76	71.28	76.05	71.77	70.30	71.57	*	72.55	73.11	75.63	61.19
21	62.18	66.89	71.83	76.71	*	69.39	72.08	75.73	73.10	73.39	75.05	59.97
22	*	†	71.83	77.01	71.71	68.84	71.69	75.11	74.22	*	75.20	58.69
23	62.37	67.32	71.56	*	71.01	69.82	*	76.00	73.86	74.61	75.50	60.57
24	61.80	67.35	71.98	76.53	70.27	69.96	71.75	75.61	*	74.31	75.80	*
25	63.05	67.52	72.40	77.28	70.76	*	72.19	75.59	72.76	74.41	*	†
26	63.83		*	77.14	70.29	69.85	71.99	75.61	72.40	74.52	†	62.00
27	64.64	66.98	73.73	77.03	69.51	70.44	72.48	75.64	72.64	74.42	75.69	64.47
28	64.87	66.78	74.70	77.10	†	70.54	72.95	75.26	72.87	74.83	75.48	64.39
29	*		74.17	76.71	†	70.18	73.00	76.04	†	*	75.55	65.73
30	65.02		74.33	*		70.38	*	75.66	†	74.37	†	66.08
31	64.35		†		67.51		73.73	76.23		74.97		*
High	65.02	67.52	74.70	77.28	76.04	73.08	73.73	76.23	77.61	74.97	75.93	75.68
Low	60.41	61.95	65.90	72.60	67.51	68.40	70.55	73.68	72.39	70.95	73.06	58.27

*Sunday

†Holiday

1899—RAILROADS

Date	Jan.	Feb.	Mar.	Apr.	May	June	July	Aug.	Sept.	Oct.	Nov.	Dec.
1	*	82.01	82.78	87.01	83.18	77.38	83.83	84.52	84.73	*	83.68	82.93
2	†	81.65	81.60	*	84.30	79.00	*	84.35	84.89	79.48	84.49	83.07
3	75.08	82.00	82.44	87.04	84.01	78.74		84.17	*	79.38	83.92	*
4	74.96	82.03	82.46	86.52	83.61	*	†	83.90	†	80.13	83.53	82.15
5	75.18	*	*	86.66	82.27	78.45	83.96	83.51	85.55	80.15	*	81.58
6	74.70	82.08	81.55	85.13	81.59	79.17	83.41	*	85.37	80.68	83.60	81.85
7	75.13	80.98	81.91	84.56	*	79.97	84.05	83.56	84.49	80.76	†	81.87
8	*	81.31	82.74	84.63	80.38	80.04	83.55	83.91	84.22	*	83.25	80.68
9	75.64	81.53	82.74	*	78.88	81.13	*	83.98	84.26	80.50	82.31	80.33
10	76.10	81.94	82.96	86.01	80.88	81.16	82.38	84.18	*	81.05	81.75	*
11	76.55	82.08	82.85	86.01	80.37	*	83.35	83.95	83.08	80.85	81.19	79.89
12	76.64	*	*	86.00	80.53	81.26	83.88	84.18	82.63	80.18	*	79.61
13	77.43	82.52	82.83	86.11	78.65	80.48	83.77	84.21	83.71	79.68	82.37	77.70
14	77.83	82.46	82.41	86.53	*	80.25	83.05	83.53	82.90	79.75	81.75	78.47
15	*	83.43	82.31	*	79.06	79.95	83.23	83.66	81.99	80.31	82.16	79.23
16	77.46	84.12	83.07	85.89	79.65	80.02	*	84.36	81.07	80.75	83.22	76.90
17	77.28	84.24	82.63	86.38	80.79	79.87	82.85	84.63	*	80.75	82.73	*
18	77.98	*	82.60	86.27	80.47	*	83.01	84.63	80.13	81.54	83.33	73.60
19	79.00	84.92	*	86.15	80.21	79.50	82.62	85.05	80.67	81.10	*	74.98
20	79.70	84.81	83.13	86.23	80.00	80.00	83.24	84.72	80.48	81.70	82.55	74.57
21	80.90	†	83.11	86.38	*	79.83	83.66	84.31	81.40	81.80	82.57	73.28
22	*	84.26	83.49	*	79.28	79.85	83.57	84.79	82.17	*	82.81	72.48
23	81.31	84.00	83.61	85.66	78.97	80.39	*	84.95	81.69	82.73	82.86	73.87
24	79.60	83.56	84.14	86.03	78.52	80.89	83.70	84.81	*	82.38	83.02	*
25	81.96		84.87	86.16	79.22	*	83.62	84.85	80.83	83.15	†	†
26	82.10	83.88	*	85.87	79.16	81.54	83.39	*	80.48	83.03	*	74.65
27	82.23	82.90	85.60	85.58	79.23	82.42	83.74	85.06	81.11	83.11	82.93	76.40
28	82.36		86.41	85.06	*	82.92	84.37	84.48	80.93	83.66	83.13	76.63
29	*		86.31		77.51	82.76	84.51	84.96		*	83.35	77.36
30	82.01		86.26	*	†	83.27	*	84.93		83.49	†	77.73
31	81.63		†		77.51		82.38	85.06		83.38		*
High	82.36	84.92	86.41	87.04	84.30	83.27	84.83	85.06	85.55	83.66	84.48	83.07
Low	74.70	80.98	81.55	84.56	77.51	77.38	82.38	83.51	80.13	79.38	81.19	72.48

*Sunday   †Holiday

1898—INDUSTRIALS

Date:	Jan.	Feb.	Mar.	Apr.	May	June	July	Aug.	Sept.	Oct.	Nov.	Dec.
1	†	49.76	47.47	44.14	*	52.87	53.00	54.60	60.50	52.52	54.94	58.16
2	*	49.54	46.58	44.60	48.60	53.36	†	55.26	60.38	*	54.51	58.14
3	49.31	49.54	46.55	*	48.30	52.77	*	55.46	†	53.62	54.95	58.45
4	48.91	49.82	46.16	45.58	†	53.13	†	55.26	*	53.80	54.75	*
5	49.53	50.23	45.73	45.06	49.43	*	52.99	55.85	†	53.76	54.93	58.30
6	50.18	*	*	46.02	49.16	53.33	52.78	55.93	60.16	53.36	*	58.52
7	50.67	50.11	44.86	45.98	50.40	53.30	53.09	*	58.92	53.08	55.57	59.04
8	50.62	49.62	45.30	45.48	*	53.15	53.25	56.31	58.54	53.27	†	59.75
9	*	49.86	45.51	45.54	51.05	53.12	53.48	56.30	57.77	*	55.30	60.11
10	50.53	50.16	45.38	*	50.46	53.71	*	56.61	58.38	52.51	56.02	60.28
11	50.33	50.14	44.44	45.95	51.63	53.26	53.35	56.55	*	51.85	56.40	*
12	50.19	†	43.29	46.32	51.09	*	53.16	56.21	58.08	51.81	57.14	59.53
13	49.85	*	*	45.19	50.82	52.61	52.61	56.83	57.55	52.87	*	59.38
14	49.63	49.49	44.73	46.06	50.68	52.20	53.15	*	57.42	52.28	57.08	58.97
15	49.15	50.04	44.41	45.37	*	50.87	52.53	57.50	58.38	51.90	56.90	58.81
16	*	48.97	45.58	44.53	50.33	51.77	52.37	58.45	58.04	*	56.77	58.74
17	49.36	49.20	44.55	*	51.26	52.13	*	58.89	58.16	52.18	56.79	58.78
18	48.81	48.59	44.86	44.92	50.55	51.53	52.27	58.08	*	51.76	56.58	*
19	49.28	47.79	44.84	44.48	51.04	*	52.32	59.09	57.61	51.56	56.82	59.11
20	49.06	*	*	44.56	50.74	51.90	52.64	†	57.23	51.80	*	59.19
21	48.92	47.11	44.50	43.27	51.40	51.73	53.13	*	58.33	52.21	56.75	59.43
22	48.88	†	43.45	43.87	*	51.38	53.01	59.39	57.73	53.01	56.97	60.09
23	*	46.16	43.22	44.55	51.73	51.74	53.21	59.63	57.63	*	56.71	
24	48.00	44.67	42.73	*	52.29	52.01	*	59.72	57.53	52.85	†	†
25	48.60	45.31	42.00	44.02	51.87	52.36	53.67	60.52	*	53.64	56.27	*
26	49.53	45.17	42.95	44.36	51.90	*	54.17	60.97	56.55	54.23	56.50	†
27	49.78	*	*	44.40	52.08	52.66	53.78	60.68	55.22	54.24	*	60.42
28	49.32	46.17	45.34	45.01	52.14	52.44	53.85	*	54.52	54.89	56.79	59.00
29	49.56		44.49	45.75	*	52.79	54.02	59.57	54.88	54.75	56.89	60.16
30	*		46.15	46.00	†	52.62	54.20	59.92	53.44	*	57.20	60.52
31	50.01		45.42		52.74		*	60.35		55.43		
High	50.67	50.23	47.47	46.32	52.74	53.71	54.20	60.97	60.50	55.43	57.20	60.52
Low	48.00	44.67	42.00	43.27	48.30	50.87	52.27	54.60	53.44	51.56	54.51	58.14

*Sunday
†Holiday

1898—RAILROADS

Date:	Jan.	Feb.	Mar.	Apr.	May	June	July	Aug.	Sept.	Oct.	Nov.	Dec.
1	†	66.00	63.01	57.90		66.53	65.47	66.00	68.59	65.95	66.58	71.59
2	*	65.76	62.05	58.34	60.61	66.56	†	66.29	68.65		66.26	71.42
3	61.86	65.70	62.24	*	60.54	65.97	†	66.60	†	66.30	66.71	71.53
4	61.24	66.15	61.51	59.16	†	66.95	†	66.85	*	66.80	66.90	*
5	62.15	66.32	60.97	58.60	62.27		65.55	67.35	†	67.11	67.05	71.21
6	63.03		*	59.49	61.90	67.23	65.31	67.88	68.78	66.91	*	71.80
7	63.53	66.08	59.56	59.19	63.22	66.93	65.71		68.20	66.57	67.63	71.97
8	63.73	65.65	59.98	58.91		66.52	65.93	68.19	67.98	66.60	†	72.05
9		65.64	60.09	59.00	63.65	66.40	66.31	68.00	67.58	*	67.83	72.70
10	63.51	66.32	59.36	*	63.13	66.90	*	68.60	67.73	66.12	68.87	73.16
11	63.82	65.94	58.46	59.62	64.40	66.48	66.46	68.43	*	65.98	68.86	*
12	64.00	* †	56.46	59.32	63.73	*	66.15	67.89	67.04	66.27	69.26	73.85
13	64.26		*	57.94	63.82	66.10	65.34	68.14	66.50	66.76	69.60	73.70
14	63.74	65.06	58.51	58.31	63.48	65.75	65.96		67.14	66.39	69.10	73.96
15	63.01	65.86	58.47	58.38		65.13	64.93	68.81	67.83	66.25	69.78	74.15
16	*	64.68	59.75	57.97	62.81	66.11	64.68	69.10	67.61	*	69.96	73.78
17	63.78	65.11	58.70	*	63.52	65.85	*	69.51	68.06	66.14	69.60	73.46
18	63.07	64.74	58.99	58.00	63.26	65.52	64.61	68.77	*	66.11	69.83	*
19	63.58	64.10	59.15	57.38	63.76	*	64.30	69.61	67.38	65.85	*	73.40
20	63.28		*	57.46	63.70	65.87	64.73	†	67.03	66.01	70.10	73.73
21	62.98	62.99	58.80	55.89	63.95	65.68	64.83		67.65	66.35	70.66	73.85
22	62.98	†	57.45	56.63		65.56	64.78	69.84	67.03	66.47	70.94	73.96
23	*	62.03	57.27	57.12	64.50	66.10	65.12	69.60	67.23	*	†	74.01
24	62.38	60.46	56.76	*	65.71	66.18	*	69.26	67.19	65.66	70.83	*
25	63.53	61.18	56.08	56.35	65.43	66.24	65.12	69.64	*	66.29	71.08	*
26	64.65	61.20	56.90	56.84	65.49	*	65.90	70.16	67.01	66.65	*	†
27	65.13		*	56.89	65.57	65.98	65.71	69.95	66.52	67.01	71.59	74.65
28	65.18	61.93	59.99	57.30	65.73	65.60	65.55	*	66.27	67.24	71.20	74.13
29	65.90		58.69	58.26	†	65.21	65.73	69.16	66.60	66.68	71.20	74.76
30			60.61	58.56		65.14	65.98	69.30	66.20	*		74.99
31	66.17		59.67		66.33		66.46	68.59		66.74		74.99
High	66.17	66.32	63.01	59.62	66.33	67.23	66.46	70.16	68.78	67.24	71.59	74.99
Low	61.24	60.46	56.08	55.89	60.54	65.13	64.30	66.00	66.20	65.85	66.26	71.21

*Sunday †Holiday

APPENDIX

1897—INDUSTRIALS

Date:	Jan.	Feb.	Mar.	Apr.	May	June	July	Aug.	Sept.	Oct.	Nov.	Dec.
1	†	42.38	41.69	39.77	38.73	40.01	44.21	*	55.44	51.54	49.11	48.41
2	40.74	42.02	41.88	39.81	*	40.22	44.18	48.84	55.77	52.59	†	48.31
3	*	41.93	42.13	39.89	38.78	40.28	43.88	50.10	55.64	*	47.67	48.31
4	40.37	41.30	41.34	*	39.48	40.52	*	50.74	55.65	52.66	47.31	48.23
5	40.87	41.23	41.45	39.74	39.18	41.04	†	51.25	*	52.26	45.73	*
6	40.95	41.42	41.31	39.57	39.54	*	43.60	51.80	†	51.79	46.32	48.79
7	40.87	*	*	39.73	39.59	41.32	44.07	51.32	55.75	51.37	*	49.46
8	40.97	41.11	41.90	40.37	39.62	41.74	43.92	*	55.60	51.64	45.65	49.39
9	40.90	40.57	41.62	40.21	*	42.21	44.16	51.73	55.81	50.88	46.53	49.60
10	*	40.57	41.79	40.29	39.95	42.38	44.37	51.80	55.82	*	47.12	49.18
11	40.75	40.27	41.94	*	39.90	42.54	*	51.97	55.71	50.64	46.19	49.48
12	41.40	†	42.05	39.95	39.69	42.57	45.05	51.50	*	48.64	46.44	*
13	41.45	39.72	42.29	40.43	39.27	*	45.61	51.97	54.61	49.35	47.12	49.81
14	41.79	*	*	39.76	38.94	42.96	45.71	52.19	55.35	48.79	*	49.67
15	42.27	39.74	42.08	39.41	38.67	42.80	45.27	*	55.62	48.42	46.47	49.02
16	42.82	40.30	41.93	†	*	42.39	45.48	51.55	55.27	48.59	47.05	48.54
17	*	40.30	41.50	39.07	38.67	42.69	45.52	51.79	55.46	*	46.83	48.14
18	42.76	40.32	41.60	*	39.20	43.07	*	51.80	55.35	49.20	46.99	48.84
19	43.25	40.28	41.12	38.49	38.80	42.89	46.45	51.65	*	49.84	47.27	*
20	42.78	40.59	41.25	38.69	38.67	*	46.76	51.84	54.66	50.39	47.23	48.45
21	42.52	*	*	38.91	38.83	42.62	46.95	52.39	52.53	49.82	*	48.25
22	42.42	†	41.39	38.57	38.98	42.80	47.73	*	53.45	50.00	46.89	48.54
23	42.02	40.69	40.86	38.49	*	43.18	47.88	52.53	53.60	49.66	46.63	48.84
24	*	40.76	40.60	38.54	39.33	43.39	47.92	52.13	52.48	*	46.21	49.39
25	41.91	40.21	40.58	*	39.20	43.28	*	52.56	52.30	48.76	†	†
26	42.22	41.29	40.07	39.22	39.55	43.70	47.71	52.92	*	49.10	46.70	*
27	42.21	41.71	39.52	†	39.21	*	47.11	53.10	52.93	48.60	47.19	49.29
28	41.88	*	*	39.02	39.64	44.61	47.86	53.23	52.31	48.46	*	49.34
29	42.06		39.13	39.01	39.91	44.27	47.70	*	51.90	48.81	46.80	49.33
30	42.56		39.86	38.96	*	44.10	47.95	54.81	50.98	49.03	47.46	49.21
31	*		39.47		†		47.88	54.81		*		49.41
High	43.25	42.38	42.29	40.43	39.95	44.61	47.95	54.81	55.82	52.66	49.11	49.81
Low	40.37	39.72	39.13	38.49	38.67	40.01	43.60	48.84	50.98	48.42	45.65	48.14

*Sunday
†Holiday

1897—RAILROADS

Date:	Jan.	Feb.	Mar.	Apr.	May	June	July	Aug.	Sept.	Oct.	Nov.	Dec.
1	†	53.46	53.15	50.21	49.05	51.22	55.04	*	63.91	62.70	60.94	61.11
2	51.71	53.09	53.40	50.58	*	51.55	55.01	58.44	64.33	63.91	†	60.78
3	*	53.22	54.07	50.46	49.44	51.35	54.68	59.21	64.83	*	59.63	60.88
4	51.24	52.92	53.32	*	49.95	51.86	†	59.46	65.04	63.94	59.20	60.76
5	51.77	52.81	53.38	49.87	49.35	52.35	54.30	59.73	*	63.61	57.90	*
6	51.85	52.77	53.19	50.10	49.79	*	54.68	60.34	†	63.00	58.14	60.96
7	52.16	*	*	50.12	49.75	52.46	54.33	61.40	65.30	62.90	*	61.64
8	51.94	52.53	53.36	50.71	49.78	52.16	54.51	*	65.32	63.13	57.45	61.96
9	52.07	52.61	53.07	50.34	*	52.39	54.50	60.79	65.60	62.15	58.55	62.28
10	*	52.66	53.11	50.15	50.07	52.73	*	61.26	66.17	*	59.50	61.68
11	51.67	52.40	53.51	*	50.16	53.06	54.45	61.94	66.18	62.06	58.57	61.90
12	52.13	†	53.82	49.78	50.20	53.10	54.83	62.08	*	60.37	59.25	*
13	52.08	*	53.96	50.52	49.77	*	55.18	61.69	65.88	61.23	59.59	62.50
14	52.39	52.06	*	50.18	49.49	53.64	55.02	62.16	66.30	60.38	*	62.35
15	52.99	51.93	54.00	49.62	49.22	53.50	55.02	*	66.83	60.30	59.15	62.26
16	53.72	52.62	54.21	†	*	53.17	55.35	62.20	66.65	60.43	59.56	62.00
17	*	52.38	53.99	49.28	49.51	53.53	55.55	61.53	67.23	*	59.06	61.68
18	53.57	52.06	53.95	48.12	40.96	53.60	*	61.67	67.03	61.41	59.25	62.58
19	53.91	52.13	53.44	49.15	49.80	*	56.06	61.53	*	62.01	59.40	*
20	53.46	52.25	53.40	49.81	49.35	53.51	55.92	61.13	66.10	62.38	59.15	62.33
21	53.01	*	*	49.59	49.57	53.58	56.07	61.20	64.15	62.00	*	61.93
22	52.80	†	53.16	49.64	49.60	54.21	56.78	*	65.51	61.83	59.03	62.04
23	52.48	52.38	52.25	49.38	*	54.57	57.15	62.45	65.68	61.53	59.30	62.40
24	*	52.18	51.88	*	50.11	54.82	57.28	62.35	64.31	*	59.08	62.75
25	52.22	51.97	51.40	50.10	50.08	54.61	*	62.32	63.93	60.11	†	†
26	52.81	52.83	51.21	†	50.47	55.12	57.12	62.68	*	60.73	59.42	*
27	52.67	53.18	50.58	49.78	50.46	*	57.15	63.24	64.61	60.13	60.06	62.64
28	52.63	*	*	49.62	50.74	55.58	57.89	63.71	63.87	60.11	*	62.49
29	52.77		49.75	49.21	50.79	55.02	57.92	*	63.38	60.71	59.61	62.20
30	53.57		50.58	*	†	54.61	58.05	63.78	62.30	60.84	60.22	62.23
31	*		49.77		50.79		58.05	63.81		*		62.29
High	53.91	53.46	54.21	50.71	50.79	55.58	58.05	63.81	67.23	63.94	60.94	62.75
Low	51.24	51.93	49.75	48.12	49.05	51.22	54.30	58.44	62.30	60.11	57.45	60.76

*Sunday   †Holiday

INDEX